The Complete International SANDWICH BOOK

Also by Sonia Uvezian:
The Cuisine of Armenia
The Best Foods of Russia
The Book of Salads
The Book of Yogurt

The Complete International SANDWICH BOOK

Hundreds of world-tested recipes
for lunch, brunch, or
breakfast, between-meal snacks,
supper, the cocktail hour,
picnics and cookouts

Sonia Uvezian

STEIN AND DAY / *Publishers* / New York

Published in the United States of America in 1982
Copyright © 1982 by Sonia Uvezian
All rights reserved.
Designed by Louis A. Ditizio
Printed in the United States of America
Stein and Day/*Publishers*
Scarborough House
Briarcliff Manor, N.Y. 10510

Library of Congress Cataloging in Publication Data

Uvezian, Sonia.
  The complete international sandwich book.

  Includes index.
  1. Sandwiches.   2. Cookery, International.
I. Title.
TX818.U93   641.8′4   80-5715
ISBN 0-8128-2787-2   AACR2

To Stan Reed, for many years food and wine editor of the Seattle *Post-Intelligencer*, a warm and generous friend who lives on in my memory, and my husband David Kaiserman, who has helped me greatly with all of my books, especially this one.

Contents

Introduction
by David Kaiserman

All the world, it seems, loves the sandwich. In every corner of the globe it turns up in a multitude of guises. So universal is its popularity that it is difficult to imagine our lives without it.

The concept of the sandwich must be at least as old as bread, and its story spans centuries and continents. Wedges of meat between thick slices of bread were enjoyed by the ancient Babylonians, Greeks, and Romans, and nearly two thousand years ago the venerable Jewish rabbi Hillel initiated the Passover ritual of placing a mixture of chopped nuts, apples, spices, and wine between two pieces of matzoh to represent the mortar the Jews were forced to use in constructing edifices for Pharoah during their slavery in Egypt. This sandwich, which was dipped in bitter herbs that symbolize the suffering the Jews endured before their deliverance, is still eaten today as part of the traditional ceremonial Passover dinner.

For many hundreds of years people in Arab lands have stuffed foods such as cheese or spit-roasted meat into pockets of pita bread, while further to the northeast Persians and Caucasians have rolled them up in *lavash*, the age-old classic thin bread of the region. And in the New World, the inhabitants of what is now Mexico have wrapped tortillas around various fillings since pre-Aztec times.

During the Middle Ages, when plates were costly items, slabs of bread called trenchers were substituted at home and at inns. The food was piled on the trenchers, which absorbed the juices. Diners worked their way down to the gravy-soaked bread and either ate it or, if no longer hungry, flung it to waiting dogs or to "trenchermen," people hanging around the table at inns who were too poor to pay for a meal. This type of repast could be construed as a sort of open-faced sandwich, although surely not the first since someone somewhere must have hit upon the idea long before.

Sandwiches have been a staple of the European peasantry, who for centuries have eaten meat or cheese between two slices of bread at their midday meal in the fields. Meat enclosed in bread slices was also given to travelers setting out on journeys.

It can readily be seen, then, that sandwiches, by whatever names they have been known in various cultures, have played a noteworthy role in gastronomy for thousands of years. But the sandwich that made history was the one put together for John Montagu (1718–1792), the fourth Earl of Sandwich, who as head of the British admiralty during the American Revolutionary War gained a reputation as a statesman of, to put it charitably, dubious virtue. In addition to this talent he was also an inveterate gambler. The sandwich was named after him in 1762 when he spent twenty-four hours straight at a gaming table. Rather than break off his card playing in order to dine, he instructed his valet to bring him a piece of meat between two slices of bread whenever he became hungry so that he could continue his mania uninterrupted. This feat made an impression, favorable or otherwise, on the Earl's companions, for word of it got out and his name was appended to this impromptu concoction. The name stuck and has been incorporated into many languages.

The Earl could not possibly have foreseen how profound an effect on Western culture his solution for simultaneously assuaging his psychological and physical hunger would have, nor did he live to see the full flowering of his idea in our time. Since his departure from this earth the sandwich has undergone many innovations while continuously gaining enthusiastic adherents. Although every region of the globe has created its own distinctive sandwiches, dependent on indigenous produce and tradition, sandwich making has reached its zenith in two places: Scandinavia, particularly Denmark, has raised the creation of the open-faced sandwich to the level of an art form, and in the United States the closed sandwich has become an indispensable element of our lifestyle, and even more of a national institution than apple pie.

The significant thing about the Earl's sandwich was that it provided a meal quickly prepared and eaten, a major reason why this category of food has since commanded such widespread popularity. This very reason, however, has often brought about its ruination. The average sandwich today is a model of mediocrity, dull and predictable. A plethora of prepackaged food products specially designed and created for the quick and easy assembly of sandwiches takes up a depressingly large amount of supermarket space. These generally bland and sterile fruits of impersonal technology are consumed daily by millions of Americans either with stoic resignation or, even worse, with alarming naiveté. Quality has all too frequently been sacrificed for convenience.

This is not to say that a sandwich must be elaborate in composition and time-consuming in preparation in order to be good or that all sandwich-related convenience foods should be shunned with disdain. On the contrary, some of the best sandwiches are simple to make and contain but a few ingredients, and careful shopping, keeping quality and good taste in mind, can yield a variety of quite serviceable prepackaged items culled from the shelves and deli cases of your supermarket. But these merely scratch the surface of a treasure chest of gastronomic treats. There is no need to have to settle only for the likes of cold cuts, processed cheese, and spongy bread. Why be in a sandwich-making rut when with just a little imagination and effort you can easily transcend such indifferent fare and, depending on your spirit of adventure, rise as high as your fancy dictates? Sandwiches, from dainty canapés to mammoth heroes, can and should provide as much opportunity for great eating as any other type of food, and the possibilities are almost without limit.

The sandwich is a highly versatile creation that can be enjoyed at any time of the day or night, either as a meal or as a snack. It is appropriate with cocktails and at teatime, it makes a satisfying breakfast, brunch, or lunch, or it can be the main event of a hearty dinner. It is flexible in that it can be a convenient resource for both casual and formal entertaining, ranging in diversity from earthy and robust to elegant and refined, and encompassing a multitude of flavors, textures, and colors. Another welcome characteristic is its adaptability to any budget. In these times of conscious thrift, a great many sandwiches can be assembled with moderately priced yet nourishing ingredients and still be made to look enticing.

The world abounds with a wealth of sandwich recipes that run the gamut from classic and subtle to innovative and exotic. With the cornucopia of foods readily available in America, we can turn these mouth-watering possibilities into delectable realities. Some of the very best await you on the following pages.

The Complete International
SANDWICH
BOOK

1

Before You Begin

What Is a Sandwich?

According to the dictionary, a sandwich consists of "two slices of bread with meat, cheese, or other filling placed between them." The venerable *Larousse Gastronomique* defines it as "foodstuff composed of two slices of buttered bread with some edible substance between." These are accurate descriptions of the conventional sandwich, which will always be with us, but limited, considering the enormous range of possibilities encompassed by this category of food. Today the term sandwich has come to mean just about any edible filling wrapped, rolled, or layered in any edible covering. The filling becomes a topping when placed on an edible base, as in open-faced sandwiches.

THE COVERING

Although most commonly bread, this can also be a pastry, pancake, vegetable, or fruit. All of these coverings are represented in this book. In addition to chapters devoted to conventional types of bread-based sandwiches, I have included special ones on pita and tortilla sandwiches since these fascinating categories have remained largely unexplored in previous sandwich cookbooks. For that same reason you

1

will find separate chapters for pastry sandwiches, filled pancakes, and vegetable- and fruit-based sandwiches.

Since bread is an essential part of the great majority of sandwiches, the importance of using the best bread possible, homemade or otherwise, cannot be overestimated. This rules out much of what passes for bread on supermarket shelves. It is encouraging to note, however, that in recent years there has been an increase in the demand for better-quality commercial breads such as French, Italian, sour rye, whole grain, pita, and firm-textured, old-fashioned white bread. Also, many more Americans are baking their own bread at home. I have included a selection of recipes for both basic and more unusual breads in chapter 12. If you have neither the time nor inclination to bake your own bread, try investigating local bakeries and specialty shops.

The bread used for sandwiches should be firm in texture. It will cut more easily if it has been chilled (you can freeze it 2 or 3 hours). Chilling is especially recommended when preparing rolled sandwiches, which must be made with very thinly sliced, freshly baked bread. Other sandwiches are easier to make if the bread is a day old. Whether or not to remove the crust depends on the type of sandwich and one's personal preference. Whenever possible, leave on the crust. Not only can it be irresistibly good, it is rich in vitamins. Trim the crusts, however, from canapés and tea sandwiches. When working with a sliced filling such as ham or cheese, the crusts and the overlapping filling can be removed at the same time.

Ordinarily, bread for sandwiches should be sliced about ¼ to ⅓ inch thick. Where densely textured bread is called for, it can be cut thinner. Hearty sandwiches, such as those for picnics and lunch boxes, can be made with ½-inch-thick slices. Bread for party sandwiches, however, should be cut very thin. Use a sharp serrated knife to cut bread.

About Butter

When used in the preparation of sandwiches made with bread, butter serves a threefold purpose: it imparts flavor, contributes texture, and prevents moist fillings from soaking into the bread. Use fresh, good butter. For easy spreading, have it at room temperature (but not melting) or cream it (page 182). Spread it evenly all the way to the edge of the bread. One-half cup (1 stick) butter is sufficient to spread

18 to 24 slices of bread, although you can be more generous if you wish. Often butter spreads (chapter 10) and, occasionally, cream cheese (also at room temperature) can be used in place of regular butter. If preferred, margarine can be substituted for butter and Neufchâtel cheese for cream cheese.

About Mayonnaise

Mayonnaise used for sandwiches should be thick, not thin, and preferably homemade. Homemade mayonnaise is far superior to the store-bought variety and can be prepared with a minimum of time and effort. You will find a recipe for it on page 262. To prevent dangerous spoilage, refrigerate mayonnaise in a tightly closed container.

About Mustard

A wide selection of imported and domestic prepared mustards is readily available, covering a broad range of flavors: sweet, mild, winy, vinegary, musty, tangy, pungent, sharp, or hot. There are European and Chinese mustards, domestic versions of the imported styles, and American varieties. In general, light-colored mustards are mild-flavored, and are most compatible with lightly seasoned fare, while dark-colored mustards tend to be more potent in flavor.

Imported mustards complement the foods of their particular country of origin. For instance, the delicate flavor of French mustards harmonizes with the skillfully blended seasonings of French cuisine, while the earthy, dark German mustards are perfect companions to strongly flavored meats and vegetables. Smooth and tangy Swedish mustards are a natural with Scandinavian specialties.

Many people consider French mustard, particularly that made in Dijon, Burgundy, the mustard capital of the world, to be the connoisseur's choice of mustards. Dijon-style mustard has an appealingly subtle and piquant flavor. Although it comes in various strengths, even the strongest is mild compared to the sharp English and fiery Chinese types. Dijon-style mustard is also available blended with such ingredients as green peppercorns, lemon, and tarragon and other herbs. Two other excellent French mustards are Savora and Meaux, which contains whole dark mustard seeds.

Among the varieties of German mustards found in this country, Düsseldorf is the best known. It is pleasantly robust in flavor, with a smooth, thick texture. English mustard, traditionally sold in powdered form and reconstituted with water, is also marketed in a prepared version. Most American mustards, unfortunately, are undistinguished.

THE FILLING

The filling of a sandwich can be one of three types: slices, strips, or the like; a salad, such as chicken or egg salad; or a spread.

Be sure that moist fillings are just that, not wet. All meats should be tender and succulent, not dried out. Have meats thoroughly cold before slicing, unless they are to be used for hot sandwiches. They should be cut thinly and trimmed of fat and gristle. When purchasing cooked sliced meats such as ham, corned beef, or tongue, ask that they be very thinly sliced (No. 2 on the slicing machine). Several thin slices of meat taste far better in a sandwich than one thick slice. Have spreads at room temperature. Apply fillings evenly all the way to the edges of the base. Meat, cheese, and other sliced fillings should not protrude over the sides but should be neatly trimmed. Such items as smoked salmon can be cut and trimmed more easily with scissors than with a knife. Store fillings in airtight containers in the refrigerator. Be sure to wrap cold sliced meats tightly before refrigerating to prevent loss of flavor and moisture.

Sandwiches are often made more appetizing and nutritious by the addition of such greens as lettuce (particularly Boston and leaf lettuce), watercress, and spinach. Two other commonly used vegetables are sliced tomato and cucumber. All of these contribute flavor as well as frequently needed moisture. They should be washed, well drained, and chilled. Another popular item is alfalfa sprouts, although I personally do not care for them.

When cucumber is called for in the recipes, use unwaxed seedless cucumber, preferably the variety known as English cucumber, or other narrow, firm cucumber.

GARNISHES AND RELISHES

Many sandwiches are enhanced by the addition of garnishes and relishes. Well-chosen ones can glorify even ordinary sandwiches. They should contrast pleasingly with the sandwiches in flavor, color, and texture without being over-elaborate, as this would defeat their purpose. For suggestions please consult chapter 11.

When preparing garnishes with fresh fruits such as apples, pears, peaches, and bananas, brush them with fresh lemon juice after cutting to prevent discoloration.

CUTTING, WRAPPING, AND STORAGE OF SANDWICHES

To cut sandwiches neatly, use a heavy, very sharp French knife. When preparing closed sandwiches ahead of time, as for picnics and lunch boxes, wrap them securely in plastic sandwich bags, clear plastic wrap, or waxed paper, label, and refrigerate. Do not hold them longer than six hours. If you enclose more than one sandwich in the same wrapping, take care not to mix different kinds; otherwise your fruit and nut sandwich will reek with the smell of sardines. If fillings for bread sandwiches are so moist that they could cause the bread to become soggy upon standing, pack them separately and assemble the sandwiches just before eating. Sandwiches that do not contain such items as mayonnaise, lettuce, or tomato can be frozen and will thaw in a few hours. Large sandwiches, such as a hero, and warm sandwiches should be wrapped in aluminum foil. It is best not to prepare open-faced sandwiches in advance but to assemble them close to serving time, since wrapping them can damage their decorations and surfaces.

Entertaining with a Sandwich Buffet

Entertaining with sandwiches can be both delightful and timesaving. For instance, if you are looking for an unusual new menu idea for your next luncheon or supper party, why not make it a sandwich buffet? It is convenient, it can be reasonable in cost, and, because everything is prepared ahead of time and guests serve themselves, you too can join in the fun. All the elements of sandwiches—breads, fillings, garnishes, and relishes—are arranged separately along with a selection of salads, beverages, and desserts for a festive and opulent buffet table. Each person can choose the ingredients he prefers in the proportions he desires, thus devising his own creations from the rich assortment provided. So many intriguing ideas present themselves! One possibility could be an international menu featuring sandwich-makings from different countries. Another could be a menu designed around Danish *smørrebrød* (chapter 2), pita bread (chapter 4), or tortillas (chapter 5).

For a sandwich spectacular that would, admittedly, involve a little more work on your part, why not go all out and plan a buffet featuring appetizer, main course, and dessert sandwiches? Before the party, arrange a buffet table with soup mugs and three sets of sandwich plates, one for the appetizer, another for the main course, and a third for dessert. At serving time, bring the appetizer sandwiches with hot or chilled soup and have guests help themselves. Next, bring the main course sandwiches with wine, beer, or the beverage of your choice. Finally, offer the dessert sandwiches with coffee or tea.

With a bit of planning and imagination, a sandwich buffet can offer a full measure of gastronomic excitement.

2

Open-Faced Sandwiches

It is only natural that a chapter on open-faced sandwiches should be launched with the famed *smørrebrød* of Denmark. Although *smørrebrød* means "buttered bread," the butter is actually a minor ingredient, not even visible under the layers of delectable toppings that cover a thin slice of bread.

While *smørrebrød* is considered a Danish invention, exactly how it originated is a matter of speculation. Possibly it may have evolved from the lowly medieval trencher. By the eighteenth century these elegantly created sandwiches had become popular among the Danish aristocracy, and today they rank as a national institution devoured for lunch as well as at other times of the day by much of the population. Actually, versions of *smørrebrød* are enjoyed throughout Scandinavia, Germany, and even Austria, but it is in Denmark that this type of sandwich has achieved its greatest fame and glory.

Smørrebrød is a feast for both the eye and the palate, satisfying a desire for beauty and order while tantalizing the senses. Its hallmark is variety—variety of color, flavor, and texture. One does not simply make these sandwiches, one composes them with the care of an artist planning a painting. It is essential to use the finest ingredients. To start with, choose the right bread, which should be firm-textured and

7

about ⅛-inch thick. As a general rule, use white bread with toppings such as chicken or mild-flavored cheese and seafood, light rye for stronger-flavored fish or meat, and dark sour rye or pumpernickel for spicy, highly seasoned toppings. Occasionally rye-krisp, both light and dark, is employed as a base for *smørrebrød*. Use the freshest butter available. Cream it and spread it evenly and thickly all the way to the edges of each bread slice in order to help insulate it against moisture. Butter spreads (chapter 10) are sometimes substituted for regular butter, contributing their own delightful flavors.

Toppings for *smørrebrød* cover a wide spectrum, including seafood, poultry, meat, eggs, vegetables, herbs, fruit, and cheese. Almost any ingredients can be used, provided they complement each other and are arranged attractively on the bread. Usually three trays of *smørrebrød* are set up: one with an assortment of fish sandwiches, another with meat and egg sandwiches, and the third with cheese sandwiches. *Smørrebrød* are customarily eaten with knife and fork, and three of them can make an ample meal. They can also be made in miniature to serve as canapés.

Because these sandwiches are such an integral part of daily life in Denmark, one finds them sold in shops everywhere, prepared by women who have undergone three years of training in how to compose them with expertise. Danish restaurants have *smørrebrød* menus that may run up to four feet in length, listing as many as two hundred different sandwiches.

Beer, the national drink of Denmark, is traditionally offered with *smørrebrød*. It is often accompanied by *akvavit*, a clear, gin-like spirit distilled from potatoes or grain and flavored with caraway seeds. *Akvavit* is drunk from very cold thimble-size, long-stemmed glasses. A swallow of *akvavit* is followed by one of beer, an ideal combination with *smørrebrød*.

Although the most celebrated open-faced sandwiches are, of course, *smørrebrød*, many others of this genre, equally delicious if less famous, are enjoyed the world over. This chapter includes recipes for some of my favorites. For additional open-faced sandwiches please consult chapters 4, 5, 6, 7, and 9.

Cold Open-Faced Sandwiches

Smørrebrød (Danish Open-Faced Sandwiches)

Nearly all of the ingredients called for in the following recipes are readily available. The few remaining ones, such as smoked eel, can be found in specialty shops.

Lobster and Caviar Sandwiches

6 slices white bread
Butter
6 small leaves Boston lettuce
8 ounces cooked lobster meat, diced
1 jar (2 ounces) red caviar

3 hard-cooked eggs
1 tablespoon mayonnaise
¼ teaspoon curry powder or dry mustard
6 parsley sprigs
6 lemon wedges

Toast the bread and spread butter on one side of each slice while still warm. Cover the buttered side of each bread slice with a lettuce leaf. Arrange about ¼ cup of the lobster meat in a ring around the outer edge of the lettuce. Spoon a ring of caviar inside the lobster ring. With a sharp-pointed knife, cut each hard-cooked egg crosswise in half, making a zigzag edge. Press the egg yolks through a fine wire strainer and mix with the mayonnaise and curry powder or dry mustard. Fill the egg whites with the yolk mixture. Place an egg half in the center of the caviar ring on each sandwich and top with a sprig of parsley. Garnish each sandwich with a lemon wedge. Makes 6.

VARIATION:

Substitute tiny cooked and shelled shrimp or flaked cooked crabmeat for the lobster. If using shrimp, substitute black caviar for the red.

Caviar Sandwich

Butter a thin slice of light rye bread. Cover with a small leaf of Boston lettuce. Top with a poached egg and a spoonful of black caviar. Decorate with mayonnaise piped through a pastry bag fitted with a small fancy tube. Garnish with leek or scallion rings.

Crab Sandwich

Spread a thin slice of white bread with Crab Butter (page 189). Cover with a small leaf of Boston lettuce. Arrange overlapping thin slices of cold boiled new potato, tomato, and/or cucumber over the lettuce. Top with cold cooked crabmeat, slices of hard-cooked egg, and cold cooked asparagus tips. Garnish with chopped parsley or chives.

Sardine, Anchovy, and Oyster Sandwich

Butter a thin slice of light or dark rye bread. Arrange 2 sardines diagonally on the bread from one corner to the other. On each side place a small tomato slice. On one side arrange 2 rolled anchovies and on the other side 2 smoked oysters. Sprinkle 1 teaspoon crumbled Danish blue cheese over each tomato slice. Garnish with a sprig of parsley or dill.

Fried Fish Sandwich

Spread a thin slice of white bread with Parsley Butter (page 183). Arrange cold fried small fish such as herring, sardines, or smelts over the bread. Place a wedge of lemon on each side of the fish. Top with a dollop of mayonnaise. Garnish with mild red or white onion rings, capers, and a sprig of dill.

Smoked Salmon Sandwich

Spread a thin slice of white bread with Dill Butter (page 183). Cover with a small leaf of Boston lettuce. Arrange overlapping thin slices of cold boiled new potato or hard-cooked egg, tomato, and cucumber over the lettuce. Top with a rolled thin slice of smoked salmon filled with Horseradish Cream (page 265) or Whipped Cream Cheese (page 191). Garnish with a sprig of dill.

Smoked Eel Sandwich

Spread a thin slice of light rye bread with Mustard Butter (page 185). Cover with thin slices of smoked eel. Top with a small spoonful of Cold Scrambled Eggs (page 227). Garnish with chopped chives.

Roast Chicken Sandwich

Spread a thin slice of white bread with Parsley Butter (page 183). Cover with thin slices of roast chicken breast. Decorate with liver pâté piped through a pastry bag fitted with a small fancy tube. Garnish with a maraschino cherry half and a small wedge of pineapple.

Turkey and Shrimp Sandwich

Spread a thin slice of white bread with Curry Butter (page 186). Arrange overlapping rows of tiny cooked and shelled shrimp and thin slices of roast turkey breast, hard-cooked egg, radishes, and cucumber attractively on the bread. Decorate with Cream Cheese and Avocado Filling (page 194) piped through a pastry bag fitted with a star tip. Garnish with sprigs of dill.

Ham Sandwich

Spread a thin slice of rye or pumpernickel bread with Mustard Butter (page 185). Cover with overlapping thin slices of cucumber. Top with thin slices of Danish cooked ham rolled to form cornucopias and filled with a mixture of Green Mayonnaise (page 262) and chopped hard-cooked egg.

Ham and Cheese Sandwich

Butter a thin slice of dark rye or pumpernickel bread. Cut 2 thin slices of Danish cooked ham the length of the bread and half its width. Fold the ham slices accordion fashion. Place one slice on the lower left-hand quarter of the bread and the other on the upper right. On the remaining quarters place 1 slice each Danish Havarti or Tybo cheese. Cut 2 purple grapes or Pickled Cherries (page 233) in half lengthwise and arrange them, cut sides down, on the cheese.

Ham, Apple, and Prune Sandwich

Spread a thin slice of light or dark rye bread with Rum Butter (page 190) or Mustard Butter (page 185). Cover with overlapping thin slices of Danish cooked ham. Garnish with a wedge of unpeeled green apple, a cooked prune, and a small leaf of Boston lettuce.

Ham, Pineapple, and Banana Sandwich

Spread a thin slice of white or rye bread with Rum Butter (page 190). Cover with overlapping thin slices of Danish cooked ham. Top with pineapple and banana slices. Garnish with a maraschino cherry and a dollop of sweetened mayonnaise.

Oliver Twist Sandwich

Butter a thin slice of pumpernickel bread. Cover with a thin folded slice of Danish cooked ham. Heap a spoonful of Horseradish Cream (page 265) in the center of the ham. Place a cooked prune on each side of the cream. Garnish with an orange twist (page 226) placed in the center of the cream.

Roast Beef Sandwich

Spread a thin slice of white or light rye bread with Horseradish Butter (page 185). Cover with overlapping thin slices of cold, tender rare roast beef. Top with crisply fried onion rings. Garnish with cooked bacon curls and pickled vegetables such as tiny gherkins, cauliflowerets, and cocktail onions.

Roast Pork Sandwich

Butter a thin slice of light rye bread. Cover with overlapping thin slices of lean roast pork. Garnish with an orange twist (page 226) placed in the center of the sandwich. Garnish each side of the twist with a cooked prune.

Steak Tartare Sandwich

Butter a thin slice of light or dark rye bread. Cover with a heaping spoonful of freshly ground lean raw beef such as tenderloin or sirloin. Garnish with a raw egg yolk placed in the center. Surround the yolk first with a ring of chopped mild red or white onion, then one of chopped pickled beets and, finally, an outside border of capers.

Sausage Sandwich

Spread a thin slice of rye or pumpernickel bread with Mustard Butter (page 185). Cover with overlapping thin slices of cold boiled new potatoes. Top with cooked cocktail sausages and a strip of crisp bacon. Garnish with slivers of tomato and chopped parsley.

Tongue Sandwich I

Spread a thin slice of light or dark rye bread with Mustard Butter (page 185) or Mixed Herb Butter (page 184). Cover with overlapping thin slices of cold cooked tongue. Top with a spoonful of cold cooked vegetable salad mixed with mayonnaise. Garnish with a small leaf of Boston lettuce and a wedge of tomato or a seedless green grape.

VARIATION:

Slices of cold, tender rare roast beef or braised veal may be substituted for the tongue.

Tongue Sandwich II

Butter a thin slice of light or dark rye bread. Cover with overlapping thin slices of cold cooked tongue. Garnish with mandarin orange sections and a dollop of Horseradish Cream (page 265).

Liver Pâté and Mushroom Sandwich

Butter a thin slice of white bread. Cover with a slice of liver pâté. Top with sautéed mushroom slices and a strip of crisp bacon. Garnish with a small leaf of Boston lettuce.

Hans Christian Andersen Sandwich

Butter a thin slice of rye or pumpernickel bread. Cover with a slice of liver pâté or liverwurst. Top with a tomato slice. Garnish with cooked bacon curls and a pickle fan (page 225). Serve this sandwich on lettuce leaves.

Egg Salad Sandwich

Spread a thin slice of rye or pumpernickel bread with Mustard Butter (page 185) or Mixed Herb Butter (page 184). Cover with a small leaf of Boston lettuce. Place a mound of Egg Salad (page 217) over the lettuce. Top with rolled thin slices of Danish or other salami, and garnish with parsley sprigs.

Lobster Salad Sandwich

Butter a thin slice of white bread. Cover with a small leaf of Boston lettuce. Arrange overlapping thin slices of cucumber and cold boiled new potatoes over the lettuce. Top with Curried Lobster Salad (page 218). Garnish with tomato slices and chopped parsley.

Danish Cheese Sandwich

Spread a thin slice of light or dark rye bread with Mustard Butter (page 185) or Paprika Butter (page 186). Cover with thin slices of Danish caraway or Havarti cheese. Garnish with green pepper rings or crisply fried onion rings.

Danish Gangplank Sandwiches

A bread board makes an excellent cutting and serving tray for these colorful and decorative platter-size sandwiches. Serve them buffet style at an informal luncheon, supper, or late evening gathering. Each diner helps himself to a serving of each kind of sandwich, which is to be eaten with knife and fork.

3 thin lengthwise slices of white or
  rye bread

¼ cup (or more) Shrimp Butter
  (page 189) or regular butter, at
  room temperature

Arrange the bread slices on a bread board and spread each slice generously with Shrimp Butter or regular butter. Put toppings on as noted below.

Lobster, Egg, and Tomato Sandwich

Topping

3 leaves Boston lettuce
2 medium firm, ripe tomatoes,
  peeled and thinly sliced
2 hard-cooked eggs, thinly sliced
6 ounces cooked lobster meat, cut
  into 1-inch pieces

2 tablespoons Green Mayonnaise
  (page 262)
1 can (2 oz.) rolled anchovy fillets
  with capers

Cover one bread slice with a layer of the lettuce leaves. Arrange the tomato slices, slightly overlapping, down one side of the bread. Arrange the egg slices on the tomatoes in a row down the center. Toss the lobster with Green Mayonnaise and arrange the mixture along the remaining side of the bread. Place a rolled anchovy on each egg slice. Cut the sandwich into 4 to 6 servings.

Cucumber and Shrimp Sandwich

Topping

½ unpeeled English cucumber, or
  1 medium narrow, firm
  cucumber, thinly sliced
2 teaspoons finely chopped fresh
  dill

¾ cup cooked, shelled, and
  deveined small shrimp
2 tablespoons mayonnaise or sour
  cream
Watercress sprigs

Arrange the cucumber slices down one side of the second bread slice and sprinkle evenly with the dill. Place the shrimp along the other side and spoon the mayonnaise or sour cream down the center. Garnish with the watercress sprigs. Cut the sandwich into 4 to 6 servings.

Crab, Avocado, and Bacon Sandwich

Topping

1 large, ripe avocado	2 tablespoons mayonnaise
Juice of 1 lemon, freshly squeezed and strained	6 slices bacon, cooked crisp and crumbled
1 cup cooked crabmeat	Finely chopped chives

Peel and slice the avocado and dip the slices in the lemon juice. Arrange them down one side of the third bread slice. Toss the crabmeat with the mayonnaise and arrange it down the other side. Sprinkle the bacon down the center. Sprinkle the chives over the crabmeat. Cut the sandwich into 4 to 6 servings.

Swedish Gangplank Sandwich I

This and the following two sandwiches each serve one person and are a meal in themselves. They are fit for a Swedish hero (or any hero) who, instead of helping himself to the buffet, has the buffet brought to him!

Cut a ¼-inch-thick slice of white or rye bread the length of the loaf and spread it with butter. Arrange rows of the following items in an attractive pattern over the bread: rolled anchovy fillets, wedges of hard-cooked egg, slices of salami rolled to form cornucopias, a rolled thin slice of roast veal, thin slices of unpeeled cucumber, and slices of Swiss or Nokkelost cheese. Decorate with mayonnaise piped through a pastry bag fitted with a small fancy tube. Place pickled cocktail onions inside the salami rolls. Tuck a parsley sprig into one end of the rolled veal, allowing it to protrude. Garnish the sandwich with a radish rose (page 224).

Swedish Gangplank Sandwich II

Cut a ¼-inch-thick slice of white or rye bread the length of the loaf and spread it with butter. Arrange rows of the following items in an attractive pattern over the bread: tiny cooked and shelled shrimp, thin slices of smoked salmon, wedges of hard-cooked egg, and thin slices of Swiss cheese. Decorate with liver pâté forced through a pastry bag fitted with a small fancy tube. Garnish with a truffle, a dill sprig, radish roses (page 224), and a small leaf of Boston lettuce.

Swedish Ring-Shaped Sandwich

Cut a slice about 6 inches in diameter from an unsliced round loaf of rye bread and spread it with butter. Arrange the following items in an attractive pattern over the bread: tiny cooked and shelled shrimp decorated with mayonnaise piped through a pastry bag fitted with a small fancy tube, and garnished with dill sprigs, overlapping slices of hard-cooked egg topped with anchovy fillets, thin slices of cold, tender rare roast beef rolled to form cornucopias and filled with pickled cocktail onions, a generous spoonful of cold cooked vegetable salad mixed with mayonnaise and garnished with sliced pimento-stuffed olives, overlapping slices of fresh or pickled cucumber, and overlapping thin slices of Swiss cheese. Place parsley sprigs in the center of the sandwich.

Tomato Sandwiches

The surprise here is the three different fillings.

Cut a hard-cooked egg crosswise in half. Mash the egg yolks until smooth and mix with enough mayonnaise to moisten and ⅟₁₆ teaspoon dry mustard. Fill the egg whites with the yolk mixture and set aside.

Peel and cut 2 thick slices from a very large tomato. Remove the seeds and juicy pulp. Put each slice on a round of buttered toast cut the same size as the tomato slice. Fill the spaces inside each tomato slice with black caviar, Cream Cheese and Chives Filling (page 193), and liver pâté. Top each sandwich with a filled egg half. Pipe a border of mayonnaise around the edge of the tomato. Makes 2.

Italian Tomato and Cheese Sandwich

Spread a slice of Italian or French bread with Anchovy Butter (page 188). Cover with a slice of mozzarella or Bel Paese cheese. Top with a thick slice of ripe tomato cut to size. Sprinkle with olive oil, salt and freshly ground pepper to taste, and a little finely chopped fresh basil. Makes 1.

Avocado, Tomato, and Cheese Sandwich

Spread a slice of toasted whole grain, rye, or onion bread with butter. Cover with a piece of Boston or leaf lettuce. Dip 2 or 3 peeled avocado slices in freshly squeezed and strained lemon juice and arrange them over the lettuce along one side. Arrange 2 slices of ripe tomato on the other side. Top each tomato slice with a mound of Herbed Cream Cheese (page 193) or Curried Cheese Filling (page 197), and sprinkle with shelled, roasted, and salted pumpkin seeds or chopped toasted blanched almonds or hazelnuts. Makes 1.

VARIATION:

Substitute Curried Egg Salad (page 216) for the cheese filling and omit the seeds or nuts.

Crab and Bacon Sandwiches

Guaranteed to produce grateful grins and clean plates.

1 small, ripe avocado
1 tablespoon freshly squeezed and strained lemon or lime juice
1 teaspoon grated or finely chopped onion
1 very small garlic clove, crushed or finely chopped
Salt to taste
4 slices egg bread or white bread
Butter
4 slices tomato
8 slices bacon, cooked crisp
4 ounces cooked crabmeat (preferably Dungeness), picked over to remove any pieces of shell
¼ cup mayonnaise
Lemon or lime wedges (optional)

Halve and pit the avocado. Peel off the skin. Place the avocado flesh in a bowl and mash it with a fork. Add the lemon or lime juice, onion, garlic, and salt and mix well. Taste and adjust the seasoning.

Toast the bread slices and butter them. Spread each slice with one-fourth of the avocado mixture. Place a tomato slice on each sandwich. Top each with 2 slices bacon. Divide the crabmeat among the sandwiches and top each with 1 tablespoon of the mayonnaise. Serve garnished with the lemon or lime wedges, if desired. Makes 4.

VARIATION:

One ounce Gorgonzola or other blue cheese, mashed with 2 tablespoons sour cream or unflavored yogurt, may be substituted for the mayonnaise.

Jewish Cream Cheese and Lox Sandwich

Cut a bagel in half lengthwise. Spread each half generously with cream cheese. Top with a thin slice of lox (smoked salmon) and, if desired, a paper-thin slice of mild red onion. Makes 1 serving.

Spanish Herring Sandwich

Spread a slice of toasted French or whole wheat bread generously with cream cheese. Cover with kippered herring fillets. Top with a whole pimento that has been marinated in Herb French Dressing (page 261). Garnish with watercress. Makes 1.

Anchovy and Egg Sandwich

Mash 1 hard-cooked egg with 1 tablespoon sour cream or mayonnaise. Spread the mixture over a slice of dark rye or pumpernickel bread. Top with a lattice of flat anchovy fillets. Makes 1.

Chicken Sandwich

A good way to recycle leftover chicken breast.

Butter
1 large slice dark rye or pumpernickel bread
1 leaf escarole or leaf lettuce
2 tablespoons shredded romaine lettuce
Remoulade Sauce with Yogurt (below)

1 slice Swiss cheese
1 slice cold cooked chicken breast
2 slices bacon, cooked crisp
½ hard-cooked egg, chopped
2 pimento-stuffed olives, sliced
Tomato wedges or cherry tomato halves

Butter the bread slice and cover it with the lettuce leaf, shredded lettuce, 1 tablespoon of the Remoulade Sauce, cheese, and chicken. Mask the sandwich with the remaining Remoulade Sauce and top with the bacon, egg, and olives. Garnish with the tomato and serve. Makes 1.

VARIATION:

Other dressings such as Thousand Island, Louis, or Roquefort can be substituted for the Remoulade Sauce, and pitted black olives for the stuffed olives.

Remoulade Sauce with Yogurt

2 tablespoons mayonnaise	⅛ teaspoon anchovy paste
2 tablespoons unflavored yogurt	½ teaspoon finely chopped parsley
2 teaspoons chopped dill pickle	⅛ teaspoon crushed dried tarragon
⅛ teaspoon Dijon-style mustard	⅛ teaspoon crushed dried basil

In a small bowl combine all the ingredients and mix well. Taste and adjust the seasoning. Cover and chill.

Marinated Beef Sandwiches

⅓ cup olive oil	1 teaspoon salt
¼ cup white wine vinegar	1 pound flank steak, trimmed of
2 tablespoons dry red wine	fat
1 small mild red onion, finely	6 slices rye or pumpernickel bread
chopped	Dijon-style mustard or mayonnaise
1 medium garlic clove, finely	Boston or Bibb lettuce leaves
chopped	Pickled beets, well drained and
1 teaspoon dry mustard	sliced
½ teaspoon crushed dried tarragon	Dill gherkins, drained and sliced

In a shallow dish mix together the oil, vinegar, wine, onion, garlic, dry mustard, tarragon, and salt. Set aside.

Broil the steak 3 to 4 inches from the heat, allowing 6 to 8 minutes on each side for rare meat. Transfer the meat to a carving board and slice across the grain into thin strips. Add the strips to the marinade in the dish and turn to coat the pieces of meat thoroughly with the mixture. Cover and chill several hours or overnight.

To assemble the sandwiches, spread each slice of bread with mustard or mayonnaise. Layer with lettuce, pickled beets, dill gherkins, and the marinated beef strips. Makes 6.

Note: One pound very tender lean roasted, boiled, or braised beef, thinly sliced, may be substituted for the broiled steak.

Ham and Papaya Sandwich

Spread a slice of egg twist bread or unsweetened brioche with Whipped Cream Cheese (page 191). Cover with 1 or 2 thin slices of Smithfield or Westphalian ham. Arrange overlapping thin slices of papaya over the ham and sprinkle with freshly ground black pepper to taste. Serve with a wedge of lime to squeeze over the fruit. Makes 1.

Braunschweiger, Bacon, and Tomato Sandwich

Spread a slice of rye bread with butter. Cover with a thick layer of Braunschweiger or liver sausage. Arrange rings of mild white onion over the Braunschweiger. Place 2 strips of crisp bacon lengthwise over the sandwich and top with 2 slices of tomato. Place overlapping thin slices of hard-cooked egg over the tomato and spoon Thousand Island Dressing (page 262) over the egg. Makes 1.

Liver Pâté and Ham Double-Deckers

6 square slices rye or pumpernickel bread	Mayonnaise
Butter	6 thin slices Danish cooked ham
3 ounces liver pâté	3 thin slices unpeeled cucumber, halved
6 small leaves Boston lettuce	3 cherry tomatoes, halved

Spread 3 of the bread slices with butter. Spread 1 ounce liver pâté on each bread slice and cover with a small lettuce leaf. Butter the remaining 3 bread slices and place them, buttered sides down, over the sandwiches. Spread the tops of the bread slices with mayonnaise and arrange 2 slices of ham on each sandwich. Garnish each sandwich with 1 of the remaining lettuce leaves, a halved cucumber slice, and a halved cherry tomato. To serve, cut each sandwich in half diagonally. Makes 3.

Cartwheel Hero Sandwiches

These platter-size sandwiches are an off-the-beaten path version of an established favorite.

1 round loaf Italian or rye bread
(8 or 9 inches in diameter)
2 recipes Parmesan Butter (page 188)
¼ cup finely chopped fresh basil (optional)
2 teaspoons grated onion
4 ounces Genoa-style salami, thinly sliced
4 ounces prosciutto or West-phalian ham, thinly sliced
4 ounces mortadella, thinly sliced
8 ounces imported provolone or Swiss cheese, thinly sliced

4 hard-cooked eggs, sliced
1 jar (6 ounces) marinated arti-choke hearts, drained (optional)
12 peperoncini (bottled hot Italian peppers) or sweet cherry peppers, drained
2 small tomatoes, cut into wedges
16 pitted black or green olives
Cucumber slices
Thinly sliced red onion rings (optional)

With a sharp knife trim off the top and bottom crusts from the bread (reserve for another use). Cut the bread into 4 even horizontal slices. Place each slice of bread on a round serving platter. Blend together well the Parmesan Butter, basil (if used), and onion and spread over each slice of bread. Arrange in pie-shaped sections on each slice a selection of meats, cheese, egg slices, marinated artichoke hearts (if used), and *peperoncini* or sweet cherry peppers. Garnish with the tomato wedges, olives, cucumber slices, and onion rings, if used. To serve, cut into wedges like a pie. Makes 4.

VARIATIONS:

Substitute Oregano Butter (page 184) for the Parmesan Butter and omit the basil.

Two jars (4 ounces each) marinated mushrooms, drained, may be substituted for the marinated artichoke hearts.

Cream Cheese, Date, and Walnut Sandwich

Spread a slice of raisin bread or whole wheat bread with a thick layer of Cream Cheese, Date, and Walnut Filling (page 209). Garnish with wedges of red apple and sprinkle with cinnamon. Makes 1.

Hot Open-Faced Sandwiches

Filled Croustades

Even a simple entrée with a sauce can take on elegance when served in buttery toasted bread cases.

Trim the crusts from a loaf of day-old unsliced white bread, then cut crosswise into 2½-inch-thick slices. Trim the slices into 2½-inch cubes. Carefully hollow out each cube, leaving a shell ½ inch thick. Cut off the sharp edges of the corners, if desired. Brush all the surfaces except the undersides with melted butter and arrange the *croustades* on an ungreased baking sheet. Bake in a preheated 400° F. oven about 12 minutes or until golden brown. Fill the croustades with any of the cream fillings on pages 213 to 215 and serve at once. Makes 8 servings.

Ratatouille and Egg Sandwiches

This will dazzle your tongue and speak to your soul.

Brush thick slices of toasted French bread with olive oil. Cover each with a few spoonfuls of hot Ratatouille (page 220). Top with a poached or fried egg and sprinkle it with freshly grated Parmesan or Romano cheese. Serve at once.

VARIATIONS:

Substitute Peperonata (page 221) for the Ratatouille.

Substitute warmed pita bread for the French bread. Slit each pita one-third of the way around to make a pocket. Fill it with hot Ratatouille and a fried egg, or fill it with cold Ratatouille or Peperonata and a cold plain omelet.

Eggs Benedict

An American classic and a popular choice for brunch. Fresh asparagus can make a splendid accompaniment.

Sauté 6 thin slices cooked ham or Canadian bacon in butter. Place each on a toasted and buttered English muffin half and top with a poached egg. Cover with Hollandaise Sauce (page 263) and, if desired, garnish with a truffle slice. Serve at once. Makes 6 servings.

Note: If you like, place a serving of cooked fresh asparagus alongside each sandwich and spoon some Hollandaise Sauce over it as well.

Bacon and Egg Sandwiches

Mexico provides the inspiration for these tempting sandwiches.

2 English muffins, split in half and toasted	4 eggs
½ recipe Guacamole (page 265)	1 tablespoon water
8 slices bacon, cooked crisp and crumbled	1 tablespoon butter
	12 thin strips Cheddar, Monterey Jack, or Swiss cheese

Arrange the toasted English muffin halves on an ungreased baking sheet. Spread each with one-fourth of the Guacamole, then sprinkle with one-fourth of the crumbled bacon. Set aside.

In a medium-sized bowl beat the eggs and water with a fork or whisk until well mixed. In a heavy skillet melt the butter over moderate heat. Add the eggs and cook over medium-low heat, stirring constantly until the eggs are set. Remove from the heat and spoon one-fourth of the eggs over each sandwich. Place 3 strips of cheese crosswise on top of each. Broil just until the cheese melts. Serve at once. Makes 4.

Creole Ham and Egg Loaf

Leftover ham makes a fresh debut in this savory loaf, equally appropriate for brunch, lunch, or supper.

2 tablespoons butter or olive oil
½ cup finely chopped onion
⅓ cup finely chopped green pepper
1 medium garlic clove, finely chopped
2 large, ripe tomatoes, peeled, seeded, and finely chopped
1 teaspoon finely chopped fresh basil, or ¼ teaspoon crushed dried basil

¼ teaspoon crushed dried oregano or thyme
Salt and freshly ground pepper to taste
1 loaf French bread (about 15 inches long)
5 eggs, well beaten
¾ cup diced cooked ham
¼ cup freshly grated Parmesan or Swiss cheese

In a heavy saucepan melt the butter or oil over moderate heat. Add the onion, green pepper, and garlic and sauté until golden, stirring frequently. Add the tomatoes, basil, oregano or thyme, and salt and pepper. Cover and cook 5 minutes. Uncover and cook 5 minutes, stirring frequently. Remove from the heat and set aside.

Cut a ½-inch-thick slice from the top of the bread. Remove most of the soft center, leaving about a ½-inch shell. Whirl enough of the soft bread in an electric blender to make 1 cup bread crumbs and reserve. (Save the remaining soft bread for another use.)

Spoon the tomato mixture evenly over the bottom of the bread shell. Mix together the eggs, additional salt, reserved bread crumbs, and ham. Turn the mixture into the bread shell. Sprinkle the cheese evenly over the top. Bake in a preheated 350° F. oven about 30 minutes or until the eggs are set. Cut crosswise into thick slices and serve at once. Makes 6 servings.

Note: If desired, you may cut the top bread slice diagonally into strips, toast them in the oven, and brush them lightly with melted butter. Use 3 of the strips to garnish the loaf, laying them across the top, about 2 inches apart. Serve the remaining strips on the side.

VARIATION:

Substitute ¾ cup diced cooked lobster meat or shrimp for the ham.

Puffed Shrimp and Cheese Sandwiches

A four-star recipe.

1 tablespoon butter	¼ teaspoon dry mustard
3 scallions, thinly sliced, including 2 inches of the green tops	¼ teaspoon dill weed
3 medium mushrooms, sliced	6 ounces diced cooked shrimp
2 eggs, separated	6 thin slices white, whole wheat, or rye bread, toasted
1½ cups shredded Gruyére or Swiss cheese	Paprika

In a small, heavy saucepan melt the butter over moderate heat. Add the scallions and mushrooms and sauté until golden and soft, stirring frequently. Remove from the heat. Stir in the egg yolks, cheese, dry mustard, dill weed, and shrimp. Beat the egg whites until stiff and fold into the shrimp mixture. Spread an equal portion of the mixture on one side of each toasted bread slice. Sprinkle evenly with the paprika and arrange on an ungreased baking sheet. Bake, uncovered, in a preheated 375° F. oven about 15 minutes, or until puffy. Serve hot or cold. Makes 6.

Scandinavian Curried Crabmeat and Sausage Sandwiches

Any Norseman will compliment you on these.

Butter	2 tablespoons brandy
½ cup finely chopped onion	8 ounces cooked crabmeat, picked over to remove any pieces of shell
2 tablespoons all-purpose flour	
1 cup half-and-half	4 slices bacon
1 teaspoon curry powder or to taste	1 can (4 ounces) Danish cocktail sausages
Salt and freshly ground pepper to taste	8 slices French bread

In a small saucepan melt 2 tablespoons butter over low heat. Add the onion and sauté until soft but not browned, stirring frequently. Add the flour and cook 1 or 2 minutes, stirring constantly. Gradually add the half-and-half, stirring, until the mixture is very thick and smooth. Stir in the curry powder and salt and pepper and simmer gently 1 minute. Add the brandy and crabmeat and simmer a few minutes. Remove from the heat. Taste and adjust the seasoning and keep warm.

Cut each slice of bacon crosswise into 4 equal pieces. Wrap a piece of bacon around each sausage and fasten with a food pick. Sauté the sausages in a heavy skillet without added fat until the bacon is browned and crisp, turning frequently. Remove from the heat and drain on paper towels. Remove the food picks.

Butter the bread slices and arrange on a heated serving platter. Spoon the crabmeat and its sauce over the bread, and top with the sausages. Serve at once. Makes 4 servings.

Chicken and Asparagus Divan Sandwiches

Easy enough for family, glamorous enough for company.

2 small chicken breasts, skinned, halved, boned, and flattened slightly
Butter
¼ cup thinly sliced scallions, including 2 inches of the green tops
2 tablespoons all-purpose flour
1 cup half-and-half

¼ cup dry white wine
Salt and freshly ground pepper to taste
¼ cup grated Swiss cheese
1 pound fresh asparagus
⅓ cup freshly grated Parmesan cheese
4 slices French bread

Wipe the chicken breasts with damp paper towels. In a heavy skillet melt 3 tablespoons butter over moderate heat. Add the chicken breasts and sauté about 4 minutes on each side, or until tender. Remove from the heat and keep warm.

In a small saucepan melt 3 tablespoons butter over low heat. Add the scallions and sauté 1 minute, stirring frequently. Add the flour and cook 1 or 2 minutes, stirring constantly. Gradually add the half-and-half and the wine, stirring, until the mixture comes to a boil and is thick and smooth. Season with the salt and pepper and simmer gently 2 or 3 minutes. Remove from the heat and stir in the grated Swiss cheese until it melts. Taste and adjust the seasoning. Keep warm.

Snap off the tough ends of the asparagus. With a vegetable parer, scrape the skin and scales from the lower part of the stalks. Tie the asparagus in bundles and drop them into a large saucepan of rapidly boiling salted water. Boil, uncovered, 10 to 12 minutes or until just tender. Drain the asparagus thoroughly. Cut and discard the strings.

Toast and butter the bread slices. Arrange them in the bottom of a buttered shallow baking dish. Cover each bread slice with half a sautéed chicken breast. Arrange the asparagus over the chicken breasts, dividing equally. Spoon the sauce evenly over the asparagus and sprinkle with the Parmesan cheese. Bake in a preheated 350° F. oven about 15 minutes or until the sauce is bubbly. Place under the broiler about 1 minute or so to brown the tops. Makes 4 servings.

VARIATION:

Eight ounces each asparagus, cooked as above, and mushrooms, sliced and sautéed in butter, may be substituted for the asparagus.

Turkey Sandwiches

The once-starring turkey makes a brilliant comeback in this role.

3 tablespoons butter	Salt and freshly ground pepper to
2 tablespoons flour	taste
1 cup hot milk	2 slices white bread, toasted
2 scallions, thinly sliced (include 2	4 slices bacon, cooked crisp
inches of the green tops)	2 slices cooked turkey breast
4 medium mushrooms, thinly sliced	2 tablespoons freshly grated
2 tablespoons dry white wine	Parmesan cheese

In a saucepan melt 2 tablespoons of the butter over low heat. Add the flour and cook about 2 minutes, stirring constantly. Gradually add the milk, stirring until the sauce is smooth and thickened. Simmer about 5 minutes, stirring occasionally.

Meanwhile, in a small, heavy skillet melt the remaining 1 tablespoon butter over moderate heat. Add the scallions and mushrooms and sauté until golden brown, stirring frequently. Stir in the hot sauce and wine. Season with the salt and pepper.

Arrange the bread slices in the bottom of a shallow baking dish. Cover with the bacon and turkey slices. Spoon the sauce evenly over the sandwiches. Sprinkle with the Parmesan cheese. Bake in a preheated 425° F. oven 5 to 6 minutes or until the top is lightly browned. Serve at once. Makes 2.

Quail Sandwiches with Cherry Sauce

What husband, when presented with this, would dare to ask his wife, "What's new?"

4 oven-ready quail, 6 ounces each
Butter
1 cup beef broth
½ cup currant jelly
½ cup port wine
1½ tablespoons freshly squeezed
  and strained lemon juice

Grated rind of ½ orange
½ cup sour cherries, pitted
4 slices French bread, each about
  ½ inch thick

Pat the quail completely dry inside and out with paper towels. In a heavy skillet melt 6 tablespoons butter over moderate heat. Add the quail and brown, turning frequently until the birds color evenly on all sides. Transfer the quail to a shallow roasting pan and roast, uncovered, in a preheated 400° F. oven about 20 minutes or until tender, basting frequently with the butter in which the birds were browned.

Meanwhile, in a small saucepan combine the broth, jelly, wine, lemon juice, and orange rind. Cover and simmer 20 minutes. Add the cherries and simmer 5 minutes. Remove from the heat and keep warm.

Butter the bread slices on both sides and toast them in a heavy skillet or griddle over moderate heat on both sides until golden. Transfer each toasted bread slice to a heated individual plate. Bone each quail and arrange it over a bread slice. Spoon the hot cherry sauce over the quail. Serve at once. Makes 4 servings.

Instead of roasting the quail, you may bone and flatten the birds, then sauté in butter until tender and lightly browned on both sides.

Filled Popovers

Golden and puffy with almost hollow insides, these big, crisp popovers make ideal receptacles for a wide variety of delicious fillings. For all their impressive appearance, they are actually quite simple to prepare.

Popovers (below)
Any of the cream fillings on pages 213 to 215

Slit the popovers open lengthwise while still warm. Remove and discard any uncooked dough. Arrange each popover on a plate and divide the filling of your choice among the popovers. Serve at once. Makes 6 servings.

VARIATION:

Allow the popovers to cool, then slit them open lengthwise in half. Remove and discard any uncooked dough. Line the insides with soft-leafed lettuce. Arrange each popover on a plate and divide either of the following salads among the popovers, mounding it in each half: Curried Shellfish Salad (page 218) or Shrimp, Asparagus, and Egg Salad (page 217).

Note: For Filled Dessert Popovers please see page 43.

Popovers

2 large eggs
1 cup unsifted all-purpose flour
1 cup milk
¼ teaspoon salt

1 tablespoon corn oil, or 1 tablespoon butter, melted and cooled
Melted butter for brushing muffin or popover cups

Combine the eggs, flour, milk, salt, and corn oil or butter in the container of an electric blender and blend until smooth. (Or, combine the ingredients in a mixing bowl and beat with an electric mixer until smooth.) Generously butter 6 muffin or popover cups, each 2½ to 3 inches in diameter, or use six 6-ounce custard cups. Divide the batter among the buttered cups. Set the custard cups on a preheated baking sheet. Bake the popovers in a preheated 400° F. oven (without peeking!) about 45 minutes or until richly browned and puffed. Remove the popovers from the oven and pierce each one in several places with a knife. Bake the popovers 5 minutes more. Remove the popovers from the cups. Use them while hot, or allow them to cool first on a wire rack. Makes 6.

Navajo Fry Bread Tostadas

Two favorite Navajo foods, fry bread and green chili stew, are combined in this Southwestern version of the *tostada*.

2 tablespoons corn oil or flavorless vegetable oil

1½ pounds boneless beef round steak, trimmed of excess fat and cut into ½-inch cubes

1 tablespoon all-purpose flour

2 cups water

2 large, ripe tomatoes, peeled, seeded, and finely chopped

2 medium garlic cloves, finely chopped

1 can (7 ounces) diced green chilies

Salt to taste

6 Navajo Fry Breads (page 251)

3 cups shredded romaine or iceberg lettuce

1½ cups shredded Cheddar, Monterey Jack, or Muenster cheese

1 large, ripe avocado, peeled and sliced

½ cup sour cream or unflavored yogurt

½ cup thinly sliced scallions, including 2 inches of the green tops

In a large, heavy saucepan or casserole heat the oil over medium-high heat. Add the meat and cook, stirring frequently, until lightly browned. Stir in the flour. Add the water, tomatoes, and garlic. Reduce the heat to low, cover, and simmer, stirring now and then, about 1 hour or until the meat is tender. Stir in the chilies, cover, and simmer 30 minutes. Season with the salt. When done, most of the liquid in the pan should have been absorbed. If not, reduce it by boiling fast, uncovered.

To serve, place each Navajo Fry Bread on an individual plate. Pass the hot stew and remaining ingredients at the table. To eat, cover the bread with the shredded lettuce, spoon the stew over the lettuce, and sprinkle with the shredded cheese. Top with the avocado slices and a dollop of sour cream or yogurt. Garnish with the scallions. Makes 6 servings.

Croque Madame

One of the most deservedly popular French sandwiches.

1 loaf French bread (about 14 inches long)
1 tablespoon instant-blending flour, such as Gold Medal Wondra
⅓ cup beer
1 tablespoon Cognac
1 egg

1 cup grated Swiss cheese
Salt, freshly ground pepper, and cayenne pepper to taste
3 tablespoons butter, melted
4 thin slices cooked ham (approximately)

Cut 3 lengthwise slices, each about ¾ inch thick, from the bread (reserve the remaining bread for another use). Put the slices on an ungreased baking sheet and place in a preheated 350° F. oven about 15 minutes or until the bread is crisp and golden.

Place the flour in a mixing bowl and gradually beat in the beer, then the Cognac and egg. Stir in the cheese, salt, pepper, and cayenne pepper. Brush the top of each slice of bread with the melted butter and cover with the ham slices. Spoon the cheese mixture over the sandwiches, covering them completely.

Bake the sandwiches in a preheated 450° F. oven about 15 minutes, or until the cheese topping has puffed and nicely browned. Cut each bread slice crosswise into 4 pieces and serve at once. Makes 12 servings.

Note: For cocktail appetizers, cut each slice of bread in half lengthwise, then crosswise into 12 pieces.

French Toast, Ham, and Pineapple Double-Deckers

A sure way to get the family out of bed on Sunday morning! A good choice, too, for late Sunday supper.

4 large slices sourdough French bread	¼ teaspoon salt or to taste
2 large, thin slices baked ham	4 tablespoons butter
2 large slices Swiss cheese	2 round slices fresh or canned pineapple
2 eggs	2 tablespoons brown sugar
½ cup half-and-half	Raspberry or currant jelly

Assemble each sandwich as follows: Cover 1 slice bread with 1 slice ham. Place 1 slice cheese over the ham, then top with another bread slice. Set both sandwiches aside.

In a bowl beat the eggs lightly, then blend in the half-and-half and salt. Pour into a shallow dish. Carefully dip each sandwich on both sides in the egg mixture. In a large, heavy skillet melt 3 tablespoons of the butter over moderate heat. Add the sandwiches and sauté slowly until the undersides are lightly browned. Turn carefully with a large spatula and brown the other sides. Remove from the heat and keep warm.

In a small skillet melt the remaining 1 tablespoon butter over moderate heat. Dip the pineapple slices in the brown sugar and sauté on both sides in the butter until glazed.

Place the sandwiches on heated individual plates and top each with a glazed pineapple slice. Fill the centers of the pineapple rounds with the jelly and serve immediately. Makes 2.

Scandinavian-Style Apple and Bacon Sandwiches

Butter	2 multi-grain English muffins, split in half
3 medium, tart apples, peeled, cored, and thickly sliced	4 slices bacon, cut in half crosswise and cooked crisp
3 tablespoons sugar or to taste	Honey

In a large, heavy skillet melt 2 tablespoons butter over moderate heat. Add the apple slices, sprinkle them with the sugar, and sauté on both sides until golden brown and glazed, adding more butter if necessary. Toast and butter the English muffins. Arrange the sautéed apple slices on the muffin halves, dividing equally. Top with the bacon slices, using 2 halves per sandwich. Drizzle honey over all and serve at once. Makes 4 sandwiches.

VARIATION:

Apple and Sausage Sandwiches

Substitute 4 small pork sausages for the bacon. Split them in half lengthwise and sauté in a heavy skillet until browned and tender, turning frequently and pouring off the fat as it accumulates in the pan. Drain the sausages on paper towels and proceed as above.

Baked Ground Beef Sandwiches

4 rectangular crusty French or sourdough rolls (3 by 5 inches)	1 medium garlic clove, finely chopped
Butter, at room temperature	1 pound lean ground beef
3 scallions, including 2 inches of the green tops, finely chopped	6 ounces Swiss or mozzarella cheese, shredded
¼ pound mushrooms, finely chopped	Salt and freshly ground black pepper to taste

Cut the rolls in half lengthwise. Spread the cut surfaces with butter. Toast until golden brown. Set aside.

In a large, heavy skillet melt 3 tablespoons butter over moderate heat. Add the scallions, mushrooms, and garlic and sauté just until the vegetables are coated with butter, not browned. Remove from the heat and allow to cool. Add the ground beef, cheese, and salt and pepper to the skillet and mix well. Spread the meat mixture on the toasted roll halves, covering them completely. Arrange them on an ungreased baking sheet and bake in a preheated 450° F. oven about 20 minutes, or until nicely browned. Serve at once. Makes 8.

Opera Sandwiches Finlandia

An almost limitless variety of unusual sandwiches are offered in Finnish cafés. Sandwiches are also eaten as part of the first course of a meal and may form the major part of breakfast or lunch. In its country of origin, this Scandinavian version of the hamburger is called *oopera-voileipä* (opera sandwich), but don't ask why. As you cut through the sandwich with a knife and fork, the still-liquid egg yolks furnish a natural sauce for every bite of succulent meat and buttered toast.

2 pounds very lean ground beef
1 medium onion, very finely
  chopped
Salt and freshly ground pepper to
  taste
Butter
6 slices French bread, about ¾ inch
  thick

6 eggs
Boston lettuce leaves
Tomato slices
Whole scallions, trimmed
Dill gherkins

In a large bowl combine the beef, onion, and salt and pepper, and mix until the ingredients are well blended. Divide the mixture into 6 equal parts and form each into an oval patty. In a large, heavy skillet melt 2 tablespoons butter over moderate heat. Add the patties and sauté on both sides until the outsides are browned but the centers are still pink. Remove from the heat and keep warm.

Butter the bread slices on both sides. Toast them on both sides in a large, heavy skillet or on a griddle until golden. Remove from the skillet or griddle and keep warm. Add the eggs and fry until the whites are set but the yolks are still soft, adding a little butter if necessary.

Put the toasted bread slices on heated individual plates. Place a cooked meat patty on each slice of bread and top with a fried egg. Garnish with the lettuce leaves, tomato slices, scallions, and dill gherkins. Serve at once. Makes 6.

Hamburger Sandwich Formidable

If you want to bring down the house, this Bunyanesque burger should do it.

1 round loaf sourdough French bread (about 10 inches in diameter)
Butter
2½ pounds lean ground beef
1 medium onion, grated
1 large garlic clove, crushed and finely chopped
Salt and freshly ground pepper to taste
Oregano Butter (page 184)

Boston or leaf lettuce leaves
1 mild red onion, thinly sliced and separated into rings
2 large, firm ripe tomatoes, thinly sliced
1 large, ripe avocado, peeled and sliced
8 pitted jumbo-size black olives
½ cup shredded sharp Cheddar or freshly grated Parmesan cheese

With a sharp knife slice the top and bottom crusts from the bread, leaving a center slice about ¾ inch thick (reserve the crusts for another use).

In a large bowl combine the beef, onion, garlic, and salt and pepper and mix until the ingredients are thoroughly blended. Form the mixture into a patty 1 inch larger than the diameter of the center bread slice to allow for shrinkage when the meat cooks. Place the meat patty in a large double-hinged wire grill. Broil over charcoal about 6 minutes or until the underside is browned. Turn over and broil about 6 minutes or until the other side is done. (If you do not have a wire grill, use 2 spatulas to transfer the meat onto a baking sheet. Place a second baking sheet on top and turn the pans over so the cooked side of the hamburger is up. Then slide the meat patty back onto the grill to broil the other side.)

Meanwhile, butter the bread slice and toast it on the grill. Transfer to a wooden board or platter and spread it with the Oregano Butter. Cover with the lettuce leaves and top with the broiled hamburger. Arrange the onion rings on the meat and lay the tomato slices on top. Arrange the avocado slices pinwheel fashion from the center. Garnish with the olives and sprinkle with the cheese. Cut into wedges and serve at once. Makes 8 servings.

Liver, Avocado, and Bacon Sandwich

Even liver skeptics will approve when they sample it cooked in this manner.

In a heavy skillet heat a small amount of butter over moderate heat. Add 1 large slice calf or beef liver, about ⅜ inch thick, and sauté on both sides about 2 minutes, or until the outside is browned but the center is still pink. Season to taste with salt and freshly ground pepper and remove from the heat. Sprinkle the sautéed liver with ½ teaspoon fresh lime juice and place it on a large buttered and oven-toasted slice of Italian or French bread. Arrange 3 slices avocado over the liver and sprinkle lightly with fresh lime juice. Top with 2 slices bacon, cooked crisp and crumbled. Serve at once with lime wedges. Makes 1.

German Chicken Liver and Apple Sandwiches

In Germany, when the main meal occurs at midday, supper is often based on toasted bread, which the Germans call *toastbrot*. Tempting varieties of "toasts," bread topped with many interesting ingredients, are favorites both at home and in cafés.

Dust ¼ pound chicken livers with flour. Sauté on both sides in butter until the outsides are browned but the insides are still slightly pink. Season to taste with salt and freshly ground pepper. Thinly spread 2 slices of toasted wheat, rye, or French bread with currant jelly. Slice the sautéed chicken livers and arrange them over the bread slices. Top with rings of peeled tart apple sautéed in butter. Bake in a preheated 475° F. oven about 5 minutes. Sprinkle with freshly ground pepper and serve at once. Makes 2.

Northern European Tongue and Egg Sandwich

Butter a slice of egg bread and spread it with liver pâté. Cover with a piece of Boston lettuce. Arrange overlapping thin slices of cold cooked tongue over the lettuce. Top with a softly fried egg and half a slice of crisp bacon. Serve at once. Makes 1.

Baked Cherry and Cream Cheese Sandwiches

2 multi-grain English muffins, split
in half and toasted
4 ounces cream cheese or Neufchâtel cheese, at room
temperature

¼ cup red currant jelly
1⅓ cups pitted dark sweet cherries
4 teaspoons chopped blanched
almonds or hazelnuts

Arrange the toasted English muffin halves on an ungreased baking sheet. Spread each half with 2 tablespoons of the cheese. Set aside.

In a small, heavy skillet melt the currant jelly over moderate heat. Add the cherries and heat, turning to glaze all over. Remove from the heat and spoon over the cheese-topped muffin halves, dividing equally. Sprinkle each with 1 teaspoon of the chopped nuts. Bake in a preheated 450° F. oven about 5 minutes. Serve at once. Makes 4.

Baked Banana and Peanut Butter Sandwiches

A "can't miss" sandwich with children of all ages.

2 multi-grain English muffins, split
in half and toasted
4 tablespoons peanut butter or
more

1 large banana
2 tablespoons Seville orange
marmalade

Arrange the toasted English muffin halves on an ungreased baking sheet. Spread each half with 1 tablespoon or more of the peanut butter.

Peel the banana. Cut crosswise into 4 equal pieces, then cut each piece lengthwise in half. In a small, heavy skillet melt the orange marmalade over moderate heat. Add the banana slices and heat, turning to glaze all over. Remove from the heat.

Arrange 2 banana slices on each muffin half. Bake in a preheated 450° F. oven about 5 minutes. Serve at once. Makes 4.

Filled Dessert Sopaipillas

6 Sopaillas (page 252)
3 cups sliced or diced fresh fruit, sweetened to taste (choose any one or more of the following:

strawberries, peaches, bananas, papayas, mangoes, or pineapple)
½ recipe Crème Chantilly (page 209)

Split the *sopaipillas* while still warm, or cool them to room temperature, then split along one side or cut in half. Spoon about ½ cup of the fruit into each sopaipilla and top with 2 or 3 tablespoons of the Crème Chantilly. Serve at once. Makes 6 servings.

Filled Dessert Popovers

Follow the recipe for Filled Dessert Sopaipillas (above), substituting 6 Popovers (page 34) for the sopaipillas. If desired, add 1 teaspoon sugar, ½ teaspoon finely grated orange rind, and ¼ teaspoon freshly grated nutmeg to the batter. Slit the popovers open lengthwise while still warm. Remove and discard any uncooked dough before filling them. Makes 6 servings.

3

Closed Sandwiches

Although we Americans cannot claim to have invented the sandwich, we have undoubtedly given the world all sorts of new versions of it. Our forte is the closed, or bivalve, sandwich, which has become firmly entrenched in our eating habits, reigning supreme over the nation at lunchtime.

Many of the sandwiches in this chapter are particularly good choices for lunch boxes and picnics since they can be made in advance. In fact, some require such preparation and taste better for it.

Cold Closed Sandwiches

Pan Bagna

This well-known Provençal sandwich, sold in the streets of Nice, is enjoyed at lunch, on picnics, and even at breakfast.

1 loaf French bread
½ large garlic clove
¼ cup olive oil
1½ tablespoons red wine vinegar
Salt and freshly ground pepper to taste
1 tablespoon finely chopped fresh basil, or 1½ teaspoons crushed dried basil
2 medium tomatoes, sliced
¼ medium cucumber, peeled, seeded (if seeds are large), and sliced
½ medium red or green bell pepper, seeded, deribbed, and cut into rings
2 scallions, thinly sliced, including 2 inches of the green tops
6 anchovy fillets, well drained
½ cup black olives, sliced
2 hard-cooked eggs, sliced
¼ cup thinly sliced celery
2 tablespoons finely chopped parsley

Halve the bread horizontally. Pull out some of the soft center from both halves (reserve for other uses, if desired), leaving a shell about ½ inch thick. Rub the cut surfaces of both halves with the garlic. In a small bowl beat together the oil, vinegar, and salt and pepper with a fork or whisk until well blended. Drizzle half the dressing over the bottom half of the bread and sprinkle evenly with the basil. Cover with half the tomato slices, followed by the cucumber, pepper rings, scallions, anchovy fillets, olives, eggs, and celery, lightly seasoning each layer with salt and pepper. Arrange the remaining tomato slices on top and sprinkle evenly with the parsley. Drizzle the remaining dressing over all. Cover with the top half of the loaf. Wrap the sandwich tightly in aluminum foil and press it down with a heavy board or weight for 2 to 3 hours. Unwrap the sandwich, cut it crosswise into 4 equal portions, and serve. Makes 4 servings.

Lavash Spirals

In the Caucasus some typically Armenian fillings for *lavash* sandwiches would include such local favorites as white goat's cheese and fresh mint leaves, hard-cooked eggs and fresh tarragon, and *shashlik* of ground or cubed lamb. But filling possibilities for this versatile bread are diverse. Here is a lavash sandwich that departs completely from tradition. Serve these spirals as snacks, with drinks, or as an accompaniment to soup or salad for a light meal.

1 round homemade Lavash (page 246) or commercial Armenian cracker bread	4 ounces thinly sliced smoked salmon
Cream Cheese and Avocado Filling (page 194)	½ cup watercress leaves 1 tablespoon finely chopped fresh dill

Sprinkle the lavash lightly with water (too much will make it soggy). Wrap the dampened bread in a kitchen towel and set aside to absorb the water and soften. When the lavash has become pliable, spread it with the Cream Cheese and Avocado Filling. Top with the smoked salmon slices and scatter the watercress leaves and dill over all. Roll up tightly like a jelly roll. Cover with a damp kitchen towel, wrap, and chill 1 to 2 hours.

To serve, with a serrated knife cut the sandwich roll into 1-inch-thick slices. Makes about 6 servings.

VARIATIONS:

Substitute ⅓ pound very thinly sliced cold, tender rare roast beef for the smoked salmon. Omit the dill.

Substitute Persian Yogurt Cheese Filling (page 195) or Caucasian Walnut, Cheese, and Herb Filling (page 197) for the Cream Cheese and Avocado Filling and ⅓ cup fresh mint leaves for the watercress leaves. Omit the smoked salmon and dill.

Salad-Stuffed Rolls

Remember these when it's time to pack a picnic and head for the great outdoors.

4 large hard rolls   **Curried Shellfish Salad (page 218),**
                                or Salade Provençale (page 218)

Cut each roll in half lengthwise. Remove the soft inside (save for another use), leaving a ½-inch shell. Spoon the salad into the shells, dividing equally. Put the stuffed rolls together, wrap each one in aluminum foil, and refrigerate until serving time. Makes 4.

VARIATIONS:

Line the hollowed rolls with leaf lettuce before filling them with the salad.

Instead of splitting the rolls lengthwise, cut off a lid from each roll and reserve. Scoop out the soft inside and fill with the salad. Replace the lid, then wrap and refrigerate as above. If desired, brush the interiors of the rolls with melted butter and toast the rolls in a pre-heated 300° F. oven about 15 minutes before filling them with the salad.

A round loaf of Italian bread can also be prepared in this same manner. To serve, cut in wedges like a pie.

Beef Sandwiches with Avocado and Cheese

⅓ cup olive oil

2 tablespoons red wine vinegar

2 tablespoons freshly squeezed and strained lemon juice

1 small mild red or white onion, finely chopped

1 medium garlic clove, finely chopped

½ teaspoon dry mustard

¾ teaspoon salt

Freshly ground black pepper to taste

1 pound flank steak (trimmed of fat) or very tender lean roasted, boiled, or braised beef

12 slices whole grain bread, lightly toasted

Cream Cheese, Gorgonzola, and Avocado Filling (page 195)

12 slices firm ripe tomato

12 slices Gruyère or Swiss Cheese (about 4 ounces)

In a shallow dish mix together the oil, vinegar, lemon juice, onion, garlic, mustard, salt, and pepper. Set aside.

If using flank steak, broil it 3 to 4 inches from the heat, allowing 6 to 8 minutes on each side for rare meat. Transfer the meat to a carving board and slice across the grain into thin strips. If using roasted, boiled, or braised beef, cut it into thin slices. Add the meat to the marinade in the dish, turning the pieces to coat them thoroughly with the mixture. Cover and chill several hours or overnight.

To assemble each sandwich, spread 6 slices of bread with an equal amount of the filling. Layer with slices of tomato, marinated beef, Gruyère or Swiss cheese, and the remaining 6 bread slices. Cut each sandwich in half and serve. Makes 6.

Ham and Ratatouille Sandwich

Split a 5- to 6-inch-long rectangular crusty French roll without cutting all the way through, leaving one edge as a hinge. Spread the roll open. Pull out most of the soft inside and reserve for another use.

Fill the bottom half with thin slices of prosciutto, Smithfield, or Westphalian ham. Top with a few spoonfuls of cold Ratatouille (page 220). Cover with the top half of the roll and serve. Makes 1.

VARIATION:

This sandwich is equally delicious made with 1 pita bread, cut crosswise in half and lightly toasted.

Swiss Salad Sandwich

Cut an onion roll in half lengthwise and spread it with butter. Cover the bottom half with an assortment of thinly sliced cold meats such as prosciutto or Westphalian ham, Italian salami, and mortadella and top with about 2 tablespoons of Swiss Cheese and Egg Salad (page 217). Add the top half of the roll and serve with *cornichons* (French sour gherkins, available at specialty shops and some supermarkets), slices of tomato, and rings of green pepper on the side. Makes 1.

Ham, Smoked Turkey, and Smoked Cheese Sandwich

Cut a French roll in half lengthwise. Spread each half with Dijon-style mustard. Cover the bottom half with thin slices of smoked turkey, Westphalian ham, and smoked Cheddar or Edam cheese. Place slices of pimento over the cheese and cover with the top half of the roll. Makes 1.

Hero Sandwiches

No sandwich repertoire would be complete without the hero, alias submarine, sub, torpedo, hoagy, poor boy, or grinder.

4 tablespoons olive oil
2 tablespoons red wine vinegar
2 whole pimentos, drained
8 thinly sliced red onion rings
¼ teaspoon crushed dried basil
¼ teaspoon crushed dried oregano
Salt and freshly ground pepper to taste
Crushed red pepper (pizza pepper) to taste (optional)

1 cup shredded romaine or iceberg lettuce
2 hero or large French rolls
4 ounces imported provolone or Taleggio cheese, very thinly sliced
4 ounces Genoa-style salami, very thinly sliced
2 ounces prosciutto or mortadella, very thinly sliced

In a small bowl combine 2½ tablespoons of the oil and 1½ tablespoons of the vinegar and mix until blended. Add the pimentos and onion rings, turn to coat them thoroughly with the mixture, and set aside to marinate. In a mixing bowl combine the remaining 1½ tablespoons oil and ½ tablespoon vinegar, basil, oregano, salt and pepper, and crushed red pepper, if used, and mix until blended. Toss the lettuce with the dressing and set aside.

Split the rolls without cutting them all the way through, leaving one edge of the bread as a hinge. Spread the rolls open. Cover the bottom halves of the rolls with the cheese, salami, and prosciutto or mortadella, dividing equally. Pile half the lettuce over each. Split the marinated pimentos and arrange 1 pimento and 4 onion rings over each sandwich. Close the sandwiches and serve. Makes 2.

VARIATION:

Omit the lettuce. Substitute rings of broiled and peeled green pepper for the pimentos. Sprinkle the cut surfaces of the bread with the dressing in the mixing bowl. Cover the bottom slice of each roll with a layer of tomato slices, then follow with the cheese, cold cuts, green pepper, and onion.

Antipasto Sandwiches

Italian Vegetable Relish (page 231)
1 can (6½ ounces) water-packed
   tuna, drained and broken into
   chunks
2 ounces Genoa-style salami, cut in
   thin strips

2 ounces Fontina or Muenster
   cheese, finely diced
6 rectangular crusty Italian or
   French rolls, each 5 to 6 inches
   long

Prepare and chill the relish as directed in the recipe. Drain and reserve the cooking liquid. Cut the vegetables into small pieces. In a large bowl combine the vegetables with the tuna, salami, cheese, and enough of the reserved liquid to moisten the ingredients. Toss gently but thoroughly. Taste and adjust the seasoning, cover, and chill.

Split the rolls without cutting all the way through, leaving one edge as a hinge. Spread them open. Pull out the soft insides (save for another use), leaving a ½-inch shell. Fill the bottom halves of the rolls with the antipasto mixture, mounding it. Cover with the top halves and serve. Makes 6.

VARIATION:

Three pita breads, halved crosswise and lightly toasted, may be substituted for the rolls.

Dutch Deli Broodjes

Broodjes are sandwiches of small, soft buttered rolls filled with thick layers of meat, cheese, fish, or salad. A great variety of broodjes are featured in Amsterdam sandwich shops known as *broodjeswinkels,* where they are traditionally washed down with milk, although Dutch beer makes an equally appropriate accompaniment.

Cut soft plain or sesame dinner rolls in half lengthwise. Spread the cut surfaces generously with butter or Mustard Butter (page 185). Cover the bottom half of each roll with a piece of Boston lettuce and top with several layers of very thinly sliced Edam, Gouda, or Swiss cheese and cold meats such as ham, mortadella, and liver sausage. Allow 2 or 3 per person.

VARIATION:

Salmon Salad Broodjes

Substitute Salmon Salad (page 219) for the cheese and cold meats, allowing about ¼ cup salad for each sandwich. Mound each portion in a Boston or Bibb lettuce cup.

Note: You can serve these sandwiches buffet style. Arrange the cheese and cold meats on a serving platter and the salmon salad, if used, scooped into lettuce leaves.

Torta

This could be described as a Mexican hero sandwich.

Split a rectangular crusty roll without cutting all the way through, leaving one edge as a hinge. Spread the roll open. Pull out most of the soft inside and reserve for another use. Fill the bottom half with about 2 tablespoons of Frijoles Refritos (page 221) and top with slices of *serrano, jalapeño,* or green chilies, thin slices of cold cooked pork, sliced meat loaf, or shredded chicken, slices of avocado and tomato, shredded romaine lettuce, slices of Cheddar, Monterey Jack, or Muenster cheese, and sour cream. Cover with the top half of the roll and serve. Makes 1.

Note: In Mexico oval-shaped *teleras* would be used instead of French rolls, and Chihuahua or Manchego cheese instead of the cheeses suggested above.

Swiss Meat Loaf Sandwich with Peperonata

Here is a happy marriage of Swiss and Italian tastes.

Split a 5- to 6-inch-long rectangular crusty Italian or French roll without cutting all the way through, leaving one edge as a hinge.

Spread the roll open. Pull out some of the soft inside and reserve for another use. Fill the bottom half with thin slices of cold Swiss Meat Loaf (page 222). Top with a few spoonfuls of cold Peperonata (page 221). Cover with the top half of the roll and serve. Makes 1.

VARIATIONS:

Thin slices of Italian sausages or cold cuts such as prosciutto or mortadella may be substituted for the meat loaf.

Substitute 1 pita bread, cut crosswise in half and lightly toasted, for the roll.

Avocado, Tomato, and Bacon Sandwiches

Cut a Kaiser roll or onion roll in half lengthwise. Spread each half generously with Curried Cream Cheese and Olive Filling (page 192). Cover the bottom half with a piece of Boston or leaf lettuce and top with 2 or 3 slices of ripe tomato. Dip 2 or 3 peeled avocado slices in freshly squeezed and strained lemon juice and arrange them over the tomato slices. Place 2 strips crisp bacon over the avocado. Cover with the top half of the roll and serve. Makes 1.

Filled Brioches

Memories are made of recipes like this one.

1 tablespoon butter
4 ounces mushrooms, finely
 chopped
2 scallions, finely chopped,
 including 2 inches of the green
 tops
¼ teaspoon crushed dried tarragon
 or to taste

2 tablespoons Madeira or sherry
Salt and freshly ground pepper
 to taste
½ recipe Chicken Liver Pâté (page
 205)
6 small Brioches à Tête (page 240)
 or small store-bought brioches

In a small, heavy skillet melt the butter over medium-high heat. Add the mushrooms and scallions and sauté until golden brown, stirring frequently. Add the tarragon and Madeira or sherry, cover, and simmer 1 minute. Uncover, increase the heat to high, and cook until the liquid in the skillet has evaporated. Season with the salt and pepper and remove from the heat. Transfer the contents of the skillet to a bowl and let cool. Add the Chicken Liver Pâté and mix until well blended. Taste and adjust the seasoning.

Cut the top off each brioche and reserve. With a small, sharp knife hollow out the inside, leaving a ½- to ¾-inch-thick shell. Fill each brioche shell with the pâté mixture and cover with the reserved top. Wrap each brioche in aluminum foil or clear plastic wrap and chill several hours before serving. Makes 6.

VARIATION:

Substitute any of the cream fillings on pages 213 to 215 for the pâté mixture above. Replace the tops of the brioches. Arrange the filled brioches on a baking sheet and bake in a preheated 350° F. oven a few minutes until heated. Serve at once. (Stale brioches or brioche shells that have been dried a few minutes in a 350° F. oven work best for this variation.)

Lefse Sandwich

Spread soft *Lefse* (page 244) with sour cream and then with lingonberry or other fruit preserves. Roll up and garnish with a dollop of additional sour cream topped with a spoonful of preserves. Serve as a dessert or snack to eat with a fork. Or serve as a brunch entrée accompanied with crisp bacon or sautéed ham slices. Makes 1.

VARIATION:

Lefse are also good spread with butter and wrapped around strips of Norwegian Gjetost or other cheese to eat out of hand.

Caribbean Brioche Sandwiches

How to become a hedonist in one easy lesson.

4 small Brioches à Tête (page 240) or small store-bought brioches
1 cup freshly squeezed and strained orange juice
⅓ cup sugar

2 tablespoons Grand Marnier
Pineapple Crème Chantilly (page 210)
2 slices cocktail orange in syrup, drained and very finely chopped

Cut the top off each brioche and reserve. With a small, sharp knife hollow out the inside, leaving a shell about ½ inch thick. Set aside.

In a heavy saucepan combine the orange juice and sugar and bring to a boil over high heat, stirring to dissolve the sugar. Reduce the heat and simmer 1 minute. Add the Grand Marnier, remove from the heat, and let cool slightly. Place the brioche shells and tops in a bowl. Spoon the syrup over them and allow to marinate in the refrigerator 3 to 4 hours, turning occasionally so that the brioches are saturated but still intact.

Combine the Pineapple Crème Chantilly with the cocktail orange. Remove the brioches from the syrup. Fill the shells with the crème Chantilly mixture and cover with the tops. Spoon a little syrup over each and serve. Makes 4.

Hot Closed Sandwiches

Mozzarella in Carrozza

Trim the crusts from 12 thin slices of Italian or French bread. Cut 6 slices of mozzarella cheese the same size and thickness as the bread and make 6 sandwiches, adding an anchovy fillet to each, if desired. Beat 2 eggs with 1 tablespoon milk and a pinch of salt. Dust each sandwich lightly with flour and dip in the beaten egg mixture. Deep-fry the sandwiches, a few at a time, in hot olive oil until golden brown on both sides. Drain on paper towels and serve at once. Makes 6.

VARIATION:

Substitute very thin slices of prosciutto for the anchovy fillets. Fry the sandwiches in a mixture of hot olive oil and melted butter (use 2 tablespoons oil and 1 tablespoon butter), burning to brown lightly on both sides. Sprinkle with freshly ground pepper, if desired, and serve.

Spinach and Cheese Loaf

Even spinach haters will succumb to the natural charms of this irresistible creation.

1 long, narrow loaf French bread   Spinach and Cheese Filling (page
                                      198)

Cut a lengthwise slit in the underside of the bread. Carefully remove the soft inside, leaving the crust shell intact (reserve the soft bread for other uses). Pack the hollowed loaf with the Spinach and

Cheese Filling and bring the bottom edges together. Wrap the stuffed loaf in aluminum foil and bake in a preheated 400° F. oven 30 minutes or until heated through. Remove from the oven and remove the foil. Allow to cool slightly, then slice and serve warm. Or cool to room temperature, wrap in foil, refrigerate, then slice and serve cold. Makes 6 servings.

Spanish Omelet Loaf

Indispensable to the enjoyment of most Spanish outings, this makes a perfect picnic dish since its advance preparation enables the flavorful and aromatic drippings of the omelet to permeate the bread, thus enhancing the taste of the loaf.

1 large, round loaf French or sourdough French bread (10 to 12 inches in diameter)
4 tablespoons olive oil
2 tablespoons butter
10 ounces serrano, prosciutto, or other lean smoked ham, diced
1 large new potato, cooked, peeled, and thinly sliced
8 ounces mushrooms, thinly sliced
1 medium onion, finely chopped
1 large garlic clove, crushed and finely chopped

1 medium green pepper, seeded, deribbed, and chopped
1 medium red bell pepper, seeded, deribbed, and chopped, or 1 jar (4 ounces) pimentos, drained and chopped
9 eggs
¾ teaspoon salt or to taste
¼ teaspoon freshly ground pepper or to taste
8 ounces Manchego or Swiss cheese, thinly sliced

With a sharp knife split the bread in half lengthwise. Remove most of the soft centers from the bread halves, leaving a 1-inch shell. (Reserve the soft bread for another use.) Brush the cut surfaces with 1 tablespoon of the oil. Reassemble the loaf by placing the 2 halves together. Wrap in aluminum foil and keep warm in a preheated 300° F. oven while you prepare the omelet.

In a large omelet pan or skillet heat 1 tablespoon of the remaining oil and the butter over medium-high heat. Add the ham, potato, mushrooms, onion, and garlic and sauté about 4 minutes, stirring frequently. Add the green peppers and red peppers or pimentos and sauté, stirring, about 4 minutes or until the ingredients are lightly browned and the liquid in the pan has evaporated. Transfer the contents of the omelet pan or skillet to a plate and keep warm.

With a wire whisk or fork beat the eggs with the salt and pepper. Return the omelet pan or skillet to moderate heat and add 1 tablespoon of the remaining oil. Return the ham and vegetables to the pan and pour in the eggs. As the edges begin to set, push the part that has set toward the center and shake the pan vigorously to allow the uncooked eggs to flow underneath. Cook the omelet about 5 minutes or until the top is just set and the underside is golden brown. To turn the omelet, run a large spatula around the edge and under it to loosen. Place an inverted plate over the pan. With one hand on the plate and the other gripping the pan handle, quickly invert the pan, turning the omelet out onto the plate. Add the remaining 1 tablespoon oil to the pan and return to medium heat. Carefully slide the omelet back into the pan. Cook about 2 minutes or until golden brown on the other side. Remove from the heat.

Remove the bread from the oven. Lift off the top half of the loaf and set aside. Invert the bottom half over the top of the omelet and quickly invert the pan, turning the omelet out onto the bread. Replace the top half of the bread and wrap the loaf in heavy aluminum foil to keep warm up to 3 hours.

To serve the loaf, cut it into wedges. Remove the top pieces of bread from the loaf. Invert them and layer with the cheese. Eat the loaf open-faced. Makes 6 to 8 servings.

VARIATION:

Substitute 10 ounces Spanish *chorizo* sausages (page 70) for the ham. Remove the casings and crumble the meat into a large, heavy skillet. Sauté, stirring, until lightly browned. With a slotted spoon remove the sausage meat from the pan. Drain and discard the drippings. When the vegetables are sautéed, stir in the meat. Beat the eggs and proceed as directed.

Curried Shrimp, Green Pepper, and Pineapple in Coconut Rolls

A sure way to achieve fame as a backyard chef without really trying.

¼ cup olive oil
¼ cup freshly squeezed and strained lemon or lime juice
1 tablespoon curry powder
1 teaspoon finely chopped fresh mint or thyme
2 scallions, finely chopped, including 2 inches of the green tops
1 medium garlic clove, crushed and finely chopped
Salt to taste

1 pound medium shrimp, shelled and deveined
1 large green pepper, seeded, deribbed, and cut into 1-inch pieces
4 rectangular French rolls
¼ cup butter, at room temperature
¼ cup grated unsweetened coconut
12 small chunks fresh or canned pineapple

Combine the oil, lemon or lime juice, curry powder, mint or thyme, scallions, garlic, and salt in a bowl. Add the shrimp and green pepper and turn the pieces about to coat them thoroughly with the marinade. Cover and refrigerate 6 hours, turning the shrimp and green pepper from time to time.

Split the rolls without cutting all the way through, leaving one edge as a hinge. Carefully open the rolls. Pull out some of the soft insides and reserve for another use. Cream the butter until soft. Gradually add the coconut, mixing until thoroughly blended. Spread the partially hollowed rolls with the coconut butter and set aside.

Remove the shrimp and green pepper from the marinade. Thread the shrimp on long skewers, leaving a few inches bare at each end. String the green pepper and pineapple chunks on separate skewers. Broil, preferably over charcoal, 4 inches from the heat until the shrimp are tender and the green pepper and pineapple are lightly browned, turning frequently and basting with the marinade. Toast the rolls, coconut sides down, until lightly browned. Remove from the fire.

Using a fork or knife, push the shrimp, green pepper, and pineapple off the skewers onto the bottom halves of the rolls, dividing equally. Cover with the tops of the rolls and serve at once. Makes 4.

Oyster, Bacon, and Tomato Sandwiches

12 slices bacon
1 pint small oysters, freshly
  shucked
½ cup all-purpose flour
½ teaspoon salt
⅛ teaspoon freshly ground pepper

⅛ teaspoon paprika or to taste
4 rectangular French rolls
Mayonnaise
Boston lettuce leaves
2 small, firm ripe tomatoes, sliced

In a heavy skillet cook the bacon over moderate heat until crisp, turning frequently. Drain on paper towels, reserving the fat. Pat the oysters dry with paper towels and roll in the flour seasoned with the salt, pepper, and paprika. Fry in the reserved bacon fat over medium-high heat, turning to brown on all sides. Drain on paper towels.

Split the rolls without cutting all the way through, leaving one edge as a hinge. Carefully open the rolls. Pull out some of the soft insides and reserve for another use. Spread the partially hollowed rolls with the mayonnaise. If desired, toast the rolls in a preheated 350° F. oven just until light gold. Line the bottom halves of the rolls with the lettuce leaves and top with the tomato slices, dividing equally. Arrange the bacon slices over the tomatoes and the fried oysters over the bacon. Cover with the top halves of the rolls and serve at once. Makes 4.

Chicken and Mushroom Sandwiches with Tomato and Cheese

2 small chicken breasts, skinned,
  halved, boned, and flattened to
  ⅛-inch thickness
Salt and freshly ground pepper
  to taste
7 tablespoons butter
1 small onion, thinly sliced
⅓ cup chopped green pepper

4 ounces mushrooms, chopped
½ teaspoon crushed dried basil
½ teaspoon crushed dried oregano
4 crusty rolls, split and toasted
8 thin slices tomato
4 slices mozzarella cheese, halved
  diagonally

Wipe the chicken breasts with damp paper towels. Cut in half crosswise. Season with the salt and pepper. Set aside.

In a heavy skillet heat 2 tablespoons of the butter over medium-high heat. Add the onion, green pepper, and mushrooms and sauté until lightly browned, stirring frequently. Transfer the vegetables to a plate and keep warm. Add 1 tablespoon of the remaining butter to the skillet and heat. Add the chicken breasts and sauté over medium heat about 1 minute on each side or until tender. Remove from the heat.

Mix the remaining 4 tablespoons butter with the basil and oregano and spread on the rolls. Place 2 chicken pieces on the bottom half of each roll. Top with the tomato, vegetables, and cheese in that order, dividing equally. Broil 4 to 5 inches from the heat about 1 minute or until the cheese melts. Cover with the roll tops and serve at once. Makes 4.

Tuscan Chicken Rolls

2 tablespoons olive oil
2 tablespoons butter
2 medium garlic cloves, finely chopped
¼ teaspoon crushed red pepper
¼ cup finely chopped parsley
4 anchovies, chopped (optional)
2½ pounds chicken breasts, skinned, boned, and cut into ¾-inch cubes

1 jar (2¼ ounces) capers, rinsed and drained
2 cans (2¼ ounces each) sliced pitted black olives, drained
¾ cup dry white wine
Salt and freshly ground pepper to taste
6 rectangular Italian or French rolls
Garlic Butter (page 185)

In a large, heavy skillet heat the oil and butter over moderate heat. Add the garlic, red pepper, parsley, anchovies (if used), and chicken and sauté 5 minutes or until golden brown, stirring constantly. Add the capers, olives, wine, and salt and pepper and simmer, uncovered, stirring now and then, about 5 minutes or until most of the liquid evaporates. Remove from the heat and keep warm.

Cut the rolls in half lengthwise. Pull out the soft centers and reserve for another use. Brush the insides with the Garlic Butter. Fill the bottoms of the rolls with the chicken mixture. Cover with the tops. Arrange the filled rolls on a baking sheet and bake in a preheated 350° F. oven about 5 minutes or until heated. Serve at once. Makes 6.

Turkey Sandwich Loaf with Mornay Sauce

1 loaf (1 pound) unsliced white or whole wheat bread	10 thin slices avocado
Mayonnaise or butter	Salt and freshly ground pepper to taste
10 thin slices cooked turkey breast	Pitted black olives
10 slices bacon, cooked crisp	Pimento-stuffed olives
10 thin slices tomato	Mornay Sauce (page 264)

With a sharp knife trim the crusts from the bread and cut the loaf into 3 even lengthwise slices. Toast in the oven or over the grill. Spread the inside surfaces of the toasted bread slices with the mayonnaise or butter. Arrange the turkey slices over the bottom slice of toast and top with the bacon slices. Arrange the tomato and avocado slices on the second slice of toast. Season with the salt and pepper and cover with the third toast slice. Gently press the layers together and place the loaf on a large serving platter. To serve, cut crosswise into thick slices. Insert 2 thin bamboo skewers vertically through each serving and impale the olives on the skewers. Pass a bowl of the hot Mornay Sauce to spoon over the sandwiches. Makes 8 servings.

VARIATION:

Substitute Cheddar cheese for the Swiss and/or Parmesan in the Mornay Sauce.

Grilled Smoked Turkey and Tilsiter Sandwich

Place 1 or 2 thin slices each of smoked turkey breast and Tilsiter cheese on a slice of white bread and spread with Curry Mayonnaise (page 262). Cover with another slice of white bread to make a sandwich. Butter on both sides and toast in a preheated sandwich grill on moderate heat until golden brown and the cheese melts. Serve immediately. Makes 1.

Corned Beef Hero Sandwich

Slice a long loaf of Italian bread in 3 lengthwise slices. Butter the bottom slice and spread with mayonnaise. Cover with Boston or leaf lettuce and arrange alternate slices of tomato and cucumber over the lettuce. Butter the second slice of bread, place it over the lettuce, and spread with Dijon-style or Düsseldorf mustard. Cover with thin slices of Swiss cheese, red onion, and dill pickle. Arrange thin slices of corned beef on top and cover with the third slice of bread spread with butter, buttered side down. To serve, cut crosswise in 4 thick slices and secure with food picks. Makes 4 servings.

Note: For individual hero sandwiches, substitute 4 large crusty rolls, sometimes called "torpedoes," for the Italian bread.

Pastrami Sandwich

Cut an onion bun in half lengthwise. Toast the bun and spread it with Mustard Butter (page 185). Cover the bottom half with a crisp lettuce leaf. Place thin slices of pastrami over the lettuce and thin slices of tomato over the pastrami. Add the top half of the bun and serve with dill gherkins. Makes 1.

Reuben Sandwich

Often featured on restaurant menus, this robust sandwich is a meal in itself.

8 large slices dark rye bread
Russian Dressing (page 262)
8 ounces cooked corned beef,
   thinly sliced

8 ounces Swiss cheese, sliced
1 cup sauerkraut, thoroughly
   drained
Butter

Spread 1 side of each bread slice with 2 to 3 teaspoons Russian Dressing. Assemble each sandwich as follows: Place 2 ounces of the corned beef on 1 slice of bread and 2 ounces of the cheese on the other. Cover the corned beef with about 2 tablespoons sauerkraut. Close the sandwiches and spread the outside surfaces with butter. Grill on a moderately hot griddle until the bread is toasted and the cheese is melted. Cut in half and serve at once. Makes 4.

VARIATIONS:

Substitute thinly sliced brisket pastrami for the corned beef.
Substitute 4 ounces thinly sliced cooked turkey breast for 4 ounces of the corned beef.

Mexican Grilled Steak Sandwiches

Satisfying enough for appetites sharpened by fresh air, these make an enticing entrée for an *alfresco* meal.

⅓ cup olive oil
3 tablespoons red wine vinegar
3 tablespoons freshly squeezed and strained lime or lemon juice
¼ cup finely chopped mild red or white onion
1 medium garlic clove, finely chopped

¾ teaspoon crushed dried oregano
¼ teaspoon cumin
½ teaspoon salt
1 pound flank steak
6 sourdough rolls
8 ounces Monterey Jack cheese, sliced
Guacamole (page 265)

In a shallow dish stir together the oil, vinegar, lime or lemon juice, onion, garlic, oregano, cumin, and salt. Add the flank steak, turning to coat thoroughly with the marinade. Cover and refrigerate several hours or overnight, turning occasionally.

Remove the steak from the marinade and broil, preferably over charcoal, 3 to 4 inches from the heat 6 to 8 minutes on each side or until it is done to your taste. Transfer the meat to a carving board and slice across the grain into thin strips.

To assemble the sandwiches, slice the rolls in half lengthwise without cutting all the way through, leaving one edge as a hinge. Arrange slices of flank steak over the bottom halves of the rolls and top with slices of cheese and a few spoonfuls of Guacamole. Close the sandwiches and serve. Makes 6.

Veal Parmigiana Sandwich

If you can't afford an Italian holiday, try this.

1½ pounds veal scallops, cut ¾
 inch thick and pounded ¼ inch
 thick
Salt and freshly ground pepper
 to taste
⅓ cup all-purpose flour
1 egg
½ cup milk
1½ cups sifted bread crumbs
⅓ cup olive oil, more if needed
4 ounces mozzarella cheese,
 thinly sliced
Tomato Sauce (page 264)
¼ cup freshly grated Parmesan
 cheese
1 loaf crusty Italian or French
 bread

Season the veal scallops with the salt and pepper. Dredge them lightly in the flour, shaking off any excess. Combine the egg and milk in a bowl and beat lightly to mix. Dip the veal scallops in the egg and milk mixture, then coat them on both sides with the bread crumbs.

In a large, heavy skillet heat the oil over medium-high heat. Add the veal scallops and sauté until lightly browned on both sides, adding more oil if necessary. Transfer the scallops to a baking dish just large enough to hold them in one layer. Top the scallops with the mozzarella slices. Cover with the Tomato Sauce. Sprinkle the grated Parmesan evenly over the top. Bake in a preheated 400° F. oven about 10 minutes, or until the cheese is melted and the sauce bubbles.

Slice the bread from one end to the other without cutting all the way through, leaving one edge as a hinge. Spread the veal *parmigiana* over the bottom half of the bread. Close the sandwich, slice it into 4 equal portions, and serve at once. Makes 4 servings.

Note: The veal parmigiana is also delicious served in lightly toasted pita bread.

Fresno Shish Kebab Sandwich

Your name doesn't have to be Aram for you to enjoy this Armenian spectacular!

2 **pounds boneless leg of lamb,**
  trimmed of excess fat and cut
  into 1-inch cubes
2 **small onions, cut lengthwise in**
  half and thickly sliced
¼ **cup chopped parsley**
¾ **teapoon crushed dried oregano**
1 **teaspoon salt or to taste**

¼ **teaspoon freshly ground pepper**
½ **cup dry red wine**
¼ **cup olive oil**
1 **warm loaf Armenian Peda Bread**
  (page 249)
1 **medium, firm ripe tomato, thinly**
  sliced

Combine the lamb, onions, parsley, oregano, salt, pepper, wine, and oil in a large bowl. Turn the pieces of meat about to coat them thoroughly with the marinade. Cover and refrigerate 6 hours or overnight, stirring from time to time.

Remove the lamb from the marinade and thread the cubes on long skewers, leaving a few inches bare at each end. Pour the marinade into a skillet. Broil the lamb, preferably over charcoal, 3 to 4 inches from the heat about 10 minutes for medium rare, turning frequently so that the meat browns evenly on all sides. Set the skillet over high heat and cook the marinade, stirring, until the onions are lightly browned. Remove from the heat and keep warm.

Split the *peda* in half lengthwise, making the bottom portion about 1 inch thick. Spoon the cooked marinade over the bottom, top with the tomato slices, and lay on the skewered lamb. Cover with the top of the bread. Press a fork against the meat on each skewer and pull out the skewer. Cut the loaf into 8 wedges and serve at once. Makes 8 servings.

Croque Monsieur

This French interpretation of a ham and cheese sandwich has achieved worldwide recognition.

2 **thin slices (¼ inch thick) firm-**
  textured white bread
2 **tablespoons butter (preferably**
  Clarified Butter, page 266),
  melted

2 **thin slices (⅛ inch thick)**
  mozzarella cheese, cut the same
  size as the bread
1 **thin slice (⅛ inch thick) cooked**
  ham, cut the same size as the
  bread

Place 1 bread slice on your work surface. Brush it with some of the butter. Cover with 1 of the cheese slices, then the ham slice, and finally the second cheese slice. Brush one side of the remaining bread slice with butter and place it buttered side down to top the sandwich. Press the sandwich together firmly with the palm of your hand. Trim off the crusts and press down again on the sandwich.

In a small, heavy skillet heat the remaining butter. Add the sandwich and sauté slowly until it is nicely browned and the cheese has begun to melt, about 2 to 3 minutes on each side. Serve at once. Makes 1.

Note: This sandwich can be cut into quarters and served as an appetizer.

Milan-Style Tostas

The conventional grilled ham and cheese sandwich takes a step up the social ladder in this Italian-inspired version, an admirable choice for informal entertaining.

1 pound Fontina, Tybo, or
  Monterey Jack cheese, sliced
8 ounces prosciutto or cooked
  ham, thinly sliced

1 loaf (1 pound) egg bread or
  French bread, sliced

CONDIMENTS:

2 jars (6 ounces each) marinated
  artichoke hearts, cut lengthwise
  in thin slices
1 jar (about 5 ounces) marinated
  mushrooms, thinly sliced

1 jar (about 8 ounces)
  peperoncini, (bottled hot Italian
  peppers)
Caponata (page 229)
Marinated Roasted Red Peppers
  (page 228)

To make each *tosta*, place 1 or 2 slices each of cheese and ham between 2 slices of bread. Toast in a preheated sandwich grill on moderate heat until golden brown and the cheese melts.

Serve the sandwiches on individual plates. Present the condiments in serving dishes. Invite diners to open their sandwiches and add to them their choice of the condiments. Makes 6 servings.

French Toast Sandwiches with Chilies, Ham, and Cheese

1 can (4 ounces) peeled green chilies	8 slices white bread
1 cup finely chopped cooked ham	6 eggs
2 cups shredded Monterey Jack, sharp Cheddar, or Muenster cheese	2 cups milk
	½ teaspoon chili powder
	½ teaspoon dry mustard
	Salt to taste

Drain and rinse the chilies and remove the seeds. Chop the chilies finely. Mix together the chilies, ham, and 1 cup of the cheese. Divide the mixture into 4 equal portions and spread over half of the bread slices. Cover with the remaining bread slices to make 4 sandwiches. Place each sandwich in a well-buttered shallow ramekin (1½- to 2-cup size), or place all the sandwiches in one layer in a 9-inch-square pan.

Beat the eggs until blended, then beat in the milk, chili powder, mustard, and salt. Pour the mixture over the sandwiches. Cover and refrigerate at least 2 hours or overnight.

Uncover the sandwiches and sprinkle them evenly with the remaining 1 cup cheese. If using ramekins, place them on a baking sheet. Bake the sandwiches in a preheated 350° F. oven about 35 minutes or until puffed and the centers are set. Serve at once. Makes 4.

Monte Cristo Sandwich

A sandwich worthy of the Count himself.

3 slices firm-textured white bread	1 thin slice Swiss cheese
2 tablespoons butter (approximately)	1 small egg
	1 tablespoon half-and-half or milk
1 thin slice baked ham	Dash salt
1 thin slice roast turkey breast	Currant jelly

Place 1 bread slice on your work surface. Spread with some of the butter, cover with the ham slice, then the turkey. Butter the second bread slice on both sides, place it on the turkey, and cover it with the cheese slice. Butter the third bread slice and place it, buttered side down, over the cheese. Press the sandwich together firmly with the palm of your hand. Trim off the crusts and cut the sandwich diagonally in half. Secure the halves with wooden picks.

Beat the egg lightly with the half-and-half or milk and salt. In a small, heavy skillet heat the remaining butter over moderate heat. Dip the sandwich halves, one at a time, in the egg mixture. Add to the skillet and sauté on both sides until golden brown. Serve with the currant jelly. Makes 1.

Note: If desired, after sautéing the sandwich you may place it on an ungreased baking sheet and bake in a preheated 400° F. oven about 4 minutes. Dust with sifted confectioners' sugar, garnish with parsley sprigs, and serve hot with the currant jelly.

Club Sandwich

This really isn't a hot sandwich, but then again it's not exactly a cold one, either.

3 slices white bread	3 or 4 slices tomato
1 to 2 tablespoons mayonnaise	1 crisp lettuce leaf
2 or 3 slices cold cooked turkey or	Parsley sprigs
chicken breast	Bread and butter pickles
3 slices bacon, cooked crisp	

Toast the bread slices and trim off the crusts. Spread each slice of toast on one side with the mayonnaise. Cover 1 of the slices with the turkey or chicken slices. Place the second slice of toast, mayonnaise side up, over the turkey or chicken. Arrange the bacon slices over the toast, lay the tomato slices over the bacon, and top with the lettuce leaf. Cover with the third slice of toast, mayonnaise side down.

Secure the sandwich with food picks and cut diagonally in half or in 4 triangles. Garnish with the parsley sprigs. Serve at once with the pickles. Makes 1.

Grilled Chorizo Rolls

Chorizos are unique reddish-brown Spanish sausages sold in links about 4 inches long. They are traditionally made of pork bits, brilliant red paprika, other spices, and herbs and cured in wood smoke. Available in Spanish groceries, they are worth tracking down.

Prick chorizos all over with a fork. Grill over charcoal about 5 minutes, turning frequently. Split small heated French rolls slightly longer than the chorizos without cutting all the way through, leaving one edge as a hinge. Place a grilled chorizo in each roll and serve at once without the addition of mustard or other relish, which would interfere with the distinctive flavor of the sausages.

Stuffed Hamburger Sandwiches

Here is an exciting alternative to conventional hamburgers.

1 pound lean ground beef	2 teaspoons freshly grated
Salt and freshly ground pepper	Parmesan or Romano cheese
to taste	⅛ teaspoon crushed dried oregano
2 slices Bermuda or red onion	or basil
2 slices pepperoni or prosciutto	2 round crusty rolls
2 slices firm ripe tomato	Garlic Butter (page 185)
2 slices mozzarella cheese	

Season the beef with salt and pepper, divide into 4 equal parts, and form each part into a patty about ¼ inch thick. Layer 1 of the patties with 1 slice each onion, pepperoni or prosciutto, tomato, and mozzarella cheese. Sprinkle with 1 teaspoon of the grated cheese and ¹⁄₁₆ teaspoon of the oregano or basil. Repeat with a second patty. Cover each with 1 of the remaining 2 patties, pressing the edges together to seal the filling. Broil, preferably over charcoal, about 7 minutes on each side or until done to your taste.

Meanwhile, cut the rolls lengthwise in half. Spread them with the Garlic Butter and toast. Place a stuffed hamburger on the bottom half of each roll and cover with the roll top. Serve at once. Makes 2.

Fresno-Style Super Cheeseburgers

A sandwich that gets talked about and deserves it.

3 pounds lean ground beef
1 medium onion, grated
1 large garlic clove, crushed and finely chopped
2 teaspoons crushed dried basil
Salt and freshly ground pepper to taste
1 warm loaf Armenian Peda Bread (page 249)

8 ounces Monterey Jack cheese, thinly sliced
2 medium, firm ripe tomatoes, thinly sliced
1 medium red onion, thinly sliced
1 cup shredded romaine lettuce
1 medium dill pickle, thinly sliced

In a bowl combine the beef, onion, garlic, basil, and salt and pepper and mix until the ingredients are thoroughly blended. Form the mixture into a patty 12 inches in diameter. Place the meat patty in a large double-hinged wire grill. Broil over charcoal about 6 minutes or until the underside is browned. Turn over and broil about 6 minutes or until the other side is done. (If you do not have a wire grill, use 2 spatulas to transfer the meat patty to a baking sheet. Place a second baking sheet on top and turn the pans over so the cooked side of the meat is up. Then slide the meat patty back onto the grill to broil the other side.)

Split the *peda* lengthwise, making the bottom portion about 1 inch thick. Place the meat on the bottom portion and cover with the slices of cheese. Broil to melt the cheese. Arrange the tomatoes, onion, lettuce, and pickle slices over the cheese. Cover with the bread top. Cut into 8 wedges and serve at once. Makes 8 servings.

VARIATION:

Eight Crusty Hamburger Buns (page 253) can be substituted for the peda loaf, in which case divide the meat mixture into 8 equal portions and shape each into a patty. Broil 4 to 6 minutes on each side or until done to your taste. Split the buns lengthwise. Place the meat patties over the bottoms and cover them with the slices of cheese. Broil, then top with the tomatoes, onion, lettuce, and pickle. Cover with the tops of the buns and serve at once.

Italian Meatball Heroes

As good as any served in an Italian restaurant.

6 to 8 hero or French rolls, heated
  and buttered if desired
Meatballs (below)
¼ cup olive oil
2 large green peppers, seeded and
  cut into ½-inch strips
2 large onions, chopped
2 medium garlic cloves, finely
  chopped

4 large, ripe tomatoes, peeled,
  seeded, and chopped
1½ teaspoons crushed dried basil
1 teaspoon crushed dried oregano
½ cup dry red wine
½ cup water
Salt and freshly ground pepper
  to taste

Split each roll lengthwise without cutting all the way through, leaving one edge as a hinge. Carefully open the rolls. Pull out enough of the soft insides to make 1 cup soft bread crumbs (to be used for the meatballs) and reserve. Prepare and bake the meatballs.

To make the sauce, in a heavy saucepan heat the oil over moderate heat. Add the green pepper strips and cook 3 minutes or until the peppers are just tender, stirring frequently. Transfer to a plate and set aside. Add the onions and garlic to the pan and cook, stirring, until the onions are soft. Add the tomatoes, basil, oregano, wine, water, and salt and pepper, and bring to a boil. Reduce the heat and simmer, uncovered, stirring now and then, about 30 minutes or until the mixture has attained the consistency of a thin sauce.

Add the meatballs and their drippings to the sauce. Cover and simmer 1 hour or until the sauce thickens. Stir in the reserved green pepper strips. Spoon the meatballs and sauce into the rolls and serve. Makes 6 to 8 servings.

VARIATION:

The meatballs are also delicious served in toasted pita halves.

Meatballs

1 cup reserved soft bread crumbs
    from the rolls
½ cup milk
2 pounds lean ground beef
1 small onion, finely chopped
2 medium garlic cloves, finely
    chopped

¼ cup finely chopped parsley
½ teaspoon crushed dried basil
¼ teaspoon crushed dried oregano
2 eggs, beaten
Salt and freshly ground pepper
    to taste

In a large bowl combine the bread crumbs and milk and let stand 5 minutes. Add the beef, onion, garlic, parsley, basil, oregano, eggs, and salt and pepper, and mix until well blended. With hands moistened in cold water, shape the mixture into 1½-inch balls. Place 1 inch apart on greased, rimmed baking sheets. Bake in a preheated 450° F. oven 15 minutes. Remove from the heat and reserve all the drippings.

VARIATION:

Substitute 1 pound each mild or hot Italian sausage (casings removed) and lean ground beef for the 2 pounds ground beef.

Curried Meatballs in Nepalese Bread

A conversation piece.

Nepalese Bread (page 251)   Curried Meatballs (below)

CONDIMENTS:

Crumbled bacon
Chopped hard-cooked egg
Thinly sliced scallions, including 2
    inches of the green tops
Coarsely chopped salted peanuts,
    cashews, or toasted blanched
    almonds

Shredded unsweetened coconut
Sliced bananas
Cubed pineapple
Chutney

Present the bread, either warm or at room temperature, in a basket. Spoon the meatballs into a heated serving dish. Fill small bowls with the condiments to pass at table. Invite diners to split each bread and stuff it with the hot meatballs and condiments. Makes 8 servings.

Curried Meatballs

2 pounds lean ground beef	1 large onion, finely chopped
1 egg	2 medium garlic cloves, finely
⅓ cup fine dry bread crumbs	chopped
2 tablespoons curry powder	2 large tomatoes, peeled, seeded,
Salt and freshly ground pepper	and finely chopped
to taste	1 red apple, peeled, cored, and
½ cup all-purpose flour	diced
(approximately)	
2 tablespoons peanut oil or	
flavorless vegetable oil	

Combine the ground beef, egg, bread crumbs, 1 tablespoon of the curry powder, and salt and pepper in a bowl. Knead until well blended and smooth. With hands moistened in water, shape the mixture into 1-inch balls. Roll lightly in the flour.

In a large, heavy skillet heat the oil over moderate heat. Add the meatballs and sauté until nicely browned on all sides. Transfer to a plate and set aside. Discard all but 2 tablespoons of the drippings. Add the onion, garlic, and remaining 1 tablespoon curry powder and cook until the onion is soft, stirring frequently. Stir in the tomatoes, apple, and salt and pepper. Return the meatballs to the skillet, cover, and simmer 20 minutes. Uncover and simmer about 10 minutes, or until the sauce is thickened.

Indian Filled Pooris

Kheema Curry (below), or West 8 Pooris (page 250)
  Indian Chicken (page 91)

Partially split each *poori* along one side and stuff it with some of the
Kheema Curry or West Indian Chicken. Serve at once. Makes 8.

Kheema Curry

3 tablespoons flavorless vegetable
  oil or butter
1 large onion, finely chopped
1 medium garlic clove, finely
  chopped
1 tablespoon finely chopped green
  pepper
½ stick cinnamon (about 1 inch
  long)
3 whole cloves
¼ teaspoon freshly ground black
  pepper
1 bay leaf
¼ teaspoon ground dried chili
  pepper or to taste

½ teaspoon cumin or to taste
1½ teaspoons coriander
½ teaspoon turmeric
1 pound lean ground lamb or beef
2 large tomatoes, peeled, seeded,
  and finely chopped
Salt to taste
¼ cup water or as needed
1 tablespoon freshly squeezed and
  strained lemon juice
1 cup green peas
3 hard-cooked eggs, chopped

In a heavy skillet heat the oil or butter over moderate heat. Add the
onion and garlic and sauté until golden, stirring frequently. Add the
green pepper, cinnamon stick, cloves, black pepper, bay leaf, chili
pepper, cumin, coriander, and turmeric and sauté 3 minutes, stirring
constantly. Add the meat and cook about 5 minutes or until browned,
stirring and breaking it up with a fork. Add the tomatoes, salt, water,
and lemon juice. Cover and simmer 30 minutes. Add the peas and a
little water if the mixture seems dry. Cover and simmer about 15
minutes or until the peas are just tender. Remove the bay leaf, cinnamon stick, and cloves. Stir in the eggs. Taste and adjust the seasoning and remove from the heat.

Note: This filling is also good served in lightly toasted pita bread.

Filled Sopaipillas

6 Sopaipillas (page 252)
Picadillo (below)
1½ cups shredded Monterey Jack
  or Cheddar cheese
2 cups shredded romaine or
  iceberg lettuce

2 medium tomatoes, chopped
4 scallions, thinly sliced, including
  2 inches of the green tops

Split the *sopaipillas* while still hot along one long side and stuff each with about ½ cup filling and some of the cheese, lettuce, tomatoes, and scallions. Serve at once. Makes 6 servings.

Picadillo

2 tablespoons corn oil or flavorless
  vegetable oil
1 medium onion, chopped
½ cup chopped green pepper
2 large garlic cloves, finely
  chopped
1 pound lean ground beef
2 medium tomatoes, peeled,
  seeded, and finely chopped

⅔ cup chopped pimento-stuffed
  olives
⅓ cup seedless raisins
2 tablespoons brown sugar
1½ tablespoons white wine vinegar
¼ teaspoon cinnamon
⅛ teaspoon cloves
Salt and freshly ground pepper to
  taste

In a heavy skillet heat the oil over moderate heat. Add the onion and sauté until soft but not browned, stirring frequently. Add the green pepper and garlic and cook, stirring, about 3 minutes. Add the ground beef and cook, stirring and breaking it up with a fork, until browned and crumbly. Add the tomatoes, olives, raisins, brown sugar, vinegar, cinnamon, cloves, and salt and pepper and cook, stirring, about 8 minutes or until most of the liquid has evaporated but the mixture is still moist. Remove from the heat. Taste and adjust the seasoning. Keep warm.

4

Pita Sandwiches

Although native to the Middle East, where it has been used to hold fillings for many centuries, pita is far more worldly than one might suspect. The versatility and adaptability of this time-honored bread can spark a cook's imagination, generating a host of internationally inspired ideas for sandwiches.

On its home ground pita has long enclosed such traditional favorites as *falafel* (page 78) and *shish kebab,* but a Mexican taco-type filling or an exotic Caribbean chicken will work equally well for an innovative snack, lunch, or supper. The chewy, absorbent texture of pita makes it an ideal bread for moist fillings, perfect for picnics and lunchboxes.

The most common way of making pita sandwiches is to cut the bread crosswise in half and stuff the pockets formed with a desired filling. Other ways, less known but just as interesting, are to slit it one-third of the way around to make an opening for fillings or to separate it into circles, either to roll around fillings or to create bases for open-faced sandwiches. Of particular interest in this last category is the novel and time-saving use of the pita circles for pizza- and quiche-type sandwiches. The following recipes cast this venerable bread in all of these tasteful roles, both old and new.

In addition to the sandwiches in this chapter, many others throughout the book are also delicious made with pita bread. I have called attention to some of them in variations to particular recipes.

Falafel Sandwiches

Throughout the Arab world and Israel one of the most common fillings for pita bread is *falafel,* which is served hot with a fresh salad, or with turnip or cucumber pickles and dressed with sesame sauce. Falafel sandwiches are as popular in that part of the Middle East as hamburgers in America.

1 pound dried white fava beans, preferably shelled (available at Middle Eastern groceries)

1 large red onion or 1 bunch scallions, very finely chopped (include 2 inches of the green tops of the scallions)

2 large garlic cloves, crushed

1 bunch parsley, finely chopped

1½ teaspoons cumin

1½ teaspoons coriander

½ teaspoon baking powder

Salt and cayenne pepper to taste

Corn oil for deep-frying

2 pita breads, halved crosswise and lightly toasted

Middle Eastern Vegetable Salad (page 216)

Sesame Sauce (below)

Soak the beans in cold water 24 hours. Drain and remove the skins if unshelled. Put through the fine blade of a meat grinder. Add the onion, garlic, parsley, cumin, coriander, baking powder, and salt and cayenne pepper. Mix well and grind again. Pound the mixture to a smooth paste and let it rest 30 minutes. Form the paste into flat round patties about 1½ inches in diameter. Arrange them on a plate and let rest 15 minutes. Fry the patties in deep hot oil, a batch at a time, until richly browned, regulating the heat as necessary and being careful not to crowd the pan. Lift out the patties with a slotted spoon and drain on paper towels.

To serve, fill each pita half with falafel patties and the vegetable salad, allowing equal portions for each sandwich. Pass a bowl of the Sesame Sauce to spoon into the sandwiches. Makes 4.

Sesame Sauce

2 medium garlic cloves or to taste

Salt

½ cup tahini (sesame seed paste, available at Middle Eastern groceries)

½ cup freshly squeezed and strained lemon juice or to taste

Cold water as needed

½ teaspoon ground cumin (optional)

In a deep bowl mash the garlic with a pinch of salt. Add the *tahini* and mix well. Gradually beat in the lemon juice and enough water (about 2 tablespoons) until the mixture attains a thick, creamy consistency. Season with ½ teaspoon salt and the cumin, if used. Taste and adjust the seasoning.

Leek and Tomato Quiche

This is my own adaptation of quiche, with pita bread substituted for the traditional pastry. It is quicker and much less complicated to prepare, considerably lower in calories, less expensive, and it makes an ideal picnic or lunch box meal since it is easy to transport and is delicious eaten cold.

1 pita bread, 6 inches or more in diameter
1 tablespoon butter
1 cup thinly sliced leek (approximately—use the white portion only of 1 large leek)
Salt and freshly ground pepper to taste
1 cup grated Swiss or Gruyère cheese

2 tablespoons freshly grated Parmesan or Romano cheese
2 teaspoons all-purpose flour
2 eggs
¾ cup heavy cream or half-and-half
1 small firm, ripe tomato, peeled, thinly sliced, and seeded
Crushed dried basil or oregano to taste (optional)

With a sharp knife carefully slit the pita all the way around to make two circles. Place one circle, smooth side down, in an ungreased 8-inch pyrex pie plate, trimming the edges as necessary to fit the bottom (reserve the second circle for another use). Set aside.

In a small, heavy skillet melt the butter over moderate heat. Add the leek and sauté until golden, stirring frequently. Season with the salt and pepper. Spread the sautéed leek evenly over the pita circle. Toss the cheeses with the flour and sprinkle them evenly over the leek.

In a mixing bowl beat the eggs just until foamy, then beat in the heavy cream or half-and-half and salt to taste until well blended. Pour over the cheese and leek. Arrange the tomato slices on top in an attractive pattern. Sprinkle the tomato with the basil or oregano and additional salt and pepper to taste. Bake, uncovered, in a preheated 400° F. oven 15 minutes. Reduce the heat to 325° F. and bake 30 minutes, or until the quiche is puffed and lightly browned and a knife inserted in the center comes out clean. Remove from the oven and let stand 10 minutes at room temperature. Serve hot or cold. Makes 4 servings.

Salade Provençale in Pita

Fill 2 pita breads, halved crosswise and lightly toasted, with Salade Provençale (page 218), allowing equal portions for each pita half. Serve at once. Makes 4.

Egyptian Fish Sandwiches

1 pound cod or haddock fillets
2 sprigs parsley
1 bay leaf
4 peppercorns
Pinch thyme
1 tablespoon freshly squeezed and strained lemon juice
2 thick slices white bread, trimmed of crusts, soaked in water, squeezed dry, and crumbled
1 small onion, grated
2 medium garlic cloves, crushed and finely chopped
2 eggs
3 tablespoons finely chopped parsley
¾ teaspoon cumin
¾ teaspoon coriander
Salt and freshly ground pepper to taste
Flour
Olive oil for deep-frying
2 pita breads, halved crosswise and lightly toasted
Tomato Sauce (page 264)

Combine the fish fillets, parsley, bay leaf, peppercorns, thyme, and lemon juice in a large, deep skillet. Pour in just enough boiling water to cover. Cover and simmer about 8 minutes, or until the fish is just firm and flakes easily when tested with a fork. Drain the fish and pat it dry with paper towels.

In a mixing bowl mash the fish with a fork. Add the bread, onion, garlic, eggs, parsley, cumin, coriander, and salt and pepper. Knead until well blended and smooth. Taste and adjust the seasoning. Form the mixture into finger-shaped patties. Coat lightly with flour and deep-fry in hot oil until golden brown. Drain on paper towels.

Fill the pita halves with the fish patties, allowing equal portions for each. Add a few spoonfuls of the Tomato Sauce to each sandwich and serve accompanied with Pickled Mixed Vegetables (page 232) or Middle Eastern Vegetable Salad (page 216), if desired. Makes 4.

VARIATION:

For an Armenian version, omit the cumin and coriander and add ¼ cup finely chopped fresh dill with the parsley.

Caribbean Chicken on Pita

A harmonious blend of Caribbean magic and Arab hospitality.

2 large chicken breasts, boned and halved
⅓ cup melted butter
2 medium garlic cloves, crushed
1 teaspoon chili powder
¼ teaspoon cumin
¼ teaspoon finely grated lime peel
2 tablespoons freshly squeezed and strained lime juice
Salt to taste

2 pita breads, separated into single layers to make 4 circles and heated*
1 medium avocado
Cherry tomatoes, halved
Pitted black olives
Lime wedges
Bibb lettuce leaves, or the tender inner leaves from 1 head romaine lettuce

Dry the chicken pieces with paper towels. In a small bowl mix together the butter, garlic, chili powder, cumin, lime peel, lime juice, and salt. Brush the chicken thoroughly with the mixture. Broil the chicken, preferably over charcoal, about 20 minutes or until nicely browned and cooked through, turning and brushing several times with the remaining butter mixture.

To serve, place the pita circles on 4 heated plates. Top each with a piece of the chicken. Peel and slice the avocado. Garnish each serving with avocado slices, cherry tomatoes, black olives, lime wedges, and lettuce leaves. Makes 4.

*To heat the pita circles, arrange them on ungreased baking sheets. Place in a preheated 350° F. oven about 3 minutes or until warm. (If grilling outdoors, place the wrapped pita on the grill alongside the chicken about 10 minutes or until warm, turning often.)

Sicilian Chicken and Eggplant in Pita

This will make an eggplant lover out of anyone.

1 medium eggplant
Salt
2 pounds chicken breasts, skinned, boned, and cut into 2-inch pieces
5 tablespoons olive oil, more if needed
½ cup chicken broth, more if needed
1 tablespoon tomato paste

1 teaspoon crushed dried oregano or to taste
1 medium onion, sliced
2 medium green peppers, seeded, deribbed, and cut into strips
2 medium, ripe tomatoes, peeled, seeded, and chopped
Freshly ground pepper to taste
4 small pita breads

Remove the stem and hull from the eggplant. Peel and cut into 1-inch cubes. Lay the eggplant cubes on paper towels. Sprinkle generously with salt and let stand 30 minutes. Rinse and dry thoroughly with fresh paper towels, squeezing with your hands to get rid of the bitter juices. Set aside.

Dry the chicken pieces with paper towels. In a medium-size, heavy saucepan heat 2 tablespoons of the oil over moderate heat. Add the chicken and sauté, turning to brown evenly on all sides. Mix together the chicken broth, tomato paste, oregano, and salt to taste and pour over the chicken. Stir well, cover, and simmer 15 minutes, adding more broth if necessary.

Meanwhile, heat the remaining 3 tablespoons oil in a large, heavy skillet over moderate heat. Add the onion, peppers, and eggplant and sauté until lightly browned, stirring frequently and adding more oil if necessary. Add the tomatoes, additional salt, and pepper and simmer 5 minutes, stirring occasionally. Transfer the contents of the skillet to the saucepan and mix gently but thoroughly. Cover and simmer about 10 minutes or until the chicken is tender. Uncover and cook, stirring occasionally, about 5 minutes or until almost all the liquid in the pan has evaporated and the sauce is thickened. Taste and adjust the seasoning. Remove from the heat.

Arrange the pita breads on ungreased baking sheets. Place in a preheated 350° F. oven 4 to 5 minutes or until heated. Remove from the oven.

With a sharp knife, slit each pita one-third of the way around to make a pocket. Fill the pitas with the chicken mixture, allowing equal portions for each sandwich. Serve at once. Makes 4.

Note: The chicken and eggplant can instead be served in pita halves.

Souvlakia

Shashlik to the Russians, *lahm mishwi* to the Arabs, and *shish kebab* to the Turks, pieces of meat roasted on skewers has been a favorite throughout the Caucasus, Central Asia, and the Eastern Mediterranean for at least three thousand years and is unquestionably one of the East's most significant contributions to world gastronomy. This Greek version provides a splendid main course for an outdoor meal.

1 pound lean boneless leg of lamb or beef sirloin, cut into ¾-inch cubes
2½ tablespoons olive oil
1 tablespoon dry red wine
1½ tablespoons freshly squeezed and strained lemon juice
1 medium garlic clove, finely chopped
1½ teaspoons crushed dried oregano
1 bay leaf
½ teaspoon salt
¼ teaspoon freshly ground black pepper
2 loaves pita, separated into single layers to make 4 circles
½ cup unflavored yogurt
1 medium tomato, seeded and chopped
1 small green papper, seeded, deribbed, and chopped
¼ cup finely chopped scallions (include 2 inches of the green tops)
2 ounces feta cheese, crumbled

Place the meat in a deep bowl. Mix together the oil, wine, lemon juice, garlic, oregano, bay leaf, salt, and pepper and pour over the meat. Turn the pieces about to coat them thoroughly with the marinade. Cover and refrigerate 5 to 6 hours, turning the meat from time to time to keep it well moistened.

Remove the meat from the marinade and thread the cubes tightly on long skewers, leaving a few inches bare at each end. Broil, preferably over charcoal, 3 to 4 inches from the heat 10 to 12 minutes or until the meat is richly browned outside and pink and juicy inside, turning and brushing frequently with the marinade.

While the meat is broiling, heat the bread: Stack and wrap the pita circles in foil and place them on the grill alongside the meat. Leave about 8 minutes or just until warm, turning often. Or place in a preheated 350° F. oven about 8 minutes.

Using a fork, push the kebabs off the skewers onto a warmed serving platter. Fill small dishes with the yogurt, tomato, green pepper, scallions, and cheese to pass at table. Present the heated bread in a basket. Invite diners to spread each pita circle with yogurt, top with the meat kebabs, and then add condiments as desired. To eat, roll up the bread and fold over one end slightly to prevent drips. Makes 4 servings.

VARIATIONS:

Omit the wine and substitute 1 small onion, grated, for the garlic.

Omit the wine. Use beef sirloin rather than lamb and substitute red wine vinegar for the lemon juice, 1 small onion, grated, for the garlic, and shredded Monterey Jack cheese for the feta.

Mexican Steak Cubes in Pita

A blissful union between our southern neighbor and the Middle East.

¼ cup olive oil
2 tablespoons white wine vinegar
2 tablespoons very finely chopped
   or grated onion
¼ teaspoon crushed dried oregano
¼ teaspoon cumin
¼ teaspoon cinnamon
⅛ teaspoon cloves
Salt and freshly ground pepper
   to taste

1 pound boneless lean top sirloin,
   trimmed of fat and cut into 1½-
   inch cubes
4 pita breads, separated into single
   layers to make 8 circles and
   heated *
Guacamole (page 265)

In a shallow bowl stir together the oil, vinegar, onion, oregano, cumin, cinnamon, cloves, and salt and pepper. Add the meat cubes, turning them to coat all sides with the marinade. Cover and refrigerate 3 to 4 hours.

Remove the meat from the marinade and thread the cubes on long skewers, leaving a few inches bare at each end. Broil, preferably over charcoal, about 4 inches from the heat, turning often until the meat is browned on all sides and done to your taste, 10 to 15 minutes for medium rare. With the side of a knife, slide the meat cubes onto a warmed platter. Present the heated pita in a basket.

Invite each diner to assemble his or her own sandwich, topping a warm pita circle with several steak cubes and a few spoonfuls of Guacamole, then rolling the bread around the filling, folding over one end slightly to prevent drips. Makes 8.

Note: If desired, the steak cubes may instead be served in pita halves.

*To heat the pita circles, stack and wrap them in aluminum foil. Place in a preheated 350° F. oven about 10 minutes or until warm. (If grilling outdoors, you may place the wrapped pitas on the grill alongside the meat about 10 minutes or until warm, turning often.)

Lebanese Hamburgers

Altogether different from ordinary hamburgers, this is a novel and exceptionally flavorful way of serving ground meat.

1½ teaspoons cinnamon
1½ teaspoons paprika
¼ teaspoon cayenne pepper or to
  taste
Salt
1½ pounds lean lamb or beef,
  ground twice
3 tablespoons cold water
4 tablespoons butter
2 large onions, cut lengthwise in
  half and thinly sliced

2 medium firm, ripe tomatoes,
  cut lengthwise in ½-inch-thick
  slices
3 pita breads, halved crosswise
  and very lightly toasted
Chopped parsley
Yogurt Sauce with Garlic and
  Mint (below)

In a small cup combine the cinnamon, paprika, cayenne pepper, and 1½ teaspoons salt. Mix well.

In a large mixing bowl combine the meat, water, and 1½ teaspoons of the spice mixture. Mix and knead vigorously until well blended and smooth. With hands moistened in water, form the mixture into 6 patties. Set aside.

In a large, heavy skillet melt 3 tablespoons of the butter over moderate heat. Add the onions and sauté until soft but not browned, stirring frequently. Sprinkle with the remaining spice mixture and continue to cook until lightly browned. Transfer the sautéed onions to a heatproof dish and place, uncovered, in a 300° F. oven.

Add the remaining 1 tablespoon butter to the skillet and melt over moderate heat. Add the tomato slices, sprinkle lightly with salt, and cook 2 minutes or so on each side. Arrange the tomato slices over the onions and pour any juices remaining in the skillet on top. Return the dish to the oven while you cook the meat.

Broil the meat patties, preferably over charcoal, about 4 to 6 minutes on each side, depending on how well done you like the meat to be.

Fill each pita half with a meat patty, a few slices of tomato, and some of the onions. Sprinkle with the parsley. Pass the Yogurt Sauce to spoon into each sandwich. Makes 6 servings.

Yogurt Sauce with Garlic and Mint

1 cup unflavored yogurt
1 medium garlic clove or to taste
¼ teaspoon salt

1 tablespoon finely chopped fresh
mint, or ½ teaspoon crushed
dried mint

Pour the yogurt into a small bowl. Mash the garlic with the salt to a smooth purée. Add to the yogurt with the mint and beat until well blended. Taste and adjust the seasoning. Cover and chill. Makes 1 cup.

Curried Meat and Apricot Burgers

Another intriguing alternative to the usual hamburger.

1 pound lean ground lamb or beef
⅓ cup finely chopped dried
apricots
1 small onion, finely chopped
¼ cup fine dry bread crumbs
1 egg
2 teaspoons curry powder or to
taste

2 tablespoons finely chopped
parsley
Salt and freshly ground pepper
to taste
4 pita breads, halved crosswise
Unflavored yogurt

Combine the meat, apricots, onion, bread crumbs, egg, curry powder, parsley, and salt and pepper in a deep bowl. Knead until thoroughly blended and smooth. With hands moistened in water, shape the mixture into 8 oval patties, each about 4 inches long. Broil, preferably over charcoal, approximately 4 inches from the heat, turning to brown on both sides, about 10 minutes or until done to your taste.

Wrap the pita in aluminum foil and heat on the grill alongside the meat, turning often. Or place in a preheated 350° F. oven about 10 minutes or until warm. Fill each pita half with a meat patty. Spoon some yogurt into each sandwich. Makes 8 servings.

Sausage and Pepper Sandwiches

Certain to bring cheers from everyone at your table.

1 pound hot Italian sausages
1 tablespoon corn oil or flavorless vegetable oil
3 medium onions, cut lengthwise in half and thinly sliced
2 cups sliced mushrooms
1½ cups chopped zucchini
1 cup thinly sliced green pepper
1 cup thinly sliced red bell pepper
3 large garlic cloves, finely chopped
¾ teaspoon ground fennel
¾ teaspoon crushed dried oregano
1 cup dry white wine
Salt and freshly ground pepper to taste
¾ pound mozzarella cheese, shredded
2 pita breads, halved crosswise and lightly toasted
4 ounces Parmesan cheese, grated

Prick the sausages all over with a fork or needle and place them in a large, heavy skillet containing ¼ inch water. Bring the water to a boil over moderate heat and boil the sausages, turning frequently, until the water is evaporated and the sausages have given up some of their fat. Continue to cook the sausages 5 minutes, turning to brown on all sides, then transfer them to a cutting board. Halve the sausages lengthwise and cut them crosswise into ¼-inch-thick slices.

Add the oil to the skillet and heat over moderate heat. Return the sausages to the skillet and sauté about 3 minutes, turning to brown lightly on both sides. Transfer them with a slotted spoon to a bowl and set aside.

Add the onions to the fat remaining in the skillet and sauté over moderate heat until soft, stirring frequently. Add the mushrooms, zucchini, green and red pepper, garlic, fennel, and oregano and cook, stirring, 5 minutes or until the vegetables are tender. Add the sausages and wine and simmer, stirring, until the liquid is evaporated. Season with the salt and pepper and keep warm.

Spoon some of the mozzarella and about ½ cup of the sausage mixture into each pita half and sprinkle it with some of the Parmesan. Serve at once. Makes 4 servings.

Mushroom, Salami, and Cheese Pizzas

Some time ago when making pizza, I hit upon the idea of substituting pita bread for the traditional yeast dough. This discovery resulted in a greatly simplified, delicious version of pizza that has become a favorite of mine.

2 pita breads, separated into single layers to make 4 circles
½ recipe Tomato Sauce (page 264)
6 ounces mozzarella cheese, thinly sliced
2 ounces Italian salami, thinly sliced
4 large mushrooms, thinly sliced
Melted butter

Arrange the pita circles, rough sides up and slightly apart, on ungreased baking sheets. Spread one-fourth of the Tomato Sauce over each circle. Cover each with one-fourth of the cheese slices and one-fourth of the salami slices. Dip the mushroom slices in the melted butter and arrange them on top, dividing them equally among the 4 pita circles. Bake in a preheated 450° F. oven about 15 minutes, or until lightly browned and crisp. Cut into wedges and serve. Makes 8 servings as a snack, 4 as a main course.

5

Tortilla Sandwiches

If you enjoy casual entertaining but are stumped for a menu for your next party, consider the multi-talented tortilla. Tacos, *tostadas,* and *burritos* are only a few of the palate-pleasing ways in which this ancient pancake-like Mexican bread can be featured at mealtime. Shaped into a variety of forms that can accommodate a myriad of fillings, the tortilla is a vehicle par excellence for a host of sandwiches ranging from traditional and classic to innovative and creative. The following selection of recipes is intended to expand the horizon of sandwich aficionados, and to offer hearty and colorful fare that can turn even an everyday meal into a fiesta.

West Indian Chicken Tacos

When one thinks of a Mexican sandwich, the taco most often comes to mind. Tacos are tortillas that are fried soft or crisp and either rolled around or folded over a filling, which can consist of just about anything hot or cold. They are finger food, especially popular as a snack but equally good as an appetizer or main course, two or three of them making a satisfying meal. Taco fillings need not be limited to Mexican fare; many international dishes, such as the West Indian Chicken below, can be utilized just as successfully.

Flavorless vegetable oil
6 flour tortillas (about 7 inches in
   diameter)
West Indian Chicken (below)
2 cups shredded romaine lettuce

Toasted chopped blanched
   almonds, peanuts, or cashews
Dark raisins
Shredded coconut
Lime or lemon wedges

To make the taco shells, in a medium-size, heavy skillet heat about ½ inch oil over medium-high heat until almost smoking. Holding a tortilla with tongs, dip it into the hot fat on both sides to soften it. Fold it in half and, holding the edges slightly apart with the tongs, fry it briefly on each side until it is golden and crisp. Drain on paper towels. Repeat with the remaining tortillas.

Fill each taco shell with a portion of the hot chicken mixture and top with some of the shredded lettuce. Pass the nuts, raisins, coconut, and lime or lemon wedges. Makes 6.

VARIATION:

This dish is also delicious served in lightly toasted pita halves.

West Indian Chicken

3 pounds chicken breasts, halved,
   boned, and skinned
3 tablespoons olive oil or corn oil
1 medium onion, finely chopped
2 medium garlic cloves, finely
   chopped
3 tablespoons freshly squeezed and
   strained lime or lemon juice
1 tablespoon curry powder or to
   taste

¾ teaspoon cumin
¾ teaspoon paprika
⅛ teaspoon crushed dried thyme
1 bay leaf
Salt and freshly ground pepper
   to taste
2 large tomatoes, peeled, seeded,
   and finely chopped

Dry the chicken pieces with paper towels. Cut into ½-inch cubes. In a heavy skillet heat the oil over moderate heat. Add the chicken cubes and sauté about 5 minutes or until golden, stirring frequently. Add the onion and garlic and sauté, stirring, about 4 minutes or until the onion is tender. Add the lime or lemon juice, curry powder, cumin, paprika, thyme, bay leaf, and salt and pepper. Cook about 2 minutes, stirring constantly. Add the tomatoes and bring to a boil while you stir. Reduce the heat and simmer, uncovered, about 20 minutes, or until the chicken is tender and the sauce is thickened. Remove and discard the bay leaf.

Picadillo Tacos

6 packaged taco shells
Picadillo (page 76)
1½ cups shredded Monterey Jack
  or Cheddar cheese

2 cups shredded romaine or iceberg lettuce

Arrange the taco shells on a pie pan and cover with aluminum foil. Place in a preheated 350° F. oven about 10 minutes, or until heated. Fill each taco shell with about ⅓ cup of the Picadillo and top with some of the cheese and lettuce. Serve at once. Makes 6.

Hamburger Tacos

1 pound lean ground beef
1 small onion, very finely chopped
¼ cup fine dry bread crumbs
1 egg
⅓ cup canned peeled and diced
  green chilies
¾ teaspoon Worcestershire sauce
¾ teaspoon cumin
Salt and freshly ground pepper to
  taste

6 corn tortillas (about 6 inches in
  diameter)
Frijoles Refritos (Refried Beans),
  (page 221)
2 medium tomatoes, thinly sliced
1 medium avocado, peeled and
  thinly sliced
Prepared taco sauce

In a mixing bowl combine the beef, onion, bread crumbs, egg, chilies, Worcestershire sauce, cumin, and salt and pepper. Mix until the ingredients are well blended. Form the mixture into 6 rectangular patties, each about ⅜ inch thick. Broil, preferably over charcoal, about 4 inches from the heat 4 minutes on each side, or until the meat is done to your taste.

Stack the tortillas and wrap them in aluminum foil. Warm them at the side of the grill, turning them over to heat evenly. Alternatively, place the wrapped tortillas in a preheated 350° F. oven about 15 minutes, or until warm.)

To serve, spread some beans on each tortilla, then place a hamburger patty and slices of tomato and avocado on one side. Add taco sauce to taste and fold over to eat out of hand. Makes 6.

Sausage and Pepper Tacos

Follow the recipe for Sausace and Pepper Sandwiches (page 88), substituting for the pita breads 4 flour tortillas (about 8 inches in diameter) that have been fried and shaped into taco shells as directed in the recipe for West Indian Chicken Tacos (page 91). Makes 4.

Avocado and Egg Tostadas

A *tostada* (Spanish for "toasted") is a thin, crisp-fried tortilla that forms the base of an open-faced sandwich of the same name. The ingredients of this savory Mexican creation are deliberately chosen to provide contrasts of textures, temperatures, and flavors. Tackle a tostada with knife and fork rather than attempting to pick it up with your hands.

4 flour or corn tortillas (about 7 inches in diameter)
2 cups shredded Monterey Jack or Cheddar cheese
¼ cup seeded and finely chopped canned peeled green chilies
1½ cups shredded iceberg or romaine lettuce

¼ cup chopped scallions (include 2 inches of the green tops)
4 poached, fried, or scrambled eggs, kept warm
1 medium avocado
Cherry tomatoes, halved
Pitted black olives

Arrange the tortillas on ungreased baking sheets. Sprinkle evenly with the cheese and chilies. Bake in a preheated 400° F. oven about 5 minutes, or until the cheese is melted. Remove from the oven and place each tortilla cheese side up on a heated dinner plate. Sprinkle with lettuce and scallions and top with an egg. Peel and cut the avocado into 12 slices. Arrange 3 avocado slices on each tostada. Garnish with the cherry tomatoes and olives. Makes 4.

VARIATIONS:

Substitute 4 individual omelets for the poached, fried, or scrambled eggs.

Add ¼ cup diced cooked ham or turkey with the lettuce and scallions. Serve the tostadas with taco sauce and sour cream, if desired.

Chile Verde Tostadas

Flavorless vegetable oil
6 corn tortillas (about 6 inches in diameter)
Frijoles Refritos (Refried Beans), (page 221)
Chile Verde (below)

Mixed Salad (below)
1 medium avocado, peeled and sliced
1 cup shredded sharp Cheddar cheese

In a medium-size, heavy skillet heat about ¼ inch oil over medium-high heat until almost smoking. Add the tortillas, one at a time, and fry them until crisp and lightly browned, turning frequently. Drain on paper towels. Transfer the tortillas to 4 large plates.

Top the tortillas with the beans, then the Chile Verde, and then the Mixed Salad, allowing equal portions for each tortilla. Garnish with the avocado and cheese. Serve at once. Makes 6.

Chile Verde

2 tablespoons olive oil or flavorless vegetable oil (more if needed)

¾ pound lean boneless beef, cut into ½-inch cubes

¾ pound lean boneless pork, cut into ½-inch cubes

1 small green pepper, seeded, deribbed, and chopped

1 large garlic clove, finely chopped

3 large tomatoes, peeled, seeded, and finely chopped

1 can (4 ounces) peeled green chilies, seeded and chopped

3 tablespoons finely chopped parsley

1 teaspoon cumin

⅛ teaspoon cloves

⅓ cup beef broth

2 tablespoons freshly squeezed and strained lemon juice

Salt to taste

In a heavy casserole or saucepan heat the oil over moderate heat. Add the beef and pork and sauté until browned, stirring frequently. Remove with a slotted spoon to a plate and reserve. Add the green pepper and garlic to the pan drippings and sauté, stirring, until soft, adding a little more oil if necessary. Add the tomatoes, green chilies, parsley, cumin, cloves, beef broth, lemon juice, reserved browned meats, and salt and bring to a boil. Reduce the heat to low, cover, and simmer 1 hour and 15 minutes, stirring occasionally. Uncover and simmer about 10 minutes or until the meat is very tender and the sauce is thickened. Taste and adjust the seasoning. Keep warm.

VARIATION:

Substitute ½ cup dry red wine for the beef broth and lemon juice.

Mixed Salad

3 cups shredded iceberg or romaine lettuce

1 medium tomato, peeled, seeded, and chopped

2 scallions, thinly sliced, including 2 inches of the green tops

12 pitted black olives, sliced

2 tablespoons chopped parsley

2 tablespoons olive oil

2 tablespoons freshly squeezed and strained lemon juice

¼ teaspoon cumin or to taste

Salt to taste

In a salad bowl combine the lettuce, tomato, scallions, olives, and parsley. In a small bowl combine the oil, lemon juice, cumin, and salt. Beat with a fork until well blended and pour over the salad. Toss gently but thoroughly. Taste and adjust the seasoning.

Salmon Burritos

A *burrito* is a warm, soft flour tortilla wrapped around a filling. In its traditional form it is substantial enough to function as an entrée that combines both salad and sandwich. The name itself means "little donkey," and it is anyone's guess as to why it has been applied to this type of dish!

2½ cups watei
1 small onion, sliced
4 whole black peppercorns
1 bay leaf
2 teaspoons freshly squeezed and strained lemon juice
½ teaspoon salt
2 salmon steaks, about 1 inch thick
2 recipes Salsa Mexicana Cruda (page 264)

6 flour tortillas (about 8 inches in diameter)
Lime wedges
Fresh coriander or parsley sprigs
1 cup sour cream or unflavored yogurt
Guacamole (page 265)
2 cups shredded iceberg lettuce

In a large, heavy skillet combine the water, onion, peppercorns, bay leaf, lemon juice, and salt. Bring to a boil over high heat. Reduce the heat to low, cover, and simmer 10 minutes. Place the salmon steaks in the skillet, cover, and simmer about 12 minutes or until the fish flakes when tested with a fork. Using a spatula, transfer the salmon to a platter. Cover and chill. Prepare the Salsa Mexicana Cruda. Cover and chill.

Stack and wrap the tortillas in aluminum foil and place in a preheated 350° F. oven about 15 minutes or until warm. Arrange the salmon on a serving platter. Garnish with the lime wedges and coriander sprigs. Place the Salsa Mexicana Cruda, sour cream or yogurt, Guacamole, and lettuce in bowls. Present the warm tortillas in a napkin-lined basket.

Invite each diner to assemble his or her own burrito, first spreading a tortilla with sour cream or yogurt, adding lettuce, chunks of salmon,

Salsa Mexicana Cruda, and Guacamole, and then rolling the tortilla around the filling, folding over one end slightly to prevent drips. Makes 6.

Note: One pound canned salmon, drained, may be substituted for the cooked fresh salmon.

Beef Burritos

You can make this excellent *burrito* with either beef or chicken or with an assortment of meats, including beef, chicken, and *chorizo* sausages.

6 flour tortillas (about 8 inches in diameter)

1 pound beef, top round or sirloin, trimmed of fat and sliced on the diagonal ⅜ inch thick into strips about 3 inches long

¼ teaspoon cumin

½ teaspoon salt

1 medium garlic clove, finely chopped

1 tablespoon butter

1 tablespoon olive oil

2 ounces Monterey Jack cheese, shredded

1 small mild red onion, cut crosswise into thin slices and separated into rings

Guacamole (page 265)

Salsa Mexicana Cruda (page 264)

Lay the tortillas one at a time in an ungreased large, heavy skillet set over medium-high heat. Heat, turning once, until softened and hot, about 15 seconds on each side. Stack at once in a dampened kitchen towel placed in a pan, then keep warm in a preheated 200° F. oven.

Sprinkle the beef with the cumin, salt, and garlic, rubbing them in with your fingertips. In a heavy skillet heat the butter and oil over moderate heat. Add the steak strips in a single layer and sauté quickly, turning once, until browned on both sides. Transfer to a heated dish and place on a warmer at the table. Place the cheese, onion, Guacamole, and Salsa Mexicana Cruda in bowls. Present the tortillas in a napkin-lined basket.

Invite each diner to assemble his or her own burrito by topping a tortilla with layers of meat, cheese, onion, Guacamole, and Salsa

Mexicana Cruda and then rolling it around the filling, folding over one end slightly to prevent drips. Makes 6.

Note: Sautéed sausage slices may be offered along with the meat. To prepare, cut ½ pound Mexican or Spanish chorizo sausages on the diagonal into ¼-inch-thick slices. Cook in a heavy skillet brushed with olive oil until lightly browned on both sides. Transfer to a heated dish and place on a warmer at the table.

VARIATIONS:

Chicken Burritos

Substitute 1½ pounds chicken breasts, skinned, boned, and sliced into ½-inch-wide strips, for the beef.

Chicken and Beef Burritos

Use ½ pound beef and 1 pound chicken breasts, skinned, boned, and sliced into ½-inch-wide strips, rather than beef alone.

Peking-Style Pork Burritos

Here is an example of the burrito's ability to go international.

1 pound lean ground pork
1 small onion, very finely chopped
¼ cup fine dry bread crumbs
1 egg
½ cup finely chopped water chestnuts
1 medium garlic clove, crushed and finely chopped
2 tablespoons soy sauce
½ teaspoon ginger
8 flour tortillas (about 8 inches in diameter)
Plum Sauce (page 265)
8 scallions, cut lengthwise in matchstick-size pieces
1½ cups fresh bean sprouts or shredded romaine lettuce
1 small bunch fresh coriander, stemmed (optional)

In a mixing bowl combine the pork, onion, bread crumbs, egg, water chestnuts, garlic, soy sauce, and ginger. Mix until the ingredients are well blended. Form the mixture into 8 logs, each about 3 inches long. Broil, preferably over charcoal, about 4 inches from the heat, turning to brown evenly until the meat is done, 12 to 13 minutes.

Stack the tortillas and wrap them in aluminum foil. Warm them at the side of the grill, turning them over to heat evenly. (Alternatively, place the wrapped tortillas in a preheated 350° F. oven about 15 minutes, or until warm.)

To serve, spread some Plum Sauce on a tortilla. Place a pork log near the lower edge and top with some scallion pieces, bean sprouts or shredded lettuce, and coriander sprigs, if desired. Fold the lower edge of the tortilla over the filling, then fold in the sides and roll up to enclose the filling. Pick up with your fingers to eat. Makes 8.

Breakfast Burrito

This interesting version of the *burrito* provides a pleasing change of pace from the usual bacon and cheese omelet.

1 flour tortilla (about 8 inches in diameter)
2 eggs
2 teaspoons water
Salt and freshly ground pepper to taste
1 tablespoon butter
1 slice bacon, cooked crisp and crumbled

2 teaspoons finely chopped scallion, including some of the green top
2 teaspoons canned peeled and diced green chilies
¼ cup coarsely grated Cheddar or Monterey Jack cheese

Heat a heavy skillet or pancake griddle over moderate heat. Put in the tortilla and turn over several times until hot and pliable. Keep hot.

In a small bowl beat together the eggs, water, and salt and pepper until the yolks and whites of the eggs are blended. In a 7-inch omelet pan or skillet heat the butter over high heat and swirl it around in the pan. Pour in the egg mixture and reduce the heat to moderate. Run a thin spatula under the egg mixture as soon as it begins to set, and lift to allow the uncooked portion to flow underneath. When the mixture no longer flows freely, remove from the heat and sprinkle evenly with the bacon, scallion, green chilies, and cheese.

Slide the unfolded omelet onto the tortilla. Fold in the ends, then roll up like a jelly roll to enclose the omelet. Serve at once to eat out of hand. Makes 1.

Crabmeat Enchiladas

An *enchilada* is a tortilla rolled around a filling, covered with sauce, and baked. The sauce is usually seasoned with chili, hence the name.

Flavorless vegetable oil
16 corn tortillas (about 6 inches in diameter)
Enchilada Sauce (below)
Crabmeat Filling (below)

1 cup sour cream
1 bunch scallions, thinly sliced, including 2 inches of the green tops

In a small, heavy skillet heat about ¼ inch oil over moderate heat. Dip 1 tortilla at a time into the hot oil for a few seconds to soften it, then dip it into the Enchilada Sauce. Stack the tortillas on a plate as you finish dipping them.

Spoon some of the Crabmeat Filling down the center of each tortilla, fold one side over the filling, and roll up into a cylinder. Arrange the enchiladas, seam sides down and slightly apart, in a 9-by-13-inch ovenproof baking and serving dish. Reheat the remaining Enchilada Sauce and ladle it over the enchiladas. Bake, uncovered, in a preheated 350° F. oven about 20 minutes, or until the cheese is melted and the sauce is bubbly. Top each enchilada with a dollop of sour cream and sprinkle with some of the sliced scallions. Serve at once. Makes 8 servings.

Enchilada Sauce

6 tablespoons butter
6 tablespoons all-purpose flour
3 cans (10 ounces each) mild red chili enchilada sauce

2¼ cups chicken broth
¼ teaspoon crushed dried oregano
¼ teaspoon cumin

In a large, heavy skillet melt the butter over low heat. Add the flour and cook about 3 minutes, stirring constantly. Remove the pan from the heat and let cool about 1 minute. Stir in the enchilada sauce and chicken broth. Return the pan to the heat and bring the sauce to a simmer while stirring with a wire whisk. Add the oregano and cumin and simmer gently, stirring frequently, 5 to 8 minutes or until the sauce is thickened. Remove from the heat and set aside, covered.

Crabmeat Filling

1 pound crabmeat, picked over and flaked
1 pound Monterey Jack cheese, coarsely grated

1 bunch scallions, thinly sliced, including 2 inches of the green tops

In a mixing bowl combine the crabmeat, cheese, and scallions. Mix until well blended.

Egg Quesadilla

2 eggs
1 tablespoon finely chopped green or red bell pepper
1 tablespoon finely chopped scallion, including some of the green top
Salt to taste
2 teaspoons flavorless vegetable oil

2 teaspoons butter
1 flour tortilla (about 7 inches in diameter)
⅓ cup coarsely grated Cheddar or Monterey Jack cheese
¼ cup Chili Con Carne (below)
Sour cream or yogurt

In a small bowl beat together the eggs, pepper, scallion, and salt until the yolks and whites are blended. Set aside.

In a medium-size, heavy skillet heat the oil and butter over moderate heat. Put in the tortilla and cook about 1 minute, or until puffy. Turn the tortilla over and slowly pour the egg mixture over it, tilting the skillet as you pour to distribute the eggs evenly and being careful that they do not run over the sides of the tortilla. Cook about 4 minutes or just until the eggs set but are still moist. Sprinkle the cheese over the top. Fold the tortilla in half and cook about 30 seconds on each side to melt the cheese. Slide onto a heated plate and spoon the hot chili over it. Top with a dollop of sour cream or yogurt. Makes 1.

Chili Con Carne

1½ tablespoons olive oil	1 tablespoon chili powder
1 medium onion, finely chopped	½ teaspoon cumin seeds, crushed
1 medium garlic clove, crushed	⅛ teaspoon crushed dried basil
½ pound lean ground beef	½ small bay leaf
1 cup water	Salt and cayenne pepper to taste
1 cup peeled, seeded, and finely chopped tomatoes	½ cup cooked kidney beans (optional)
½ medium green pepper, seeded, deribbed, and chopped	

In a heavy saucepan heat the oil over moderate heat. Add the onion and garlic and sauté until golden, stirring frequently. Add the beef and cook, stirring and breaking it up with a fork, until browned. Add the water, tomatoes, green pepper, chili powder, cumin seeds, basil, bay leaf, and salt and cayenne pepper. Simmer, uncovered, stirring from time to time, about 1 hour or until the mixture is thickened. Stir in the beans, if desired, and cook until heated through. Taste and adjust the seasoning.

Mexican-Style Ham and Cheese Sandwiches

These make ordinary grilled ham and cheese sandwiches seem a little pale in comparison.

12 corn or flour tortillas (about 7 inches in diameter)	1 small, mild onion, finely chopped
6 ounces cooked ham, thinly sliced	1½ cups shredded romaine lettuce, lightly dressed with French Dressing (page 261)
6 ounces Cheddar or Monterey Jack cheese, thinly sliced	6 radishes, sliced
Flavorless vegetable oil	
¾ cup sour cream	
¾ cup Guacamole (page 265) or Salsa Mexicana Cruda (page 264)	

Spread 6 of the tortillas flat. Cover each one with some of the ham and cheese. Top each with another tortilla to make a sandwich and fasten each pair of tortillas together with 2 wooden food picks, one on each side.

In a large, heavy skillet heat about ¼ inch oil over moderate heat. Fry 1 sandwich at a time in the hot oil, turning once, until crisp and golden on both sides. Drain on paper towels. Transfer the fried sandwiches to individual heated plates and garnish them with the sour cream, Guacamole or Salsa Mexicana Cruda, and chopped onion. Decorate each plate with the lettuce and radishes. Serve at once. Makes 6.

Pupusas

El Salvador is the home of this unusual sandwich, which is enjoyed both as a snack and as a light main course. The *masa harina* called for in the recipe can be found in Mexican groceries, specialty shops, and some supermarkets.

4 cups dehydrated masa harina (corn tortilla flour)
1½ teaspoons salt
1 teaspoon chili powder
2½ cups water (approximately)
Meat Filling (below)
3 cups shredded romaine or iceberg lettuce

2 carrots, scraped, trimmed, and shredded
1 cup sour cream or unflavored yogurt
4 limes, quartered

In a bowl combine the masa harina, salt, chili powder, and water. Mix together with a spoon until a dough is formed. Divide the dough into 24 equal pieces and roll each piece into a ball. Place each ball on a piece of waxed paper about 6 inches square and cover with another square of waxed paper. With a rolling pin, gently roll each ball until it is about 5 inches in diameter. (Alternatively, form circles with a tortilla press.)

To make each *pupusa*, peel the top paper from 1 circle of dough.

Place about ¼ cup of the Meat Filling in the center of the circle, then spread it evenly to within ½ inch of the edge. Peel the paper from a second circle and turn the dough over onto the filling. Peel off the top paper. Carefully pinch and flute to seal the edges of each pupusa.

Heat a large, heavy skillet or ungreased griddle over moderate heat. Place the pupusas on the pan ½ inch apart and cook about 5 minutes on each side or until golden brown and heated through. Keep warm until all the pupusas are cooked.

Meanwhile, mix the shredded lettuce with the carrots and place in a serving bowl. Spoon the sour cream or yogurt into a small bowl and arrange the quartered limes on a small serving plate.

To eat, carefully squeeze a pupusa to make it pop open along one edge. Spoon some of the lettuce mixture and sour cream or yogurt inside. Squeeze lime juice into the filling and eat with your fingers. Makes 12.

Meat Filling

1 pound lean ground beef
1 small onion, finely chopped
1 can (10 ounces) red chili sauce
½ medium green pepper, seeded, deribbed, and finely chopped
½ teaspoon cumin
2 teaspoons beef stock base
2 cups finely shredded dry Monterey Jack cheese or freshly grated Parmesan cheese

In a heavy skillet cook the ground beef over moderate heat, stirring and breaking it up with a fork until browned and crumbly. Add the onion and cook until soft, stirring frequently. Spoon off and discard excess fat. Stir in the red chili sauce, green pepper, cumin, and beef stock base and cook over high heat, stirring, until all of the liquid in the pan has evaporated. Remove from the heat and cool to room temperature. Stir in the cheese until well mixed. Taste and adjust the seasoning.

Southeast Asian-Style Sandwiches

Flour tortillas provide an excellent substitute for the flat, unleavened Indian bread used in the original version of these sandwiches.

1 tablespoon peanut oil or corn oil
1 pound lean ground beef
1 large onion, finely chopped
2 garlic cloves, finely chopped
1 cup chopped mushrooms
1 teaspoon curry powder
1 teaspoon salt
⅛ teaspoon cayenne pepper or to taste

¼ cup finely chopped fresh coriander leaves or parsley
6 eggs
2 tablespoons water
10 flour tortillas (about 8 inches in diameter)

In a large, heavy skillet heat the oil over moderately high heat. Add the beef and cook, stirring and breaking it up with a fork until browned and crumbly. Add the onion, garlic, mushrooms, curry powder, salt, and cayenne pepper. Cook, stirring, until the vegetables are soft. Stir in the coriander or parsley and remove from the heat. Taste and adjust the seasoning. Beat the eggs lightly with the water.

Lightly grease a griddle or heavy skillet and heat over moderate heat. For each serving, place 1 tortilla on the griddle or in the skillet. Spread one-fifth of the meat mixture over the tortilla. Cook until the tortilla begins to brown on the bottom, then drizzle ⅓ cup of the egg mixture over it. Top with a second tortilla, pressing down lightly. Cook until the tortilla on the bottom is golden and the egg is almost set. Carefully turn to brown the other tortilla. Repeat with the remaining tortillas. Serve at once, cut into wedges. Makes 5 servings.

Blintz-Style Chimichangas

⅔ cup ricotta or dry small-curd
  cottage cheese
2 tablespoons sugar
¼ teaspoon finely grated lemon
  rind
¼ teaspoon cinnamon

2 flour tortillas (about 7 inches in
  diameter)
2 teaspoons flavorless vegetable oil
2 teaspoons butter
Sour cream or unflavored yogurt
Strawberry or cherry preserves

In a small bowl combine the ricotta or cottage cheese, sugar, lemon peel, and cinnamon and mix well. Set aside.

Heat a heavy skillet or pancake griddle over moderate heat. Put in the tortillas, one at a time, and turn over several times until hot and pliable. Spoon half of the cheese mixture down the center of each tortilla. Turn up the ends, fold one side over the filling, and roll up into a cylinder.

In a small, heavy skillet heat the oil and butter over moderate heat. Place the rolled tortillas seam sides down in the skillet and sauté 2 to 3 minutes, turning them until they are crisp and golden brown on all sides. Drain on paper towels. Transfer to a heated plate. Top each *chimichanga* with a dollop of sour cream or yogurt and a spoonful of preserves. Serve at once. Makes 1 serving.

6

Canapés and Tea Sandwiches

Some of the most delightful finger foods ever created are canapés and tea sandwiches. A canapé (literally, a "sofa" in French) is, in classic cuisine, an appetizer consisting of a bread or thin pastry base and a topping such as cheese, seafood, or meat. In much of Europe little open-faced sandwiches, really types of canapés, are enjoyed as hors d'oeuvre, as an accompaniment to tea or coffee, and even as the main event at lunch. Canapés are perfect for serving at parties and receptions. The American institution known as the cocktail hour is the ideal showcase for a tempting assortment of canapés, the number and variety of which offer virtually limitless possibilities to spark the artistic imagination of the cook.

The bread used for canapés should be firm-textured, sliced ¼ inch thick, and trimmed of crusts. Some breads, such as dark pumpernickel, will hold up under a moist topping; less sturdy ones should be toasted. Canapé shapes can range from simple squares, circles, and triangles to fanciful forms made with canapé- or small cookie-cutters. The size of a canapé is usually about 1 or 2 inches in diameter, if a circle, or the equivalent in other shapes, although it can be larger. Allow 6 to 8 canapés per person, depending on what other appetizers are being offered. Canapé decorations include nuts, olives, pimento, radishes, pickles, unwaxed seedless cucumber, hard-cooked egg, capers, parsley, dill, chives, seedless grapes and other fresh fruit, Mimosa (page 227), and truffles. If you care to invest in a set of truffle cutters, you can fashion tiny tulips, rosettes, hearts, stars, or other charming shapes from some of these. Another tool that will lend a professional look to canapés is a pastry bag with assorted tubes through which various creamy mixtures can be piped.

Although the pleasant custom of afternoon tea seems to be disappearing from our lives, tea sandwiches are, fortunately, here to stay, to be enjoyed with the beverage of your choice and other accompaniments, such as a selection of cookies and pastries. They can be made in an assortment of shapes, including rounds, squares, triangles, fingers, crescents, stars, diamonds, and hearts. For variety you can create color contrasts by combining light and dark bread. Use firm-textured, very thinly sliced bread with crusts removed.

Tea sandwiches are smaller than regular sandwiches. The exact size will depend on the shape; for example, two slices of bread with a filling will make about four tiny sandwiches when cut into squares, triangles, or fingers. Count on four to six sandwiches per person, depending on what else is being served.

As a general rule, in order to present canapés and tea sandwiches in prime condition, have all of the ingredients ready beforehand so that they can be assembled in a minimum of time at the last possible moment. Some exceptions, such as ribbon and pinwheel sandwiches, are best made a day in advance, wrapped in aluminum foil or waxed paper, and chilled. They then become more moist and easier to slice than if assembled just before serving. It is often convenient to make small sandwiches in quantity by cutting a whole loaf of bread into thin lengthwise slices that are then spread and shaped. Some bakeries will slice bread this way for you. Alternatively, you can butter the bread and then slice it off. If tea sandwiches are prepared several hours ahead of time, cover them with a dampened tea towel or clear plastic wrap and refrigerate until ready to serve. When storing, it is best not to mix different kinds.

When planning a selection of canapés or tea sandwiches, include some containing cheese, seafood, or meat as well as some with fruit or vegetables. If offering canapés as a prelude to a meal, emphasize piquant foods in order to stimulate the appetite rather than sweet foods, which tend to have a cloying effect.

A variety of breads and bread shapes adds interest to any sandwich tray. In some of the following recipes other types of bread, bread shapes, and butter spreads (chapter 10) can be used if desired instead of those suggested. Also, many sandwiches in other chapters can serve as appetizers when made in miniature.

Cold Savory Canapés and Tea Sandwiches

Swedish Cheese Canapés

Spread small squares of dark rye or pumpernickel bread with butter. Border each square with Swedish Cheese Filling (page 196) piped through a pastry bag fitted with a small fancy tube. Place a small radish rose (page 224) or seedless grape in the center of each square.

Cream Cheese and Olive Stars

Cut thin slices of dark rye or pumpernickel bread into small star shapes. Using a pastry bag fitted with a plain tube, pipe Cream Cheese and Nut Filling (page 191) into pitted black olives. Place a stuffed olive in the center of each star and pipe a line of the spread along each tip of the star.

Persian Yogurt Cheese Canapés

Spread small toasted triangles of pita bread, cocktail-size rounds of *lavash* (page 246), or crisp wheat crackers with Persian Yogurt Cheese Filling (page 195).

Caucasian Walnut, Cheese, and Herb Canapés

Spread cocktail-size rounds of *lavash* (page 246) or small toasted triangles of pita bread with Caucasian Walnut, Cheese, and Herb Filling (page 197). Garnish with tiny wedges of unpeeled cucumber or tomato.

Cheese Cornucopias

Trim the crusts from a chilled loaf of thinly sliced white bread. With a 3-inch cookie cutter cut a circle in the center of each bread slice. Flatten each circle with a rolling pin. Lightly butter both sides of each circle, then roll it into a cone shape and press the overlapping edges together, securing with a food pick if necessary. Arrange the bread cones on an ungreased baking sheet and bake in a preheated 350° F. oven about 12 minutes or until lightly browned. Remove from the oven, cool, and remove the food picks, if used. Fill the cornucopias with Curried Cheese Filling (page 197) or Cream Cheese, Gorgonzola, and Avocado Filling (page 195) piped through a pastry bag fitted with a fluted tube.

Onion, Cheese, and Apple Canapés

Spread small rounds of whole wheat toast or unsweetened brioche with mayonnaise. Cover each round with a paper-thin slice of red onion and top with a thin slice of Port Salut or Gruyère cheese, both cut to size. Garnish with a wedge of unpeeled tart apple and a sprig of mint.

Dutch Cheese and Grape Canapés

Spread small rectangles of rye Melba toast with butter. Cover each rectangle with a piece of Boston lettuce cut to size. Arrange thin wedges of Edam or Gouda cheese over the lettuce and top with a few halved and seeded red grapes, cut sides down.

Pear and Cheese Canapés

Spread small rectangles of whole wheat toast with Roquefort and Walnut Filling (page 196). Cover with overlapping thin slices of unpeeled pear that have been brushed with fresh lemon juice to prevent discoloration. Garnish with sprigs of watercress or mint.

Curried Egg Salad Canapés

Spread small rounds of white, whole wheat, or rye bread with butter. Cover each round with a piece of Boston lettuce cut to size. Place a thin tomato slice over the lettuce and top with a spoonful of Curried Egg Salad (page 216). Garnish with a parsley sprig.

Artichoke Canapés

Spread small rounds of dark rye or pumpernickel bread with Anchovy Butter (page 188). Place a small drained marinated artichoke heart, bottom side up, in the center of each round. Using a pastry bag fitted with a small star tube, pipe Whipped Cream Cheese (page 191) in a circle around each artichoke.

Hearts of Palm Canapés I

Spread small rounds of toast with *pâté de foie gras* or Chicken Liver Pâté (page 205). Sprinkle with sieved hard-cooked egg yolk and finely chopped parsley. Top each round with a small slice of heart of palm.

Hearts of Palm Canapés II

Spread small rounds of toast with Cream Cheese and Chives Filling (page 193). Border each round with a ribbon of caviar and center a small slice of heart of palm on each.

Olive Canapés

Fill the cavities of pitted jumbo black olives with *pâté de foie gras* or Chicken Liver Pâté (page 205). Spread small rounds of toast with Smoked Salmon Butter (page 189) and top each round with a stuffed olive. Decorate the canapés with mayonnaise piped through a pastry bag fitted with a small fancy tube. Sprinkle with finely chopped chives.

Danish Shrimp Canapés

Spread small squares of white bread with Shrimp Butter (page 189). Cover each square with a piece of Boston lettuce cut to size. Arrange a row of overlapping tiny cooked and shelled shrimp along the bottom and right side of the square. Decorate the top left corner with mayonnaise piped through a pastry bag fitted with a small tube. Garnish with a cucumber rose (page 225) or dill sprigs.

Curried Shrimp and Cucumber Canapés

Spread small rounds of white toast with Curried Shrimp Filling (page 199). Top each round with a slice of unpeeled cucumber.

Shrimp and Pineapple Canapés

Spread small triangles of white toast with Avocado Butter (page 187). Top each triangle with a thin slice of pineapple cut to size and spread with a thin layer of mayonnaise that has been mixed with an equal amount of stiffly whipped cream. Arrange 3 tiny cooked and shelled shrimp on each triangle and pipe a rosette of Avocado Butter at the top.

Crabmeat Canapés

Spread small triangles of white toast with Shrimp Butter (page 189). Cover with flaked cooked crabmeat. Decorate each triangle with a border of Shrimp Butter piped through a pastry bag fitted with a small fancy tube. Garnish with a dot of caviar or a slice of pimento-stuffed olive.

Curried Lobster Canapés

Follow the recipe for Curried Egg Salad Canapés (page 112), substituting Curried Lobster Filling (page 200) for the egg filling.

Lobster and Mussel Canapés

Spread small squares of white toast with Chive Butter (page 185). Cover with thin slices of cooked lobster meat. Top with small cooked mussels dipped in sherry. Decorate with mayonnaise piped through a pastry bag fitted with a small fancy tube. Dust lightly with paprika.

Swedish Smoked Salmon Canapés

Spread slices of white bread with Dill Butter (page 183). Sprinkle with freshly ground black pepper and cover with thin slices of smoked salmon. Stamp out canapés with a fluted round cutter. Top each canapé with a slice of hard-cooked egg and garnish with a sprig of dill.

VARIATION:

Omit the egg and dill. Cut the canapés into crescents, stars, diamonds, or hearts.

Rolled Smoked Salmon Canapés

Spread thin slices of smoked salmon with Whipped Cream Cheese (page 191) flavored with finely chopped dill or Cream Cheese and Avocado Filling (page 194). Roll the salmon like a jelly roll. Wrap the rolls securely in aluminum foil and chill thoroughly. Cut the rolls into ½-inch-thick slices and serve them on small rounds of white toast.

Smoked Salmon Bagelettes

Split and toast Miniature Bagels (page 256) or frozen Lender's Bagelettes, thawed. Spread with Lemon Cream Cheese (page 191) or Cream Cheese and Chives Filling (page 193). Top with diced smoked salmon. Garnish with finely chopped fresh dill.

Salmon, Sturgeon, and Caviar Canapés

Cover one-third of a small square of white toast with a thin slice of smoked sturgeon, the second third with one of smoked salmon, and the remaining third with caviar. Garnish with a border of Mimosa (page 227).

Caviar Canapés

Spread small crescents of white toast with black caviar. Sprinkle one end of each crescent with sieved egg white, the other with sieved egg yolk. Place a tiny cooked shrimp or a slice of pimento-stuffed olive in the center.

Swedish Smoked Cod Roe Canapés

Spread slices of white bread with butter and cut into small heart shapes. Cover with smoked cod roe. Garnish with chopped chives.

Greek Tarama Croustades

Trim the crusts from thinly sliced white bread. Flatten each slice with a rolling pin. Using a 2¼-inch round cutter, cut 2 circles from each slice. Fit each circle carefully into a buttered 1¼-inch muffin tin. Brush the circles with melted butter and bake them in a preheated 400° F. oven about 8 minutes or until golden brown. Remove the croustades from the tins and cool on a wire rack. Fill the croustades with Greek Taramasalata (page 202) and garnish each with a pitted black olive.

Cream Cheese, Anchovy, and Caper Canapés

Spread small ovals of white toast with cream cheese mixed with a little heavy cream and seasoned with anchovy paste. Using a pastry bag fitted with a plain tube, pipe a strip of the cream cheese mixture down the length of each oval. Sprinkle with finely chopped parsley and scatter drained capers on both sides of the strip.

Spanish Anchovy, Pimento, and Olive Canapés

Spread small squares of white toast with Anchovy Butter (page 188) and cover with alternating strips of anchovy fillets and pimento. Garnish with slices of green olives.

Danish Anchovy Canapés with Potato and Sour Cream

Spread small rounds of white bread with butter. Border each round with a ring of anchovy fillets. Fill the ring with cold cooked diced potato in sour cream. Garnish with a tiny wedge of cherry tomato, a parsley sprig, and a few drained capers.

Sardine and Egg Canapés

Spread small rounds of white toast with Tuna Butter (page 189). Top each round with a slice of hard-cooked egg and garnish with a small sardine.

Oysters and Caviar in Croûtes

Cut 1-inch-thick slices of crustless white bread into 1½-inch rounds. Carefully hollow out the center of each round with a sharp knife, leaving a shell about ⅛ inch thick. Brush the bread on all surfaces except the bottom with melted butter. Arrange the croûtes on a baking sheet. Bake in a preheated 400° F. oven 8 to 10 minutes, or until golden brown. Remove from the oven and cool. Place a small raw oyster in each croûte and top with black caviar.

Swedish Smoked Eel and Cucumber Canapés

Spread small rectangles of dark rye or pumpernickel bread with Dill Butter (page 183). Cover each rectangle with 3 overlapping thin slices of unpeeled cucumber. Top with a thin strip of smoked eel and garnish with a dill sprig.

Smoked Turkey Canapés

Spread small squares of white toast with Whipped Cream Cheese (page 191). Cover each square with a paper-thin slice of smoked turkey breast cut to size and garnish with a watercress sprig.

Danish Ham Canapés

Spread small triangles of white bread with Rum Butter (page 190). Cover each triangle with a thin slice of Danish cooked ham but to size. Garnish with a tiny piece of Boston lettuce, a small wedge of pineapple, and a maraschino cherry.

Prosciutto and Melon Canapés

Cover small rounds of buttered brioche or egg twist bread with thin slices of prosciutto cut to size. Top each round with a small circle of cantaloupe, honeydew, or casaba melon. Sprinkle with freshly ground pepper, if desired.

VARIATION:

Papaya may be substituted for the melon.

Ham and Pâté de Foie Gras Canapés

Trim the crusts from very thin slices of fresh white bread. Spread the slices with Ham and Pâté de Foie Gras Filling (page 204). Roll them in cigarette shapes and chill 1 hour. Cut the cigarettes into 1-inch-thick slices, spread the tops with butter, and sprinkle with sieved hard-cooked egg yolk or with finely chopped parsley.

Middle Eastern Steak Tartare Canapés

Spread small toasted triangles of pita bread with Kibbeh (page 173). Sprinkle with a mixture of very finely chopped parsley, scallion, and green pepper. Garnish each triangle with a wedge of cherry tomato.

Danish Liver Pâté Canapés

Spread small ovals of white bread with butter. Cover each oval with a thin slice of liver pâté cut to size. Garnish with a cucumber twist (page 225) and place a slice of pimento-stuffed olive on each side of the twist.

Liverwurst Canapés

Spread small rounds of dark rye or pumpernickel bread with liverwurst. Place a ring of mild red onion on each round. Put a dab of sour cream in each ring and top with lumpfish caviar. Garnish with a tiny piece of lemon rind.

VARIATION:

Substitute liver pâté for the liverwurst.

Chicken Liver Pâté and Pistachio Rolls

Trim the ends from small rectangular hard French rolls and carefully remove the soft insides, leaving a ¼-inch-thick shell. Stuff the shells with Chicken Liver Pâté (page 205) mixed with chopped skinned pistachio nuts. Wrap each stuffed roll in aluminum foil and chill several hours or overnight. To serve, cut the rolls crosswise into ¼-inch-thick slices.

Chicken Liver, Ham, and Bacon Canapés

1 tablespoon butter
8 ounces chicken livers, cleaned
   and dried with paper towels
1 slice bacon
1 tablespoon thinly sliced scallions,
   including 2 inches of the green
   tops

2 teaspoons finely chopped parsley
2 tablespoons finely chopped lean
   cooked ham
Small rounds of crustless rye
   bread or toast, buttered
Mayonnaise
Black olives

In a large, heavy skillet melt the butter over medium-high heat. Add the chicken livers and sauté until lightly browned, stirring frequently. Remove them from the pan, drain on absorbent paper, and chop finely. Set aside.

In a small skillet cook the bacon until crisp. Lift from the skillet and chop finely. Add the scallions and parsley to the bacon fat remaining in the skillet and sauté about 1 minute, stirring constantly.

Combine the sautéed livers, bacon, scallions, parsley, and ham in a bowl and mix well. Spread the mixture on the bread rounds. Garnish each round with mayonnaise piped through a pastry bag fitted with a small fancy tube. Top with a black olive.

Salami Canapés

Spread small rounds of rye bread with Herbed Cream Cheese (page 193). Cover with thin slices of salami cut to size.

Italian Rolled Mortadella Canapés

Spread very thin slices of mortadella with Whipped Cream Cheese (page 191). Spread over the cream cheese a seeded, grated, and well-drained cucumber mixed with just enough mayonnaise to bind. Roll the mortadella like a jelly roll. Wrap the rolls securely in aluminum foil and chill thoroughly. Cut the rolls into ½-inch-thick slices and serve them on small rounds of white toast.

VARIATION:

Substitute smoked salmon for the mortadella and flavor the mayonnaise with finely chopped dill.

Swedish Fruit Salad Canapés

Spread small rounds of dark rye or pumpernickel bread with butter. Cover each round with a thin slice of orange cut to size. Top with a spoonful of diced apple, celery, and chopped walnuts mixed with mayonnaise. Garnish with a tiny piece of Boston lettuce, a wedge of red apple, and a walnut half.

Mushroom Sandwiches

Spread thin slices of whole wheat bread with Cream Cheese and Mushroom Filling (page 194). Top each with another bread slice.

Gently press each sandwich, trim the crusts, and cut into 4 squares. Brush all 4 sides of each square lightly with mayonnaise and dip each side into finely chopped parsley.

Tomato Sandwiches

Spread 2-inch rounds of white bread with Green Mayonnaise or Curry Mayonnaise (page 262). Top half of the rounds with thin slices of tomato cut to size, and sprinkle with salt and freshly ground pepper to taste. Cover with the remaining bread rounds, mayonnaise sides down.

Cream Cheese and Avocado Sandwiches

With a canapé or small cookie cutter, cut diamond shapes out of thin slices of light and dark bread trimmed of crusts. Spread half of the diamonds with butter and Cream Cheese and Avocado Filling (page 194). Using a tiny diamond cutter, cut out a diamond from the center of each of the remaining bread diamonds and cover the sandwiches. The fillings will show through.

VARIATION:

Use dark bread for the bottom diamonds and light bread for the tops or vice versa.

Checkerboard Sandwiches

Trim the crusts from 3 thin slices each of white and dark bread. Spread a slice of the white bread with butter and a cold creamy filling (chapter 10) and top with a slice of dark bread. Spread the dark bread with butter and filling and cover with a slice of white bread. Repeat this procedure, starting instead with dark bread so that you end up with a slice of dark bread on the top. Gently press each sandwich and cut crosswise into ½-inch-thick slices. Spread each slice with butter and filling and stack them in piles of three, with strips of dark bread directly over strips of white bread. Press gently, wrap in a damp kitchen towel, and chill several hours. To serve, cut into thin slices.

Curried Egg Sandwiches

Butter thin slices of white or whole wheat bread. Spread half of the slices with Curried Egg Filling (page 199). Cover with the remaining bread slices, buttered sides down. Gently press each sandwich, trim the crusts, and cut into 4 squares, triangles, or fingers.

Smoked Salmon and Cucumber Sandwiches

Spread thin slices of white bread with Smoked Salmon Filling (page 200). Cover half of the slices with very thin slices of peeled cucumber and top them with the remaining bread slices, filling sides down. Gently press each sandwich, trim the crusts, and cut into 4 triangles.

Swedish Anchovy and Egg Sandwiches

Spread Swedish Anchovy and Egg Filling (page 201) between thin slices of white bread. Gently press each sandwich, trim the crusts, and cut into 4 triangles.

Sardine and Cucumber Sandwiches

Follow the recipe for Smoked Salmon and Cucumber Sandwiches (above), substituting Sardine and Cream Cheese Filling (page 201) for the Smoked Salmon Filling.

Finger Rolls with Chicken and Almond Filling

Split finger rolls almost through and spread the insides with butter. Sandwich the rolls with Chicken and Almond Filling (page 203).

Turkey and Avocado Sandwiches

Spread thin slices of white and dark bread with Curry Butter (page 186). Place very thin slices of cold roast turkey on each slice of white bread and cover with a layer of very thinly sliced avocado. Top with a slice of dark bread. Gently press each sandwich, trim the crusts, and cut into 4 triangles.

VARIATION:

Slices of cold roast chicken may be substituted for the turkey.

Ham Rounds

With a canapé or small cookie cutter, cut circles out of thin slices of white, whole wheat, or pumpernickel bread trimmed of crusts. Using a very small round cutter or large thimble, cut holes in the center of half of the circles to form rims. Spread the whole circles with Mustard Butter (page 185). Place the rims on top of the whole circles. Fill the centers with Ham Filling (page 203) or Deviled Ham and Cream Cheese Filling (page 204).

VARIATION:

Use dark bread for the bottom circles and white bread for the tops and substitute Ham and Pâté de Foie Gras Filling (page 204) for the Ham Filling.

Ham and Apricot Sandwiches

Spread very thin slices of white, whole wheat, or light rye bread with almond or hazelnut butter (see Nut Butter, page 186) seasoned with a little dry mustard. Spread half of the slices with a layer of apricot jam and top with thin slices of Smithfield or Westphalian ham cut to size. Cover with the remaining bread slices. Gently press each sandwich, trim the crusts, and cut into 4 fingers.

Rolled Prosciutto and Watercress Sandwiches

Spread very thin slices of white or whole wheat bread, crusts removed, with a thin layer of Whipped Cream Cheese (page 191). Cover with a thin layer of watercress sprigs, then a thin layer of prosciutto. Grind a little pepper over the prosciutto. Roll the slices into cylinders. Tuck watercress sprigs into both ends of each cylinder, allowing them to protrude. Arrange the sandwiches seam sides down on a serving tray. If necessary, secure them with food picks. Cover with clear plastic wrap and chill. Remove the food picks, if used, before serving.

VARIATION:

You may substitute paper-thin slices of Westphalian ham, Italian salami, smoked turkey, or smoked salmon for the prosciutto.

Stuffed Pinwheel Sandwiches

Trim the crusts from a chilled unsliced loaf of white bread. Spread one long side of the loaf with butter and cut off a very thin slice. Spread the slice with Ham and Pâté de Foie Gras Filling (page 204). Arrange a row of pimento-stuffed olives along one narrow end. Beginning at the same end, roll up the bread tightly like a jelly roll. Following this same procedure, prepare as many rolls as needed. Wrap the rolls in a damp cloth and chill them several hours. Close to serving time, cut the rolls crosswise into ⅓- to ½-inch-thick slices. Each sandwich will have a slice of olive in the center of the pinwheel.

VARIATION:

Pinwheel Sandwiches

Substitute Mixed Herb Butter (page 184) for the Ham and Pâté de Foie Gras Filling and omit the olives.

Rolled Cream Cheese, Avocado, and Bacon Sandwiches

Spread very thin slices of white or whole wheat bread, crusts removed, with Cream Cheese and Avocado Filling (page 194). Sprinkle evenly with bacon, cooked crisp and crumbled, and roll the slices into cylinders. Arrange the sandwiches, seam sides down, on a serving tray. If necessary, secure them with food picks. Cover with clear plastic wrap and chill. Remove the food picks, if used, before serving.

Tongue and Ham Sandwiches

Spread thin slices of rye bread with Tongue and Ham Filling (page 206). Top each with another bread slice. Gently press each sandwich, trim the crusts, and cut into 4 fingers.

VARIATION:

Spread the filling between slices of white and whole wheat bread. Cut each sandwich into 4 squares or triangles.

Pâté de Foie Gras Sandwiches

Spread small rounds of unsweetened brioche or white bread with Whipped Pâté de Foie Gras (page 206). Top each with another round. Lightly brush the edge of each sandwich with mayonnaise and dip it into finely chopped parsley.

Ribbon Sandwiches

Chicken Liver Pâté and Mushroom Filling (page 205)

Cream Cheese, Green Pepper, and Pimento Filling (page 195)

1 loaf (1 pound) unsliced white bread, chilled

1 loaf (1 pound) unsliced whole wheat bread, chilled

Prepare the fillings. With a sharp knife trim the crusts from the loaves. From each loaf cut 2 lengthwise slices, each ¼ inch thick. (Reserve the remaining bread for other uses, or use 4 slices from each loaf and double the amounts of the filling ingredients to make 64 sandwiches). Spread a white bread slice with half of the Chicken Liver Pâté and Mushroom Filling. Top with a whole wheat bread slice. Spread with all of the Cream Cheese, Green Pepper, and Pimento Filling. Top with the second white bread slice. Spread with the remaining Chicken Liver Pâté and Mushroom Filling. Cover with the second whole wheat bread slice. Press the layers together firmly. Wrap the loaf thus formed in aluminum foil and refrigerate at least 3 hours or overnight.

To serve, use a serrated knife to cut the loaf into 16 slices, then cut each slice in half crosswise. Makes 32.

Sandwich Loaf

1 loaf (1 pound) unsliced whole wheat bread, chilled
1 loaf (1 pound) unsliced white bread, chilled
½ cup butter, at room temperature
½ cup Cream Cheese and Avocado Filling (page 194)
½ cup Deviled Ham Filling (page 204)
½ cup Chicken Liver Pâté and Bacon Filling (page 206)
Cream Cheese Frosting (below)
Watercress sprigs

With a sharp knife, trim the crusts from the loaves. From each loaf cut two ½-inch-thick slices lengthwise. (Reserve the remaining bread for another use.)

To assemble the loaf, spread one of the whole wheat bread slices with butter, then with an even layer of Cream Cheese and Avocado Filling. Cover with one of the white bread slices. Spread with butter, then with an even layer of Deviled Ham Filling. Cover with the second whole wheat bread slice. Spread with butter, then with an even layer of Chicken Liver Pâté and Bacon Filling. Top with the second white bread slice. Press the layers together gently. Wrap the loaf in aluminum foil or clear plastic wrap and refrigerate several hours or overnight. Unwrap and place on a platter. Frost the top and sides with the Cream Cheese Frosting. Chill about 1 hour or until the frosting has set.

Transfer the loaf to a chilled serving platter. Garnish with the watercress sprigs. Present the loaf whole, then cut it in thick slices to serve. Makes 1 loaf (about 8 servings).

VARIATION:

Omit the food coloring from the Cream Cheese Frosting. Sprinkle the frosting with sieved hard-cooked egg yolk. Decorate the loaf with watercress sprigs, radish roses (page 224), cucumber twists (page 225), and tomato wedges.

Cream Cheese Frosting

16 ounces cream cheese, at room temperature
¼ cup heavy cream

Few drops green food coloring (optional)

In a mixing bowl beat the cream cheese, gradually adding the heavy cream until the mixture is light and fluffy. Add the food coloring, if desired, to tint the frosting a delicate green.

Sandwich Torte

1 round loaf white bread, about 7 inches in diameter
Cream Cheese, Olive, and Nut Filling with Mayonnaise (page 192)
Shrimp Butter (page 189)

Curried Egg Filling (page 199)
Mayonnaise
Thin slices of cucumber
Cherry tomato halves
Watercress sprigs

With a sharp knife, slice the top third from the bread. Trim off the bottom and side crusts. Cut the bread into 4 even horizontal slices. (Reserve the top of the loaf and the crusts for another use.) Spread the bottom slice with the Cream Cheese, Olive, and Nut Filling with Mayonnaise. Cover with the second slice of bread and spread it with the Shrimp Butter. Cover with the third slice of bread and spread it with the Curried Egg Filling. Cover with the fourth slice of bread.

Press the torte together gently, wrap it in aluminum foil or clear plastic wrap, and chill several hours or overnight.

Transfer the torte to a chilled serving platter and spread the top with a thin coating of mayonnaise. Garnish the top with the cucumber slices and cherry tomato halves. Surround the base of the torte with the watercress sprigs. Cut into wedges to serve. Makes 1 loaf (about 8 servings).

Cocktail Brioches

Bake and cool 1 recipe Tiny Brioches à Tête (page 241). Remove the heads and reserve. Carefully hollow out the brioches. Arrange the brioche shells on a baking sheet and place in a preheated 350° F. oven about 3 minutes to dry the interiors. Remove from the oven and cool to room temperature. Fill the brioche shells with caviar, or with any of the fillings given below, piped through a pastry bag fitted with a ¼-inch tube. Cover the shells with the reserved heads and serve. Makes about 30.

Fillings for Cocktail Brioches

Cream Cheese and Mushroom
   Filling (page 194)
Cream Cheese, Gorgonzola, and
   Avocado Filling (page 195)
Curried Cheese Filling (page 197)
Curried Shrimp Filling (page 199)

Curried Lobster Filling (page 200)
Ham Filling (page 203)
Chicken Liver Pâté (page 205)
Whipped Pâté de Foie Gras (page
   206)

Hot Savory Canapés and Tea Sandwiches

Cheddar Cheese and Olive Canapés

Spread lightly toasted whole grain English muffin halves with Cheddar Cheese and Olive Filling (page 198). Arrange them on a baking sheet and place under a preheated broiler about 4 inches from the heat until the tops are bubbly and lightly browned. Quarter each muffin half and serve the canapés at once.

Mushroom Croustades

12 thin slices white bread
3 tablespoons butter
1 cup finely chopped mushrooms
⅓ cup finely chopped shallots or scallions (include 2 inches of the green tops of the scallions)
¼ cup heavy cream
Freshly grated Parmesan cheese

2 tablespoons fresh bread crumbs
⅛ teaspoon crushed dried thyme
⅛ teaspoon crushed dried oregano
Salt and freshly ground pepper to taste
Butter

Prepare croustades with the bread as directed in the recipe for Greek Tarama Croustades (page 116). Set aside.

In a small, heavy skillet melt the butter over medium-high heat. Add the mushrooms and shallots or scallions and cook, stirring, about 10 minutes or until most of the liquid has evaporated. Add the cream, ⅓ cup Parmesan cheese, the bread crumbs, thyme, oregano, and salt and pepper and cook gently about 2 minutes. Divide the mixture among the croustades and arrange them on a baking sheet. Sprinkle the croustades with Parmesan cheese, dot with butter, and place under a preheated broiler about 4 inches from the heat until the cheese is melted. Serve at once. Makes 24.

Crostini Alla Napoletana

Arrange small triangles of white bread on a baking sheet and toast under a preheated broiler about 4 inches from the heat until they are golden brown on one side. Cover the untoasted side of each triangle with a thin slice of Bel Paese cheese cut to size. Place 2 anchovies over the cheese and top with a thin slice of Italian plum tomato. Sprinkle with freshly ground pepper and crushed dried oregano to taste and dribble ½ teaspoon olive oil over each triangle. Bake in a preheated 375° F. oven about 10 minutes or until the cheese is melted. Serve at once.

Angels on Horseback

Wrap shucked oysters in lean bacon slices, using half a bacon slice for each oyster. Secure with food picks. Arrange the oysters on a wire rack over a baking pan and broil about 4 inches from the heat, turning them occasionally with tongs until the bacon is crisp, about 5 minutes. Remove the food picks and serve at once on small buttered rounds of white toast.

Chinese Shrimp Toast

6 slices white bread
½ pound shrimp, shelled, deveined, and ground
2 tablespoons fresh pork fat, ground
2 tablespoons finely grated onion
1 teaspoon salt
½ teaspoon monosodium glutamate (optional)

1 tablespoon cornstarch
1 large egg, lightly beaten
24 leaves fresh coriander (cilantro or Chinese parsley) or flat-leaf Italian parsley (optional)
Peanut oil or flavorless vegetable oil for deep-frying

Trim the crusts from the bread. Cut each slice into 4 squares or triangles. Spread out on a tray and set aside.

Combine the shrimp, pork fat, onion, salt, monosodium glutamate (if used), cornstarch, and egg in a bowl. Mix thoroughly until they form a paste. Spread the mixture on the bread squares or triangles, mounding them slightly in the center. If desired, gently press a coriander or parsley leaf into the center of each mound.

Heat the oil to 375° F. Drop in the bread squares or triangles a few at a time, shrimp sides down. Deep-fry until golden brown. Drain on paper towels and serve hot. Makes 6 servings.

Spinach, Cheese, and Ham Canapés

1 pound spinach
¼ cup cold water
Butter
¼ cup finely chopped shallots or scallions (include 2 inches of the green tops of the scallions)
1 medium garlic clove, finely chopped
½ teaspoon crushed dried rosemary
Freshly grated nutmeg to taste
Salt and freshly ground pepper to taste
4 ounces cream cheese
¼ cup diced cooked ham
1 teaspoon Dijon-style mustard
2 rectangular hard French rolls
Freshly grated Parmesan or Gruyère cheese

Wash the spinach thoroughly under cold running water, discarding the stems and bruised leaves. Drain. Chop the spinach and combine it with the water in a large saucepan. Bring to a boil over high heat. Reduce the heat to low, cover, and simmer 5 minutes or until the spinach is wilted. Transfer to a colander and allow the spinach to drain and cool. Squeeze it dry and chop finely. Reserve.

In a heavy skillet melt 2 tablespoons butter over moderate heat. Add the shallots or scallions and garlic and sauté about 3 minutes or until golden, stirring frequently. Add the reserved spinach, rosemary, nutmeg, and salt and pepper and cook, stirring, 5 minutes. Add the cream cheese, ham, and mustard and cook, stirring, about 5 minutes or until the mixture is thickened and the cheese is melted. Remove from the heat and keep warm.

Trim the ends from the rolls and cut the rolls into ¼-inch-thick slices. Toast the slices lightly. Butter each slice, spread it with a layer of the spinach mixture, and sprinkle with the grated cheese. Arrange the canapés on a baking sheet and place under a preheated broiler about 4 inches from the heat until lightly browned and bubbly. Serve at once. Makes about 24.

Miniature Hamburger and Bagel Appetizers

½ pound lean round steak, ground
  twice
Salt and freshly ground pepper
  to taste
8 Miniature Bagels (page 256) or
  frozen Lender's Bagelettes,
  thawed

Tomato Relish (page 231)
1 to 2 leaves Boston or Bibb
  lettuce

Season the meat with the salt and pepper and form into miniature hamburger patties, using 1 to 1½ tablespoons for each hamburger. Broil the patties in a preheated broiler about 4 inches from the heat about 2 minutes on each side or until they are nicely browned.

Split and toast the miniature bagels. Place a hamburger patty on the bottom half of each bagel. Top with a spoonful of the Tomato Relish and a tiny piece of lettuce. Cover with the top half of the bagel and serve at once. Makes 8.

VARIATIONS:

Instead of broiling the hamburger patties, you may roll them lightly in flour and sauté them in ½ tablespoon each butter and olive oil.

Thin slices of Italian plum tomato and mild red onion may be substituted for the Tomato Relish. Top each hamburger with a slice of onion and a slice of tomato.

Chinese Chicken Liver, Pork, and Mushroom Half-Moons

2 chicken livers, cleaned
3 tablespoons peanut oil or flavorless vegetable oil
2 scallions, thinly sliced, including 2 inches of the green tops
4 ounces lean ground pork
1¾ cups finely diced mushrooms
½ cup finely chopped water chestnuts
2 tablespoons soy sauce
1 tablespoon pale dry sherry
1½ tablespoons water

1 tablespoon cornstarch
¼ teaspoon salt
⅛ teaspoon freshly ground pepper
¼ teaspoon sugar
¼ teaspoon five-spice powder
½ teaspoon Oriental sesame oil
12 thin slices homemade-type white bread
1 egg yolk
Peanut oil or flavorless vegetable oil for deep-frying

Drop the chicken livers into boiling water 20 seconds. Drain well on paper towels and cut into small cubes. Set aside.

Heat a wok or skillet over high heat 30 seconds. Pour in the 3 tablespoons oil and heat. Add the scallions and pork and stir-fry over medium-high heat until the pork is cooked. Add the mushrooms and cook 30 seconds. Add the chicken livers and stir-fry until they lose their redness. Add the water chestnuts and mix well. Remove the wok or skillet from the heat for a moment. Stir together the soy sauce, sherry, water, cornstarch, salt, pepper, and sugar until the cornstarch is dissolved. Return the wok or skillet to the heat, add the cornstarch mixture, and cook 20 seconds. Add the five-spice powder and sesame oil and mix thoroughly. Remove from the heat and transfer the contents of the wok or skillet to a bowl. Cool to room temperature.

Trim the crusts from the bread slices. Flatten each slice with a rolling pin. Cover the bread with a barely dampened kitchen towel. Prepare each half-moon as follows: Place about 1½ tablespoons of the chicken liver mixture on the lower half of each bread slice. Moisten the edges with the egg yolk. Fold over the other half and press the edges together to seal. Trim with scissors into a half-moon shape.

Heat the oil to 375° F. Lower the half-moons, a few at a time, into the hot oil and deep-fry until golden brown. Drain on paper towels and serve. Makes 12.

Finger Rolls with Pâté

Split finger rolls almost through and sandwich them with Chicken Liver Pâté (page 205) or Whipped Pâté de Foie Gras (page 206). Arrange the rolls on a baking sheet and bake in a preheated 350° F. oven about 10 minutes or until heated. Serve at once.

Cold Sweet Canapés and Tea Sandwiches

Italian Cream Cheese Canapés

Spread small thinly sliced rectangles of pound cake, fruit bread, or thin cookies with Italian Cream Cheese Filling (page 207). Garnish each with a mandarin orange section or an apricot wedge.

Dessert Cornucopias

Follow the recipe for Cheese Cornucopias (page 111), substituting Italian Cream Cheese Filling (page 207) or Lemon-Honey Cheese Filling (page 207) for the Curried Cheese Filling. If desired, garnish each cornucopia with a raspberry or a small stemmed strawberry.

Lemon-Honey Cheese Canapés

Spread small rounds of white or whole wheat toast with Lemon-Honey Cheese Filling (page 207). Garnish each round with a small stemmed Bing cherry.

VARIATION:

Substitute small thinly sliced rectangles of pound cake, fruit bread, or thin cookies for the toast. Omit the Bing cherries.

Cream Cheese and Marmalade Canapés

Spread small diamonds of white or whole wheat toast with Cream Cheese and Marmalade Filling (page 208). Garnish each diamond with a toasted blanched almond or hazelnut.

Cream Cheese, Nut, and Jelly Bagelettes

Split and toast Miniature Bagels (page 256) or frozen Lender's Bagelettes, thawed. Spread with Cream Cheese and Nut Filling (page 191) and cover with currant, quince, or grape jelly.

Sweetened Yogurt Cheese Canapés

Spread small triangles of toasted pita bread, cocktail-size rounds of *lavash* (page 246), or crisp wheat crackers with Sweetened Yogurt Cheese Filling (page 209). Garnish each canapé with a tiny piece of glacéed orange peel or fruit paste or a tiny wedge of peach, apricot, or preserved kumquat.

Whipped Honey Butter Canapés

Spread small diamonds of white or whole wheat toast with Whipped Honey Butter (page 190). Sprinkle with chopped toasted blanched almonds or toasted sesame seeds.

Pink Hearts

With a canapé or small cookie cutter, cut heart shapes out of thin slices of white or dark bread trimmed of crusts. Spread half of the hearts with Bar-le-Duc Filling (page 207). Using a tiny heart cutter, cut out a heart from the center of each of the remaining bread hearts and cover the sandwiches. The fillings will show through.

VARIATION:

Use dark bread for the bottom hearts and white bread for the tops.

Cream Cheese and Jelly Rounds

With a canapé or small cookie cutter, cut circles out of thin slices of white or whole wheat bread trimmed of crusts. Using a very small, round cutter or large thimble, cut holes in the center of half of the circles to form rims. Spread the whole circles with Cream Cheese and Nut Filling (page 191). Place the rims on top of the whole circles. Fill the centers with currant or other jelly.

Ladyfinger Sandwiches

Split small ladyfingers and sandwich them with a thick layer of Crème Chantilly (page 209) or one of the variations piped through a pastry bag fitted with a fluted tube. Serve chilled.

Fruit and Nut Sandwiches

Spread thin slices of whole wheat bread with cream cheese, using about 2 tablespoons for each slice. Cover with a thick layer (about 3 tablespoons per slice of bread) of Apricot-Almond Filling, Date-Nut Filling, or Prune-Nut Filling (pages 211-212). Top each sandwich with a thin slice of whole wheat bread. Trim the crusts and cut the sandwiches into triangles, squares, or strips.

Miniature Dessert Brioches

Follow the recipe for Cocktail Brioches (page 128), substituting any of the following fillings for the ones suggested in that recipe:

Italian Cream Cheese Filling (page 207)
Lemon-Honey Cheese Filling (page 207)

Bar-le-Duc Filling (page 207)
Cream Cheese and Marmalade Filling (page 208)

Makes about 30.

7

Pastry Sandwiches

The world's cuisines encompass a rewarding repertoire of pastry sandwiches. Armenian *lahmajoon*, Russian *pirozhki*, Italian *calzoni*, Latin American *empanadas*, and Indian *parathas* all belong to a vast family of glorious pastries that come in numerous shapes and accommodate themselves to a wide assortment of fillings. Various doughs are used, ranging from simple bread and pie dough to flaky pastry.

Many pastry sandwiches can be prepared in different sizes to suit the occasion, and are equally appetizing hot or cold. They are perfect for buffets and parties, particularly in their smaller versions, which can also be served as hors d'oeuvre or as accompaniments to soups or salads. Some make excellent main-course dishes, and a large number provide ideal fare for lunch boxes and picnics.

Almost anything, it seems, tastes delicious in a pastry, to which the universal popularity of pastry sandwiches attests.

Cheese Pastry Rounds

Roll out 1 recipe Cheese Pastry (below) on a lightly floured board to ⅛-inch thickness and cut into 1½-inch rounds. Arrange the rounds on ungreased baking sheets and bake in a preheated 425° F. oven about 15 minutes, or until lightly browned. Transfer to wire racks and cool.

Put 2 rounds together, sandwich fashion, with any of the fillings given below. Repeat with the remaining rounds and filling. Makes about 30.

Note: Instead of cutting the dough into rounds, you may cut it into squares, triangles, or strips. One teaspoon sesame seeds may be added to the dough before rolling it out.

Fillings for Cheese Pastry Rounds

Cream Cheese, Olive, and Nut
  Filling (page 192)
Cream Cheese, Olive, and Bacon
  Filling (page 193)
Curried Cream Cheese and Olive
  Filling (page 192)

Deviled Ham and Cream Cheese
  Filling (page 204)
Ham, Cream Cheese, and Almond
  Filling (page 203)

Cheese Pastry

Follow the recipe for Pâte Brisée (page 140) with these changes: Use 1⅔ cups flour, ½ teaspoon salt, ¼ cup each butter and vegetable shortening, and ¼ to ⅓ cup ice water. Toss 1 cup grated Swiss or sharp Cheddar cheese with the flour and salt before cutting in the butter and shortening.

Pirozhki

These extremely popular Russian pastries are traditionally offered with vodka along with other appetizers, at teatime, and as an accompaniment to soup.

1 tablespoon butter
1 medium onion, finely chopped
8 ounces lean ground beef
1 hard-cooked egg, finely chopped
1 tablespoon finely chopped fresh
  dill

Salt and freshly ground pepper
  to taste
1 recipe Pâte Brisée (below)
1 egg
1 teaspoon water

In a heavy skillet melt the butter over moderate heat. Add the onion and sauté until soft but not browned, stirring frequently. Add the meat and, breaking it up with a fork, cook until browned and crumbly. Remove from the heat. Add the egg, dill, and salt and pepper and mix well. Taste and adjust the seasoning.

On a lightly floured board roll out the pastry to ⅛-inch thickness or less. Cut into 3-inch circles or squares. Place about 1½ teaspoons of the meat mixture in the center. Moisten the edges of the dough with cold water. Fold over to make half-moons or triangles and press the edges together to seal.

Arrange the *pirozhki* on a greased baking sheet. Beat the egg with the water and brush the tops of the pirozhki with the mixture. Bake in a preheated 400° F. oven about 20 minutes or until golden brown. Serve hot. Makes about 40.

Note: One loaf (1 pound) frozen bread dough, defrosted, may be substituted for the Pâte Brisée.

Pâte Brisée
Short Crust Pastry

2 cups sifted all-purpose flour	⅓ cup vegetable shortening
¾ teaspoon salt	5 tablespoons ice water
⅓ cup butter	(approximately)

Sift the flour and salt into a mixing bowl. Cut in the butter and shortening with a pastry blender or 2 knives, working quickly until the mixture resembles very coarse cornmeal. Sprinkle with the water, a little at a time, mixing well with your fingers or a fork after each addition, until a soft dough is formed. Gather the dough into a ball. Wrap in waxed paper and chill 1 hour.

Hamburgers en Croûte

3 pounds lean ground beef
½ cup very finely chopped onions
Salt and freshly ground pepper
   to taste
6 tablespoons butter
1 pound mushrooms, chopped
8 scallions, finely chopped,
   including 2 inches of the green
   tops
2 green peppers, seeded, deribbed,
   and finely chopped

2 medium cloves garlic, finely
   chopped
1 tablespoon finely chopped fresh
   tarragon, or ¼ teaspoon crushed
   dried tarragon (optional)
2 recipes Cream Cheese Pastry
   (below)
1 egg
1 teaspoon water
4 ounces mushrooms, thinly sliced
3 tablespoons Cognac

In a large mixing bowl combine the beef, onions, and salt and pepper and mix well. Taste and adjust the seasoning. Form into 6 patties, each about 4 inches in diameter and 1 inch thick. Broil quickly, preferably over charcoal, until both sides of the patties are seared but the insides are still uncooked. Place on a rack set over a roasting pan, cover with aluminum foil, and chill.

Meanwhile, in a large, heavy skillet melt 4 tablespoons of the butter over medium-high heat. Add the chopped mushrooms, scallions, green peppers, garlic, and tarragon, if used, and sauté until the vegetables are soft, stirring frequently. Season with salt and pepper. Transfer to a bowl, cover, and chill.

On a lightly floured board roll out the pastry to ⅛-inch thickness. Cut into six 8-by-10-inch rectangles. Spoon the vegetables into the centers of the rectangles, dividing equally. Top each rectangle with a hamburger.

Beat the egg with the water and brush the edges of each pastry rectangle with some of the mixture. Fold the pastry over the meat, making certain that the hamburger is completely enclosed. Press the edges together to seal. Trim off the excess pastry, reserving the scraps for decoration. Arrange seam sides down on an ungreased baking sheet and brush with more of the egg mixture. Roll out the pastry trimmings and cut into decorative shapes. Arrange the cutouts over the pastries and brush with the remaining egg mixture. Bake in a preheated 400° F. oven about 20 minutes or until the pastry is lightly browned.

Meanwhile, in a medium-size skillet melt the remaining 2 tablespoons butter over moderate heat. Add the sliced mushrooms and sauté until lightly browned, stirring frequently. Season with salt and pepper. Keep warm.

Place the hamburgers on a heated platter. Warm the Cognac, add it to the mushrooms, and ignite, shaking the pan until the flame subsides. Spoon over each hamburger and serve. Makes 6 servings.

Note: Twelve frozen patty shells, defrosted but still chilled, may be substituted for the Cream Cheese Pastry. Combine 2 patty shells and roll into 8- by-10-inch rectangles.

Cream Cheese Pastry

4 ounces cream cheese, at room
   temperature
½ cup butter, at room temperature

1 cup sifted all-purpose flour
   (approximately)
¼ teaspoon salt

Combine the cream cheese and butter in a bowl and beat until well blended and smooth. Gradually mix in the flour and salt until the dough holds together. Wrap the dough in waxed paper and chill 1 hour.

Artichoke and Pepper Pizza

Bread Dough (page 143)
Tomato Sauce (page 264)
1 jar (6 ounces) marinated
   artichoke hearts, drained and
   halved lengthwise
2 medium red or green bell
   peppers, seeded, deribbed, and
   cut into thin strips

3 ounces thinly sliced prosciutto or
   cooked ham, cut into strips
1½ cups freshly shredded
   mozzarella or Monterey Jack
   cheese

Prepare the dough and let rise. Meanwhile, prepare the Tomato Sauce and set aside to cool.

Punch down the dough and roll into a large circle on a lightly floured board. Transfer to a greased 14-inch pizza pan and pat evenly to fit over the bottom and sides. Spread the Tomato Sauce over the dough, then arrange the artichoke hearts, pepper strips, and prosciutto or ham in an attractive pattern on top. Sprinkle evenly with the cheese.

Bake the pizza on the lowest rack of a preheated 450° F. oven about 20 minutes, or until the crust is nicely browned and crisp. Cut into wedges and serve. Makes 4 to 6 servings.

Note: One loaf (1 pound) frozen bread dough may be substituted for the homemade dough. Defrost as directed on the package. Or, for a really quick and delicious pizza, use pita bread instead (see page 247).

VARIATION:

Mushroom and Pepper Pizza

Substitute 1 jar (4 ounces) marinated mushrooms, drained and sliced, or 4 ounces fresh mushrooms, sliced, for the artichokes and 3 ounces Italian-style hard salami, cut in strips, for the prosciutto or ham.

Calzoni

Italian Turnovers

A specialty of southern Italy, *calzoni* are an interesting version of pizza.

Bread Dough

1 cup warm water (110° F.)
1 package active dry yeast
1 tablespoon olive oil
½ teaspoon salt
2¾ cups unsifted all-purpose flour
　(approximately)

Sausage Filling or Vegetable
　Filling (below)
Olive oil

To make the dough, pour the warm water into a mixing bowl and sprinkle with the yeast. Let stand 4 to 5 minutes, then stir to dissolve the yeast. Stir in the oil and salt, then gradually mix in enough flour to make a soft dough. Turn out the dough onto a lightly floured board and knead thoroughly, sprinkling occasionally with just enough flour to keep it from sticking. When it is smooth and elastic in texture, form into a lump and place in a lightly greased bowl. Turn the dough over to grease the top. Cover loosely with a kitchen towel and let rise in a warm place free from drafts about 1½ hours, or until doubled in size.

Meanwhile, prepare either the Sausage Filling or Vegetable Filling. Set aside. Punch down the dough and divide into quarters. On a lightly floured board form each quarter into a ball. Roll each ball of dough into an 8½-inch circle. Brush the surface of each circle lightly with olive oil. Spread ¼ of the filling on the lower half of each circle to within ½ inch of the edge. Fold over the other half to make a half-moon and press the edges together to seal. Roll the ½-inch edge up and over, seal, and crimp. With a wide spatula transfer the turnovers to lightly greased baking sheets. Prick the tops with a fork and brush lightly with olive oil. Bake in a preheated 475° F. oven about 18 minutes, or until golden brown. Serve hot. Makes 4.

Sausage Filling

3 mild Italian sausages (about 10 ounces), sliced	½ teaspoon crushed dried oregano
1 small onion, thinly sliced	½ teaspoon crushed dried basil
1 medium garlic clove, finely chopped	¼ teaspoon crushed red pepper or to taste
4 ounces mushrooms, sliced	2¼ cups (about 8 ounces) freshly shredded mozzarella cheese
1 medium green pepper, seeded, deribbed, and sliced	¾ cup (2½ ounces) freshly grated Parmesan or Romano cheese
1 cup Tomato Sauce (page 264)	Salt and freshly ground pepper to taste
1 can (2¼ ounces) sliced black olives, drained	

In a large, heavy skillet sauté the sausages over moderate heat until browned, stirring frequently. Add the onion, garlic, mushrooms, and green pepper and cook, stirring, until the vegetables are soft. Stir in the Tomato Sauce, olives, oregano, basil, and red pepper and simmer, uncovered, 5 minutes. Remove from the heat and cool. When ready to assemble the *calzoni*, stir in the cheeses and salt and pepper. Taste and adjust the seasoning.

Vegetable Filling

Follow the recipe for Sausage Filling (above) with these changes: Omit the sausage and cook the vegetables in 3 tablespoons olive oil.

Lahmajoon
Armenian Meat Pies

The popularity of *lahmajoon* in the Middle East can be compared to that of its relative, pizza, in America. Since lahmajoon (or *lahm bi ajeen* or *sfeeha*, as it is known in its Arabic version) is equally delicious eaten hot or cold, it is most likely to be included among the main attractions at an Armenian picnic. It can be baked in advance, frozen, and reheated in a warm oven before serving.

Dough

¾ cup warm water (110° F.)
1 package active dry yeast
2¼ cups sifted all-purpose flour
   (approximately)

½ teaspoon salt
½ teaspoon sugar
¼ cup butter, melted

Topping

1 pound lean ground lamb
2 medium onions, finely chopped
¼ cup finely chopped green
   pepper
1 medium ripe tomato, peeled,
   seeded, and finely chopped
¼ cup finely chopped parsley
1 teaspoon finely chopped fresh
   mint
1 small garlic clove, finely
   chopped

2 tablespoons tomato paste
3 tablespoons freshly squeezed and
   strained lemon juice
⅛ teaspoon cayenne pepper
Salt and freshly ground pepper
   to taste
Paprika

Lemon wedges or unflavored
   yogurt

To make the dough, pour ½ cup of the water into a small bowl and add the yeast. Let stand 3 minutes, then stir to dissolve the yeast. In a deep bowl combine the flour, salt, and sugar. Make a well in the center and pour in the yeast mixture, melted butter, and remaining ¼ cup water. Using a large spoon, gradually blend the liquids into the flour mixture, working from the center out. Beat until the ingredients are well blended and form a soft dough.

Place the dough on a lightly floured board and knead thoroughly, sprinkling occasionally with just enough flour to keep it from sticking. When it is smooth and elastic in texture, form into a lump and place in a lightly greased bowl. Turn the dough over to grease the top. Cover loosely with a kitchen towel and let rise in a warm place free from drafts 2 to 3 hours or until doubled in size.

Meanwhile, combine all the topping ingredients except the paprika in a deep bowl and knead well until thoroughly blended. Taste and adjust the seasoning and set aside.

Punch down the dough and divide into 14 equal pieces. Form each into a ball and place on a lightly floured board. Cover with a kitchen towel and let rest 15 minutes.

On a lightly floured board roll out each of the balls into a circle approximately 5 inches in diameter. Place ⅓ to ½ cup of the topping in the center of each circle, then spread it evenly to within about ¼ inch of the edge.

Arrange the pies on ungreased baking sheets. Bake in a preheated 450° F. oven about 12 minutes or until lightly browned. If desired, place the pies briefly under the broiler to brown the tops. Sprinkle with the paprika and wrap immediately in aluminum foil, with meat sides against one another. Set aside 10 minutes. Serve hot or cold, with lemon wedges or unflavored yogurt. Makes 14.

VARIATIONS:

Another way to serve the lahmajoon is to top it with Middle Eastern Vegetable Salad (page 216). Roll up and eat out of hand.

Lahmajoon with Pita Bread

For a simplified version of these meat pies, substitute 4 or 5 pita breads, separated into single layers to make 8 or 10 circles, for the yeast dough.

Lebanese Meat Pastries

One is likely to encounter fascinating versions of these admirable pastries in the smallest of Middle Eastern hamlets.

Dough

1 cup warm water (110° F.)
1 package active dry yeast
1 teaspoon sugar
¼ cup olive oil
1½ teaspoons salt
½ cup unsifted whole wheat flour
2¼ cups unsifted all-purpose flour
   (approximately)

Lamb or Beef Filling (below)
1 egg
1 tablespoon water
Sesame seeds

To make the dough, combine the warm water, yeast, and sugar in the large bowl of an electric mixer. Let stand 4 to 5 minutes, then stir to dissolve the yeast. Stir in the oil, salt, and whole wheat flour, then gradually mix in 1¾ cups of the all-purpose flour. Beat on medium speed 5 minutes. Using a heavy-duty mixer or a wooden spoon, gradually beat in the remaining ½ cup all-purpose flour or enough to make a soft dough. Turn out the dough onto a lightly floured board and knead thoroughly, sprinkling occasionally with just enough flour to keep it from sticking. When it is smooth and elastic in texture, form it into a lump and place in a lightly greased bowl. Turn the dough over to grease the top. Cover loosely with a kitchen towel and let rise in a warm place free from drafts 1 to 1½ hours or until the dough has almost doubled in size.

Meanwhile, prepare the filling and set aside.

Punch down the dough and divide into 12 equal pieces. Form each piece into a ball and place on a lightly floured board. Cover with a kitchen towel and let rest about 30 minutes.

Roll out each ball of dough into a 5½-inch circle. Place 3 tablespoons filling in the center of each circle. Bring up the edges at 3 points to make a triangular-shaped pie and pinch the dough securely together at the top. Arrange the filled pies 1 inch apart on lightly greased baking sheets. Cover loosely with a kitchen towel and let rise in a warm place about 40 minutes or until puffy.

Beat the egg with the water and brush the pastries with the mixture. Sprinkle with the sesame seeds. Bake in a preheated 400° F. oven about 18 minutes or until golden brown. Serve hot or warm. Makes 12.

Lamb or Beef Filling

2 tablespoons olive oil or butter	Salt and freshly ground pepper
3 tablespoons pine nuts	to taste
1 large onion, finely chopped	¼ cup beef broth or water
1 medium garlic clove, finely	2 tablespoons finely chopped
chopped	parsley
1 pound lean ground lamb or beef	
1 teaspoon cinnamon, or ½	
teaspoon each cinnamon and	
allspice	

In a heavy skillet heat 1 tablespoon of the oil or butter over moderate heat. Add the pine nuts and sauté until lightly browned, stirring constantly. Remove the nuts with a slotted spoon and set aside. Add the remaining 1 tablespoon oil or butter to the skillet and heat. Add the onion and garlic and sauté until soft but not browned, stirring frequently. Add the meat and, breaking it up with a fork, cook until browned and crumbly. Add the cinnamon or cinnamon and allspice, salt and pepper, and broth or water. Cook, stirring, until most of the liquid in the skillet has evaporated. Mix in the parsley and pine nuts, and remove from the heat. Taste and adjust the seasoning and cool.

Indian Stuffed Parathas

This spicy sandwich with a crisp, chewy texture is eaten primarily in northern India, where wheat is grown.

Dough

4 cups unsifted whole wheat flour	1 cup water or as needed
½ cup butter, melted and cooled	

Filling

2 tablespoons butter or corn oil	1 teaspoon chili powder
1 pound lean ground beef or lamb	1 tablespoon finely chopped fresh
1 medium onion, finely chopped	mint leaves (optional)
1 medium garlic clove, finely	1 tablespoon freshly squeezed and
chopped	strained lime juice
1 teaspoon cumin	Salt and freshly ground pepper
1 teaspoon coriander	to taste

Prepare the dough: In a large mixing bowl combine the flour with ¼ cup of the melted butter and blend well. Gradually stir in enough water to make a soft dough. Transfer the dough to a lightly floured board and knead about 5 minutes or until smooth. Cover with clear plastic wrap and let rest about 30 minutes.

Prepare the filling: In a heavy skillet heat the butter or oil over moderate heat. Add the remaining ingredients and cook, stirring and breaking the meat up with a fork until it is browned and finely crumbled. Remove from the heat, taste and adjust the seasoning, and cool.

Divide the dough into 24 equal pieces. On a lightly floured board roll out each piece into a 5-inch circle (or larger for thinner parathas). Lightly brush one circle with some of the remaining melted butter. Spread with about ¼ cup filling to within ¼ inch of the edge. Top with a second circle and pinch the edges to seal. Roll out until 8 inches in diameter. Repeat this procedure with the remaining circles of dough and filling, making 12 stuffed parathas.

Heat an ungreased skillet or griddle over moderate heat. Bake the stuffed parathas slowly and without crowding until crisp and browned, about 6 minutes on each side. Keep warm until all are baked. Makes 12.

Note: For hors d'oeuvre, cut each stuffed paratha into 4 to 6 wedges before serving.

VARIATION:

Three cups whole wheat flour and 1 cup all-purpose flour may be substituted for the whole wheat flour.

Chinese Chicken and Vegetable Buns

Frozen bread dough is used in this simplified version of the hearty, ginger-flavored buns which are customarily steamed rather than baked. Serve them as a luncheon entrée or as a snack.

2 loaves (1 pound each) frozen
  bread dough
Peanut oil or flavorless vegetable
  oil
½ ounce dried Chinese mushrooms
2 chicken breasts (about 1 pound
  each)
4 tablespoons soy sauce
2 medium garlic cloves, finely
  chopped
2 teaspoons peeled and finely
  chopped ginger root

1 tablespoon cornstarch
½ teaspoon sugar
¼ teaspoon salt
2 tablespoons dry sherry
⅓ cup water
2 stalks celery, thinly sliced
4 scallions, cut into 1½-inch
  lengths, including 2 inches of the
  green tops
1 can (8 ounces) water chestnuts,
  drained and sliced
2 tablespoons melted butter

Defrost the frozen bread loaves just until pliable, about 1½ hours at room temperature. Brush them with oil and cover with clear plastic wrap.

Meanwhile, rinse and soak the mushrooms in hot water about 20 minutes, or until soft. Drain. Cut off and discard the tough stems. Cut the mushrooms into thin strips and reserve. Skin and bone the chicken breasts. Cut the meat in ½-inch-thick strips, each about 2 inches long. Combine the chicken with 2 tablespoons of the soy sauce, garlic, and ginger root. Set aside. Stir together the cornstarch, sugar, salt, remaining 2 tablespoons soy sauce, sherry, and water. Set aside.

In a wok or skillet heat 2 tablespoons oil over high heat. When the oil is hot, add the chicken and cook 3 minutes, stirring constantly. Add the celery and cook, stirring, 1 minute. Stir the cornstarch mixture to recombine it. Add the reserved mushrooms, scallions, water chestnuts, and the cornstarch mixture and cook, stirring, until the sauce thickens. Remove from the heat and cool.

With a lightly floured knife cut each defrosted loaf into 4 equal pieces. Roll each piece into a ball. On a lightly floured board roll each ball into a circle about 7 inches in diameter. Place ½ cup of the chicken mixture in the center. Gather the edges of dough up around the filling, being careful not to stretch the dough. Pleat in the edges and pinch together tightly to seal. Place the buns, pinched sides down and 2 inches apart, on a lightly greased baking sheet. Cover loosely with a kitchen towel and let rise in a warm place about 40 minutes or until puffy. Brush with melted butter and bake in a preheated 350° F. oven about 30 minutes or until lightly browned. Serve warm. Makes 8.

Empanadas

Latin American Turnovers

Pastry turnovers or pies known as *empanadas* are the most popular sandwiches in Latin America. They come in various sizes, shapes, and flavors to enjoy as appetizers, snacks, or light main courses.

Meat Filling (below) or Shrimp   1 egg
   or Crab Filling (below)   1 tablespoon water
Pâte Brisée (page 140)

Prepare the filling of your choice and set aside. On a lightly floured board roll out the pastry to ⅟₁₆-inch thickness or less and cut into 5-inch circles. Place about 1 tablespoon of the filling on the lower half of each circle. Moisten the edges of the circle with cold water. Fold over the other half to make a half-moon and press the edges together to seal. Arrange the empanadas slightly apart on ungreased baking sheets. Prick the tops with a fork. Beat the egg with the water and brush the empanadas with the mixture. Bake in a preheated 400° F. oven about 15 minutes or until golden brown. Serve hot or warm. Makes about 36.

Meat Filling

2 tablespoons butter or olive oil
1 medium onion, finely chopped
¾ pound lean ground beef, or ¾
  pound lean boneless sirloin or
  round steak, cut into ¼-inch
  cubes
1 large tomato, peeled, seeded,
  and finely chopped
½ cup finely chopped green
  pepper
⅛ teaspoon cayenne pepper or to
  taste

½ teaspoon each paprika and
  cumin or crushed dried oregano,
  or ½ teaspoon each chili powder
  and coriander
Salt to taste
2 hard-cooked eggs, chopped
3 tablespoons seedless raisins
½ cup chopped pimento-stuffed
  olives

In a heavy skillet heat the butter or oil over moderate heat. Add the onion and sauté until golden brown, stirring frequently. Add the beef and cook, stirring, until browned. (If using ground beef, break it up with a fork until browned and crumbly.) Spoon off and discard excess fat. Add the tomato, green pepper, spices, and salt and cook, stirring, about 10 minutes or until most of the liquid in the skillet has evaporated. Remove from the heat and mix in the eggs, raisins, and olives. Taste and adjust the seasoning and cool.

Shrimp or Crab Filling

3 tablespoons olive oil
1 medium onion, finely chopped
1½ cups peeled, seeded, and finely
  chopped tomatoes
¾ pound cooked shrimp or
  crabmeat, diced
Salt and freshly ground pepper to
  taste

2 hard-cooked egg yolks, chopped
¼ cup chopped black olives or
  pimento-stuffed olives
2 tablespoons finely chopped
  parsley

In a heavy skillet heat the oil over moderate heat. Add the onion and sauté until golden, stirring frequently. Add the tomatoes and cook gently 10 minutes, stirring occasionally. Mix in the shrimp or crabmeat and salt and pepper and cook 5 minutes. Remove from the heat and stir in the egg yolks, olives, and parsley. Taste and adjust the seasoning and cool.

Semlor

Swedish Dessert Buns

Offered on Shrove Tuesday and the remaining Tuesdays during Lent.

⅔ cup milk
6 tablespoons butter
1 package active dry yeast
¼ cup warm water (110° F.)
3¼ cups unsifted all-purpose flour
¼ cup sugar
½ teaspoon salt

1 teaspoon cinnamon
1 egg, lightly beaten
8 ounces homemade or canned
  almond paste
Crème Chantilly (page 209)
Confectioners' sugar

Scald the milk, stir in the butter, and let stand until lukewarm. In a small bowl sprinkle the yeast over the water. Let the mixture rest a few minutes, then stir to dissolve the yeast. Sift the flour, measure, and sift again with the sugar, salt, and cinnamon into a large mixing bowl. Add the milk mixture, dissolved yeast, and egg, and beat thoroughly until a soft dough is formed. Transfer the dough onto a lightly floured board and knead until smooth and elastic. Shape into a ball. Place in a lightly buttered bowl and turn over to grease the top. Cover loosely with a kitchen towel and let rise in a warm place free from drafts about 1½ hours or until doubled in bulk.

Punch down the dough. Pinch off pieces of dough and form smooth, round balls about 1½ inches in diameter. Arrange the balls on a greased baking sheet about 2 inches apart. Cover loosely with a kitchen towel and let rise about 45 minutes or until doubled in size. Bake in a preheated 400° F. oven about 15 minutes, or until golden brown. Transfer the buns to wire racks and let cool.

To serve, cut a thin top off each bun. Spread the inside of the bottom part with the almond paste and cover with about 3 tablespoons Crème Chantilly. Replace the top and sift confectioners' sugar over it. Makes about 10.

Piirakka

Finnish Sweet Cheese Buns

Piirakka is a well-known oval or round open pastry from the region of Karelia. It can have either a savory or sweet filling and is a popular lunchbox item.

Dough

¼ cup warm water (110° F.)

1 package active dry yeast

1 cup milk, scalded and cooled to lukewarm

1 teaspoon salt

¼ cup sugar

2 eggs, well beaten

5½ cups sifted all-purpose flour (approximately)

½ cup butter, melted

Filling

2 eggs

⅓ cup sugar

½ cup sour cream

8 ounces cream cheese, at room temperature

1 tablespoon freshly squeezed and strained lemon juice

1 tablespoon finely grated lemon rind

1 egg

1 teaspoon water

Raspberry or other jam or Cranberry Topping (below)

To make the dough, pour the warm water into a large mixing bowl and add the yeast. Let stand about 5 minutes, then stir to dissolve the yeast. Stir in the milk, salt, sugar, and eggs. Add 2 cups of the flour and beat until smooth. Add the melted butter and mix well. Gradually beat in enough of the remaining flour (approximately 3½ cups) to make a stiff dough. Cover loosely with a kitchen towel and let rest 15 minutes. Turn out the dough onto a lightly floured board and knead thoroughly, sprinkling occasionally with just enough flour to keep it from sticking. When the dough is smooth and elastic in texture, form it into a lump and place in a lightly greased bowl. Turn the dough over to grease the top. Cover loosely with a kitchen towel and let rise in a warm place free from drafts about 1½ hours, or until doubled in size.

Pinch off small pieces of dough and shape them into 2-inch balls. Arrange the balls 3 inches apart on buttered baking sheets. Cover and let rise about 10 minutes in a warm place until puffy. Flatten each ball of dough with your fingers to about ⅜-inch thickness. Let rise again about 10 minutes or until puffy.

Meanwhile, prepare the filling: In the small bowl of an electric mixer combine the eggs, sugar, sour cream, cream cheese, lemon juice, and lemon rind. Beat until well blended and smooth.

Flatten the centers of the dough rounds, leaving the edges slightly higher to enclose the filling. Beat the egg with the water and brush the rounds with the mixture. Spoon about 2½ tablespoons of the filling into the center of each round. Bake in a preheated 375° F. oven about 20 minutes, or until the filling is set and the crust is lightly browned. Spoon the jam or Cranberry Topping over the filling and serve hot (preferably) or cold. Makes about 24.

Cranberry Topping

1½ cups cranberries
¼ cup freshly squeezed and
   strained orange juice
¾ cup sugar
1½ teaspoons cornstarch

1 tablespoon water
½ teaspoon grated lemon rind
1 tablespoon cranberry liqueur
   (optional)

In a saucepan combine the cranberries, orange juice, and sugar. Cover and cook over moderate heat about 6 minutes or until the cranberry skins burst. Mix the cornstarch with the water and add to the cranberries. Cook, stirring, 2 minutes or until the mixture thickens. Remove from the heat, stir in the lemon rind and cranberry liqueur, if used, and chill.

8

Filled Pancakes

Some of the most delectable sandwiches ever invented are made with pancakes. French crêpes, Hungarian *palacsinta*, Jewish blintzes, Philippine *lumpia*, and Chinese Mandarin pancakes are but a handful of the vast number of tempting international creations in this category of food.

Filled pancakes take many forms, from simple and unpretentious to elegant and refined. With a savory filling they can be served either as hors d'oeuvre or entrées; with a sweet filling they become splendid desserts.

Shellfish Crêpes

2 tablespoons butter	Béchamel Sauce (page 263)
2 scallions, thinly sliced, including 2 inches of the green tops	Salt to taste
	12 Crêpes (below)
8 ounces mushrooms, sliced	⅓ cup half-and-half
¼ cup sherry or Madeira	1½ cups shredded Swiss cheese
8 ounces cooked and shelled small shrimp, crabmeat, or lobster meat, or 4 ounces each shrimp and crabmeat or lobster meat	Freshly grated nutmeg

In a heavy saucepan melt the butter over moderate heat. Add the scallions and mushrooms and sauté, stirring frequently, until most of the liquid in the pan has evaporated. Stir in 2 tablespoons of the sherry or Madeira, the shellfish, half of the Béchamel Sauce, and salt, and remove from the heat. Divide the mixture among the crêpes. Roll up each crêpe to enclose the filling and arrange side by side in a greased 9-by-13-inch baking pan.

Add the half-and-half and remaining 2 tablespoons sherry or Madeira to the rest of the Béchamel Sauce and reheat over low heat, stirring constantly. Spoon evenly over the crêpes, sprinkle with the cheese, and dust lightly with the nutmeg. Bake, uncovered, in a preheated 425° F. oven about 10 minutes, or until lightly browned and bubbly. Makes 6 servings.

Crêpes

2 cups sifted all-purpose flour
4 eggs
1 cup milk
1 cup water
½ teaspoon salt

4 tablespoons butter, melted
2 tablespoons butter
   (approximately), melted, for
   brushing the crêpe pan

Put the flour, eggs, milk, water, salt, and 4 tablespoons butter in the container of an electric blender. Cover and blend at high speed 1 minute. Scrape down the sides of the container with a rubber spatula and blend again about 15 seconds or until smooth. (Or in a mixing bowl, blend the eggs and flour with an electric beater or wooden spoon, then beat in the milk, water, melted butter, and salt.) Cover and refrigerate the batter 2 hours.

Warm a 6- to 7-inch crêpe pan or heavy skillet over high heat, testing it with a drop of cold water. When it splutters and evaporates instantly, the pan is ready. Brush the pan lightly with melted butter. Reduce the heat to medium. Stir the crêpe batter with a wire whisk or spoon. Remove the pan from the heat and, using a small ladle, immediately pour about 2 tablespoons of the batter into the pan (just enough to coat the bottom of the pan thinly). Tilt the pan quickly in all directions to allow the batter to cover the bottom completely. The batter will adhere to the pan and begin to firm up almost instantly. At once pour off any excess batter back into the bowl and note the correct amount for the next crêpe. The cooked crêpes should be no more than ⅟₁₆ inch thick. If the batter seems too heavy (that is, if it spreads too slowly in the pan), thin it by stirring in a little more milk or water. Place the pan over medium heat and cook about 1 minute or until the underside of the crêpe is very lightly browned. If any holes appear in the crêpe, spoon on a little batter just to cover. Turn it over with a narrow spatula, using your fingers to help, and cook 30 to 60 seconds, or until very lightly browned on the other side. Slide the crêpe onto a plate. Repeat with the remaining batter, greasing the pan lightly each time if it seems necessary and stacking the crêpes as they are cooked. Makes about 24.

Peking-Style Duck

Based on a famed Chinese classic.

2 ducklings (4½ to 5 pounds each), defrosted
1 teaspoon ginger
1 teaspoon cinnamon
½ teaspoon nutmeg
¼ teaspoon cloves
⅛ teaspoon freshly ground pepper

2 tablespoons soy sauce
1 tablespoon honey
Mandarin Pancakes (below), prepared in advance and reheated
12 Scallion Flowers (below)
Plum Sauce (page 265)

Reserve the duck giblets for another use. Rinse the ducks inside and out and pat dry with paper towels. Mix together the ginger, cinnamon, nutmeg, cloves, and pepper. Dust ½ teaspoon of the mixture inside each duck, then rub the remaining spices evenly over the exterior of the birds. Close the abdominal cavities with small skewers. Wrap each duck separately in aluminum foil, folding the edges to seal securely. Place the ducks side by side in a large baking pan and bake in a preheated 425° F. oven 1 hour. Remove from the oven and allow to cool 15 minutes at room temperature. Carefully open the foil at one end and, protecting your hands with hot pads, drain out the accumulated juices and fat. Discard the foil.

Place the ducks slightly apart on a rack in the baking pan and prick the skin lightly all over with the tines of a fork. Bake in a preheated

375° F. oven 30 minutes. Blend the soy sauce with the honey and brush the ducks with the mixture. Raise the oven temperature to 500° F. Return the ducks to the oven and bake about 5 minutes or until the skin is richly browned but not charred.

Carve the ducks in thin strips, leaving a portion of skin on each strip. Alternatively, with a small, sharp knife and your fingers, remove the crisp skin from the breast, sides, and back of each duck. Cut the skin into bite-size morsels and arrange them on a heated platter. Cut the meat into bite-size pieces and arrange them on another heated platter.

Place the duck, the heated pancakes, the Scallion Flowers, and Plum Sauce on the table. Spread a pancake flat on a plate, dip a scallion in the sauce, and brush the pancake with it. Place the scallion in the middle of the pancake with a strip of the duck (or with a piece each of duck skin and meat). Fold the lower end of the pancake over the filling, then bring both sides over to enclose. Roll up the pancake cigarette fashion. Pick up with your fingers to eat. Makes 6 servings.

VARIATION:

Substitute 24 flour tortillas (each about 6 inches in diameter) for the Mandarin Pancakes. Lightly dampen the tortillas, then stack and wrap them in aluminum foil. Heat in a preheated 350° F. oven 10 to 15 minutes, or until moist. Serve in a napkin-lined basket to keep warm.

Mandarin Pancakes

2 cups sifted all-purpose flour	1 to 2 tablespoons Oriental sesame
¾ cup boiling water	oil

Sift the flour into a mixing bowl and make a well in the center. Pour the boiling water into the well. Using a wooden spoon, gradually mix together the water and flour until a soft dough is formed. Transfer the dough to a lightly floured surface and knead about 10 minutes, or until smooth and elastic. Cover with a damp kitchen towel and let rest 15 minutes. On a lightly floured board roll out the dough into a circle about ¼ inch thick. With a 2½-inch cookie cutter cut the dough into circles. Knead scraps together, roll out again, and cut more circles. Brush half of the circles lightly with the sesame oil. Top them, sandwich fashion, with the remaining unoiled circles. With a rolling pin flatten each pair into a 6-inch circle, rotating the sandwich as needed in a clockwise direction as you roll so that the circle keeps its shape. Turn it once to roll both sides. Take care not to allow creases to form in the pancakes as you roll. Cover the pancakes with a dry towel.

Heat an ungreased 8-inch skillet over medium-high heat. Cook the pancakes, one at a time, in the skillet, turning them over as they puff up and little bubbles appear on the surface. Cook them on the other side in the same manner. Do not allow the pancakes to brown, although a few light brown spots will do no harm. If overcooked, however, they become dry and brittle. As each pancake is done, gently separate the halves while still warm. Stack and keep covered while you make the remaining pancakes. Serve the pancakes at once, or wrap them in aluminum foil and refrigerate up to 2 days.

To reheat the pancakes for serving, either steam them in a steamer for 10 minutes or warm them, still wrapped in foil, in a preheated 350° F. oven about 10 minutes. Serve in a napkin-lined basket to keep warm. Makes 24.

Scallion Flowers

Trim off the roots and green tops of the scallions, leaving 3-inch lengths. Make 4 intersecting cuts 1 inch deep in both ends of the scallions and drop them into ice water. Refrigerate until the ends curl into flower shapes. Drain well on paper towels before using.

Lumpia

In the Philippines this intriguing and flavorful concoction enjoys immense popularity both as a streetcorner snack and as a banquet attraction.

Lumpia Pancakes (below)   Lumpia Filling (below)
Dipping Sauce (below)   ½ bunch scallions, trimmed and
18 small leaves romaine or Boston   cut lengthwise into slivers
   lettuce (approximately)   (optional)

Assemble the lumpia in the kitchen, or let each diner put together his or her own, as follows: Spread a Lumpia Pancake with about 1 teaspoon Dipping Sauce. Cover with a lettuce leaf. Spoon about 2 tablespoons filling on the lettuce and add a sliver of scallion, if desired. Fold the lower half of the pancake over the filling, then bring both sides over to enclose. Pick up with your fingers to eat. Makes 6 servings.

Lumpia Pancakes

3 eggs   ½ teaspoon salt
¾ cup cornstarch   Flavorless vegetable oil
1⅓ cups water

In the container of an electric blender combine the eggs, cornstarch, water, salt, and 1½ tablespoons of the oil. Blend about 1 minute, or until smooth.

Heat a 7-inch crêpe pan or skillet over medium heat and add 1 teaspoon oil. Quickly stir the pancake batter and pour 2 to 3 tablespoons into the pan, tilting and rotating the pan to cover the bottom evenly with the batter. Cook the pancake until the edges start to curl and the top looks dry. Slide out of the pan onto paper towels to cool. Continue making pancakes in this manner until all the batter is used. Stack the pancakes after they have cooled slightly. Makes about 18.

Dipping Sauce

2 tablespoons cornstarch   3 tablespoons soy sauce
¼ cup packed brown sugar   1 tablespoon flavorless vegetable
½ cup cold water   oil
½ cup freshly squeezed and   2 medium garlic cloves, finely
  strained orange juice   chopped
3 tablespoons white wine vinegar

In a small bowl combine the cornstarch with the brown sugar. Add the water, orange juice, vinegar, and soy sauce and mix well.

In a small saucepan heat the oil over moderate heat. Add the garlic and sauté until lightly browned. Add the sauce mixture and cook, stirring, until it boils and thickens. Before serving, stir in the juices drained from the Lumpia Filling.

Lumpia Filling

¾ pound lean ground pork
1 medium onion, chopped
3 medium garlic cloves, finely
   chopped
6 ounces shelled and deveined raw
   shrimp, chopped

2 tablespoons chopped cooked
   ham
½ cup coarsely chopped bean
   sprouts
⅓ cup chopped water chestnuts
2 tablespoons soy sauce

Crumble the pork into a heavy skillet. Add the onion and garlic and sauté 6 minutes, stirring constantly. Add the shrimp and ham and cook, stirring, 2 minutes. Add the bean sprouts and water chestnuts and cook, stirring, 2 minutes. Add the soy sauce, mix well, and remove from the heat. Before serving, drain and add the juices to the Dipping Sauce. Stir ¼ cup of the sauce into the filling.

Crêpe Sandwich Gâteau

Admittedly something of a production, but this *gâteau* is worth it.

7 Crêpes (page 157)

Ingredients for Fillings

4 large stalks broccoli
5 tablespoons butter
Salt and freshly ground pepper to
   taste
1½ pounds mushrooms, finely
   chopped

4 tablespoons finely chopped
   shallots or scallions (include 2
   inches of the green tops of the
   scallions)
1½ pounds mild-cured ham, diced
¼ cup Madeira or port

Cheese Sauce

½ cup all-purpose flour
1¼ cups milk, or more if needed
¼ cup butter
1 egg
2 egg yolks
Salt, white pepper (preferably
   freshly ground), and Tabasco
   sauce to taste

⅓ cup plus 3 tablespoons freshly
   grated Parmesan cheese
⅓ cup grated Swiss cheese
Tomato Sauce (page 264)
   (optional)

Make the crêpes and set aside.

To make the fillings, cut the broccoli into flowerets. Trim the stalks and peel the stems of the flowerets and the stalks. Cook in boiling salted water about 4 minutes or until just tender. Drain and cool, then chop into ³⁄₁₆-inch pieces. In a heavy skillet heat 1 tablespoon of the butter over moderate heat. Add the broccoli and sauté briefly, stirring. Season with the salt and pepper. Transfer to a plate and set aside.

Add 2 tablespoons butter to the skillet and heat. Add the mushrooms and 2 tablespoons of the shallots or scallions and sauté a few minutes, stirring frequently. Transfer to a plate and set aside.

Add the remaining 2 tablespoons butter to the skillet and heat. Add the ham and sauté, stirring, until lightly browned. Add the Madeira or port and the remaining 2 tablespoons shallots or scallions and boil, stirring, several minutes until the liquid is reduced by half. Remove from the heat and set aside.

To make the Cheese Sauce, place the flour in a medium, heavy saucepan. Gradually beat in the milk with a wire whisk. Add the butter and stir over moderate heat until the sauce comes to a boil. Beating vigorously, add the whole egg, then the yolks, one at a time. Season with the salt, pepper, and Tabasco sauce. Fold in ⅓ cup of the Parmesan cheese and all of the Swiss cheese.

Reserve ¼ cup of the Cheese Sauce in a small saucepan and drain the ham cooking juices into it. Fold just enough of the remaining sauce into the broccoli, mushrooms, and ham to coat them. Taste and adjust the seasoning.

Place a crêpe, browned side up, in the center of a buttered shallow round baking-and-serving dish. Top with half of the broccoli filling, being careful not to hump it in the middle but spreading it evenly to within ¾ inch of the edges of the crêpe. This will prevent the finished gâteau from being lopsided. Cover with a crêpe, pressing it gently but firmly, and spread it with half of the ham filling. Cover with another crêpe, then with half of the mushrooms. Continue with alternating layers of crêpes and fillings, ending the mound with a crêpe, browned side up.

Reheat the reserved Cheese Sauce in the small saucepan. If it is too thick to pour, stir in a little milk to thin it out to spreading consistency. Spoon it over the mound of crêpes, letting it dribble down the sides. Sprinkle the remaining 3 tablespoons Parmesan cheese on top and bake in a preheated 375° F. oven about 30 minutes or until the gâteau is bubbling and the top is nicely browned.

To serve, cut into pie-shaped wedges and spoon a little of the Tomato Sauce around each wedge, if you like. Makes 4 to 6 servings.

Soufflé Roulade

Worthy of an honored place in your repertoire, this is actually a soufflé rather than a pancake, rolled up like a jelly roll around a savory filling.

Butter	Spinach and Cheese Filling (page
All-purpose flour	198), Ham Filling (page 203), 2
2 cups warm milk	recipes Cream Cheese and
4 eggs, separated	Mushroom Filling (page 194), or
Salt to taste	Tarama and Caviar Filling (page
	202)

Butter a 10-by-15-inch jelly roll pan and line it with waxed paper. Butter the paper and sprinkle it with flour, shaking off the excess. Set aside.

In a heavy saucepan melt 4 tablespoons butter over low heat. Add 6 tablespoons flour and cook about 1 minute, stirring continuously. Remove from the heat and gradually add the warm milk, stirring the mixture with a wire whisk until well blended and smooth. Return to the fire and cook over moderate heat, stirring constantly until the batter is very thick. Remove from the heat and stir in the egg yolks thoroughly, one at a time. Season with the salt. Beat the egg whites until stiff. Fold gently but thoroughly into the batter. Spread the batter evenly into the prepared jelly roll pan. Bake in a preheated 325° F. oven about 35 minutes or until the soufflé is golden brown and firm. Turn the soufflé out onto a sheet of aluminum foil. Peel off the waxed paper, cool about 3 minutes, then spread with one of the fillings and roll up lengthwise, jelly roll fashion. With 2 large spatulas transfer the roll to a rectangular serving platter. Cut the roll into thick slices. Makes 8 servings.

Note: If using the Ham Filling or Tarama and Caviar Filling, you may pass a bowl of lightly salted sour cream to spoon over each serving.

Cheese Blintzes

This Jewish specialty has earned an international reputation, and when you taste it you will know why.

1 egg yolk	16 Crêpes (page 157), browned on
3 tablespoons sugar	one side only
8 ounces cream cheese, at room	Confectioners' sugar
temperature	1 cup sour cream or whipped
1 pound pot cheese or cottage	cream
cheese	1 cup cherry or strawberry
½ teaspoon vanilla extract	preserves
2 tablespoons butter or as needed	

In a mixing bowl combine the egg yolk and sugar and beat with an electric mixer until thick and yellow. Add the cheeses and vanilla extract and mix well.

To make each blintz, place a rectangular mound of about 3 table-spoons cheese filling across the lower third of the browned side of each crêpe. Fold over once, turn the sides in, and fold over once or twice more to form a small rectangular package.

In a large, heavy skillet melt the butter over moderate heat. Add the blintzes and sauté, seam sides down and without crowding, until golden brown on the undersides. Turn carefully and sauté until lightly browned on the other sides, adding more butter as necessary. Transfer to a platter and keep warm while you cook the rest. Sprinkle with the confectioners' sugar and serve hot with the sour cream or whipped cream and preserves. Makes 8 servings.

Quince Palacsinta

Palacsinta are thin Hungarian pancakes, not unlike French crêpes. This dessert version (using crêpes) features a delightful filling of cream cheese, quince jam, and toasted nuts.

12 **Crêpes (page 157), adding 1½ tablespoons sugar to the batter**
Lemon Cream Cheese ﹐(page 191) or Whipped Cream Cheese (page 191)

½ **cup finely chopped toasted almonds or walnuts**
½ **cup quince jam or apple jelly**
½ **tablespoon butter**
Confectioners' sugar

Place 1 crêpe on a buttered baking dish and spread with a thin layer of the cream cheese. Cover with a second crêpe and sprinkle it evenly with some of the nuts. Cover with a third crêpe and spread it with a layer of jam. Continue to layer the crêpes in this manner until all are used, ending with a plain crêpe. Dot the top with the butter. Bake in a preheated 350° F. oven 10 minutes or until thoroughly heated. Transfer the stacked palacsinta to a serving dish and sift confectioners' sugar evenly over the top. Cut into wedges and serve at once. Makes 6 servings.

Gâteau of Crêpes with Cherries

To eat this *gâteau* without giving due praise would be unthinkable.

12 **Crêpes (page 157), adding 2 tablespoons sugar to the batter**
1½ **pounds tart cherries, pitted**
Sugar
2 **strips lemon rind, very finely chopped**
2 **tablespoons kirsch or cherry-flavored brandy**

¼ **cup unsalted butter, melted**
1 **cup heavy cream**
Pinch cinnamon
¼ **cup slivered blanched almonds, toasted**

Make the crêpes and set aside.

In an enameled or stainless steel saucepan combine the cherries, ¼ cup sugar, and lemon rind. Cook, stirring, over moderate heat until the sugar is melted, then simmer gently about 5 minutes or until the cherries are tender. With a slotted spoon remove the fruit to a heat-proof mixing bowl. Raise the heat to high and boil the juices until reduced to about ¼ cup. Remove from the heat and stir in the kirsch or cherry-flavored brandy. Add to the cherries.

Place a crêpe, browned side up, in the center of a buttered shallow round baking-and-serving dish. Spoon some of the cherries with syrup over the top, being careful not to hump them in the middle but spreading them evenly to within ¾ inch of the edge of the crêpe. This will prevent the finished gâteau from being lopsided. Cover with another crêpe, pressing it gently but firmly, and brush it with some of the melted butter. Continue layering, ending with a crêpe, browned side up. Brush the top with melted butter and sprinkle evenly with 2 tablespoons sugar. Bake in a preheated 350° F. oven about 12 minutes, or until heated through.

Meanwhile, in a small, heavy saucepan combine the cream, 1½ tablespoons sugar, and cinnamon. Cook over medium-high heat, stirring, until the sugar dissolves, then boil until the mixture is reduced to about ¼ cup. Remove the gâteau from the oven and spoon the cream over the top, letting it dribble down the sides. Sprinkle evenly with the nuts. Serve warm, cut into wedges. Makes 4 servings.

Viennese Strawberry and Ice Cream Crêpes

There are times when it's best to forget about calories.

12 Crêpes (page 157), adding 2 tablespoons sugar to the batter
Orange Sauce (below)
1 pint vanilla ice cream

3 cups strawberries, hulled and halved
Crème Chantilly (page 209)
¼ cup toasted sliced almonds

Dip the crêpes, one at a time, into the hot Orange Sauce. Transfer, one at a time, to 6 individual dessert plates, allowing 2 crêpes per plate. Place 2 large spoonfuls of ice cream and some strawberries along the center of each crêpe (reserve 6 strawberry halves for garnish). Fold over the two sides of each crêpe, enclosing the filling. Spoon over additional Orange Sauce and top each serving with a dollop of Crème Chantilly and almonds. Garnish with a strawberry half and serve at once. Makes 6 servings.

Orange Sauce

1 orange
6 tablespoons sugar
1 cup freshly squeezed and strained orange juice
2 tablespoons freshly squeezed and strained lemon juice

3 tablespoons butter
2 tablespoons Grand Marnier or other orange-flavored liqueur

With a vegetable peeler peel a few long strips from the orange. Cut in julienne to make 1 teaspoon slivered peel. Set aside.

Place the sugar in a small, heavy saucepan and heat over moderate heat until the sugar melts and turns light gold. Watch closely to prevent burning. Cover the pan and do not stir. Add the orange peel, orange juice, lemon juice, and butter to the caramelized sugar. Cover and simmer gently just until the ingredients are blended together. Stir in the orange liqueur.

Note: If you wish, you may flame the sauce at serving time with 2 tablespoons each warm Grand Marnier and brandy.

9

Vegetable- and Fruit-Based Sandwiches

A welcome departure from the conventional sandwich is one based on a vegetable or fruit rather than on bread. Although hardly a new idea, this type of sandwich is rarely encountered and so remains a novelty. Recipes such as Lebanese Kibbeh in Romaine Leaves, Stuffed Grape Leaves, and Chinese Pork and Shrimp Lettuce Rolls have been popular for centuries. Others, such as Armenian Lentil and Bulghur Patties in Romaine Leaves, are my own adaptations of traditional dishes and offer a new way of enjoying them. Still others feature familiar ingredients in refreshing and imaginative combinations.

The recipes that follow show the ample assortment of vegetable- and fruit-based sandwiches available as well as their adaptability. Tempting hors d'oeuvre, intriguing luncheon and supper dishes, and unique desserts are just some of the palate-pleasing ways in which these sandwiches can be savored at mealtime.

Armenian Lentil and Bulghur Patties in Romaine Leaves

Don't think about it, try it! Mundane-sounding ingredients can sometimes produce extraordinary results.

Romaine lettuce leaves (use the
tender inner leaves)
1 cup lentils, washed and drained
2½ cups water
Salt to taste
4 tablespoons butter
¾ cup fine bulghur
¼ cup olive oil or butter
1 medium onion, finely chopped
Freshly ground black pepper or
cayenne pepper to taste

¼ cup finely chopped green or
red bell pepper
¼ cup finely chopped scallions,
including 2 inches of the green
tops
⅓ cup finely chopped parsley
Paprika
2 tablespoons finely chopped
fresh mint leaves (optional)
2 medium tomatoes, cut into
small pieces
1 lemon, cut into wedges

Wash the lettuce leaves under cold running water. Drain, pat dry
with paper towels, and chill.

Combine the lentils, water, and salt in a heavy saucepan. Bring to a
boil over high heat, stirring to dissolve the salt. Reduce the heat and
simmer 45 minutes, or until the lentils are very tender and the water is
absorbed. Stir in the butter and the bulghur and simmer gently about
2 minutes. Remove from the heat, cover, and set aside 15 minutes.

Meanwhile, in a heavy skillet heat the oil or butter over moderate
heat. Add the onion and sauté until lightly browned, stirring frequently. Combine the lentil and bulghur mixture with the contents of
the skillet in a large mixing bowl. Season with salt and black pepper or
cayenne pepper. With hands moistened by occasionally dipping them
in a bowl of lightly salted warm water, knead the mixture 2 minutes.
Add 3 tablespoons each of the green or red pepper, scallions, and
parsley, and knead about 1 minute or until well blended. Taste and
adjust the seasoning.

Keeping your hands moist, form the mixture into finger-shaped
patties. Arrange them on a serving platter and sprinkle with the
paprika and remaining green or red pepper, scallions, and parsley and
the mint, if used. Garnish with the tomatoes. Serve at once, accompanied with the lemon wedges and a bowl of the lettuce leaves.

To eat, place 1 or 2 finger patties in the center of a lettuce leaf and
top with a few pieces of tomato. Squeeze a little lemon juice over and
eat out of hand. Makes 6 servings.

Note: Larger romaine or leaf lettuce leaves cut in 2 or 3 pieces can be
substituted for the smaller leaves, in which case wrap them around the
finger patties and tomatoes.

Chinese Pork and Shrimp Lettuce Rolls

You don't have to be Chinese to savor these delicious rolls.

6 large leaves Boston or iceberg
  lettuce
4 cups peanut oil or flavorless
  vegetable oil
1 ounce bean thread noodles°
8 ounces lean ground pork
4 ounces cooked small shrimp,
  shelled and deveined

2 large dried Chinese black
  mushrooms, soaked, drained,
  and chopped
12 water chestnuts, chopped
2 tablespoons soy sauce
¾ cup plus 2 teaspoons water
2 teaspoons cornstarch
1 scallion, chopped, including 2
  inches of the green top

Wash the lettuce leaves under cold running water. Drain, dry with paper towels, and chill.

In a wok or deep, heavy skillet heat the oil to 375° F. Loosen the bean thread noodles by pulling them apart and plunge them into the oil. The noodles will immediately become a white nest. Turn the nest over and fry the other side. This will take about 10 seconds. Transfer the noodles to paper towels to drain. Break into small pieces and arrange them in the center of a serving platter. Set aside.

Remove all but 1 tablespoon of the oil from the skillet. Heat the remaining oil over moderate heat. Add the pork and cook, stirring, about 5 minutes or until browned. Pour off any excess drippings. Add the shrimp, mushrooms, water chestnuts, soy sauce, and ¾ cup water. Cover and simmer gently about 5 minutes. Blend the cornstarch and remaining 2 teaspoons water, mix into the liquid in the skillet, and cook, stirring, until slightly thickened. Remove from the heat and spoon over the noodles. Sprinkle with the scallion and surround with the lettuce leaves.

To eat, place 2 or 3 spoonfuls of the meat mixture and noodles slightly below the center of a lettuce leaf. Fold the bottom edge of the leaf up over the filling, then fold in the sides and roll up to enclose the filling. Pick up with your fingers. Makes 6.

°Sometimes known as cellophane noodles, these are available in Oriental groceries and some supermarkets.

Hawaiian Beef Lettuce Rolls

Pleasing to both Oriental and Occidental palates alike.

8 large leaves Boston or iceberg lettuce
2 tablespoons peanut oil or flavorless vegetable oil
1 medium garlic clove, finely chopped
12 ounces lean ground beef
4 large mushrooms, chopped
4 ounces green peas
2 tablespoons oyster sauce
1 tablespoon dry sherry
1½ tablespoons soy sauce
Salt and freshly ground pepper to taste
6 water chestnuts, diced
1 tablespoon cornstarch
3 tablespoons water
1 scallion, finely chopped, including 2 inches of the green tops, and/or toasted slivered blanched almonds

Wash the lettuce leaves under cold running water. Drain, dry with paper towels, and chill.

In a wok or heavy skillet heat 1 tablespoon of the oil over moderate heat. Add the garlic and beef and sauté, stirring and breaking up the meat with a fork, until browned and crumbly. Transfer to a plate. Add the remaining 1 tablespoon oil to the skillet and heat. Add the mushrooms and peas and sauté, stirring, until tender. Add the oyster sauce, sherry, soy sauce, and salt and pepper and mix well. Return the meat to the skillet, add the water chestnuts, and cook, stirring, until heated through. Blend the cornstarch and the water. Mix into the liquid in the skillet and cook, stirring, until thickened. Remove from the heat and transfer the mixture to a heated serving dish. Garnish with the scallions and/or almonds. Serve at once, accompanied with a bowl of the lettuce leaves.

To eat, place 2 or 3 spoonfuls of the meat mixture slightly below the center of a lettuce leaf. Fold the bottom edge of the leaf up over the filling, then fold in the sides and roll up to enclose the filling. Pick up with your fingers. Makes 8.

Lebanese Kibbeh in Romaine Leaves

Kibbeh, a mixture of bulghur (cracked wheat) and, usually, ground lamb, is considered to be the national dish of Lebanon, where its popularity borders on a passion. Here is a classic way of serving it as an appetizer.

Romaine lettuce leaves (use the tender inner leaves)
Kibbeh (below)
1 tablespoon olive oil
1 tablespoon freshly squeezed and strained lemon juice
2 tablespoons finely chopped green pepper
2 tablespoons finely chopped red bell pepper

2 tablespoons finely chopped scallions, including 2 inches of the green top
¼ cup finely chopped parsley
2 medium tomatoes, cut into small pieces
1 lemon, cut into wedges

Wash the lettuce leaves under cold running water. Drain, dry with paper towels, and chill.

Form the kibbeh into finger shapes and arrange them on a serving platter. Sprinkle with the olive oil, lemon juice, green pepper, red pepper, scallions, and parsley. Garnish with the tomatoes. Serve at once, accompanied with the lemon wedges and a bowl of the lettuce leaves.

To eat, place 1 or 2 kibbeh fingers in the center of a lettuce leaf and top with a few pieces of tomato. Squeeze a little lemon juice over and eat out of hand. Makes 6 servings.

Note: Larger romaine lettuce leaves cut in 2 or 3 pieces can be substituted for the smaller leaves, in which case wrap them around the kibbeh fingers and tomatoes.

Kibbeh

1½ to 2 cups fine bulghur
8 ounces very lean boneless leg of lamb, ground 3 times

1 small onion, finely chopped
Salt, freshly ground pepper, and cayenne pepper to taste

Soak the bulghur in cold water to cover 10 minutes. Drain and squeeze out as much moisture as possible with your hands. Combine the bulghur, lamb, onion, salt, pepper, and cayenne pepper in a mixing bowl. With hands moistened by occasionally dipping them into a bowl of lightly salted ice water, knead the mixture about 10 minutes, or until it is well blended and smooth. Taste and adjust the seasoning.

Stuffed Belgian Endive

Separate the leaves of 1 or 2 heads Belgian endive. Using a pastry bag fitted with a small fluted tube, pipe Herbed Cream Cheese (page 193) down the center of each leaf. Serve chilled, sprinkled with lemon pepper (available in the spice departments of supermarkets).

VARIATIONS:

Substitute Caucasian Walnut, Cheese, and Herb Filling (page 197) for the Herbed Cream Cheese, and finely chopped fresh mint leaves for the lemon pepper.

Substitute Roquefort and Walnut Filling (page 196) for the Herbed Cream Cheese, and finely diced radishes for the lemon pepper.

Substitute Tongue and Ham Filling (page 206) or Ham Filling (page 203) for the Herbed Cream Cheese, and paprika for the lemon pepper.

Stuffed Grape Leaves

One of the finest expressions of Armenian culinary skills, famous the world over.

2 cups grated onion
½ cup uncooked long-grain white rice
2 tablespoons pine nuts
2 tablespoons dried currants
2 tablespoons chopped parsley
2 tablespoons finely chopped fresh dill
1 tablespoon finely chopped fresh mint leaves (optional)

6 tablespoons olive oil
2½ tablespoons freshly squeezed and strained lemon juice
Salt and freshly ground black pepper to taste
60 fresh, tender leaves from a grapevine, or 60 preserved grape leaves (a 1-pound jar)
1 cup water
1 lemon, cut into wedges

Place the onion, rice, pine nuts, currants, parsley, dill, mint (if used), olive oil, 1 tablespoon of the lemon juice, and the salt and pepper in a bowl and mix well. Taste and adjust the seasoning and set aside.

If using fresh grape leaves, soak them in boiling salted water 2 minutes to soften, then rinse under cold water. Rinse preserved grape leaves in hot water to remove brine. Spread the washed leaves on absorbent paper to drain.

Cover the bottom of a heavy casserole with 10 of the leaves to prevent the stuffed leaves from burning during cooking. Stuff each of the remaining 50 leaves as follows: Remove the stem, if any, and spread the leaf on a plate, stem end toward you, dull side up. Place about 1 teaspoon (or more for larger leaves) of the rice mixture near the stem end. Fold the stem end over the stuffing, then fold over the sides to enclose the stuffing securely. Beginning at the stem end, roll the grape leaf firmly away from you toward the tip, forming a cylinder.

Layer the stuffed leaves seam sides down and close together in neat rows in the casserole. Sprinkle the remaining 1½ tablespoons lemon juice over them and add the water. Gently place an inverted plate over the top to keep the stuffed leaves in place while cooking. Bring to a boil over moderate heat, reduce the heat to low, cover, and simmer about 50 to 60 minutes or until the stuffing is very tender. If necessary, more water may be added. Remove from the heat and cool to room temperature. Remove the plate and arrange the stuffed leaves on a serving platter. Cover and chill. Serve garnished with the lemon wedges. Makes about 50.

Cucumber Canapés

Select an unwaxed seedless cucumber, preferably the variety known as English cucumber, or other narrow, firm cucumber. Cut crosswise into ¼-inch-thick slices. Place about 1 teaspoon Pistachio Cheese Filling (page 196) on each cucumber slice. Spread the filling to the edge of the cucumber, smoothing it on top (or pipe the filling through a pastry bag fitted with a small fancy tube). Serve chilled.

VARIATIONS:

Substitute Herbed Cream Cheese (page 193) for the Pistachio

Cheese Filling. Cover each canapé with a thin slice of Italian salami cut to size.

Substitute Smoked Salmon and Cream Cheese Filling (page 201) for the Pistachio Cheese Filling. Garnish each canapé with a dill sprig.

Substitute Caucasian Walnut, Cheese, and Herb Filling (page 197) for the Pistachio Cheese Filling. Garnish each canapé with a mint sprig.

Substitute Swedish Anchovy and Egg Filling (page 201) for the Pistachio Cheese Filling. Garnish each canapé with a dill sprig.

Substitute Cream Cheese and Nut Filling (page 191) for the Pistachio Cheese Filling. Cover each canapé with a thin slice of prosciutto, Smithfield ham, or mortadella cut to size.

Substitute Greek Taramasalata (page 202) for the Pistachio Cheese Filling. Garnish each canapé with half a black olive, cut side down.

Substitute Curried Shrimp Filling (page 199) for the Pistachio Cheese Filling.

Substitute Ham Filling (page 203) for the Pistachio Cheese Filling. Garnish each canapé with paprika and very finely chopped parsley.

Stuffed Cucumber Boats

Peel 2 small cucumbers with a fluted vegetable knife, or run the prongs of a fork down unpeeled ones. Cut the cucumbers in half lengthwise. Scoop out the seeds with a grapefruit spoon and discard. Fill the cucumber boats with one of the fillings given for Cucumber Canapés (above) and garnish as directed. Serve chilled. Makes 2.

Zucchini Appetizer

Trim the ends from medium zucchini and cut the zucchini in half lengthwise. Place in boiling salted water to cover and simmer, uncovered, about 5 minutes, or until just tender. Rinse with cold water. Drain, dry with paper towels, and cool. Place the zucchini cut sides up on a platter. Using a pastry bag fitted with a star tube, pipe Smoked Salmon and Cream Cheese Filling (page 201) or Deviled Ham and Cream Cheese Filling (page 204) on top of the zucchini (or spread on the filling with a spatula). Cover and chill 2 to 3 hours. Serve whole or cut in 1-inch-thick slices.

Zucchini Canapés

Follow the recipe for Cucumber Canapés (page 175), substituting zucchini slices for the cucumber slices.

Guacamole and Tomato Sandwich

Peel 1 medium firm, ripe tomato and cut it horizontally into 4 thick slices. Spread Guacamole (page 265) between the slices and stack them on a salad plate lined with lettuce leaves. Cover and chill about 2 hours. Serve with corn chips or tortilla chips and eat with knife and fork. Makes 1.

VARIATIONS:

Finely chopped hard-cooked egg, chopped crisp-cooked bacon, or diced shrimp marinated in French Dressing (page 261) may be mixed with the Guacamole.

Shrimp and Avocado Filling (page 200), Shrimp, Asparagus, and Egg Salad (page 217), Curried Shellfish Salad (page 218), or Salmon Salad (page 219) may be substituted for the Guacamole.

Basil, Cheese, and Tomato Sandwiches

¼ cup chopped parsley
1 cup fresh basil leaves
2 tablespoons freshly squeezed and
  strained lemon juice
Salt
⅓ to ½ cup olive oil
1 cup freshly grated Parmesan
  cheese

¼ cup pine nuts
8 large tomato slices, cut about ⅓
  inch thick
Freshly ground pepper to taste
Pine nuts for garnish
Parsley sprigs for garnish

Put the parsley, basil, lemon juice, ½ teaspoon salt, and oil in the container of an electric blender and blend until smooth. Add the cheese and whirl until blended, adding additional oil if needed to make a smooth paste. Stir in the ¼ cup pine nuts. Sandwich the tomato slices together in pairs with 1½ to 2 tablespoons of the basil mixture and arrange on a serving platter. Sprinkle with salt and pepper to taste, and top each sandwich with a little of the remaining basil mixture and additional pine nuts. Garnish with the parsley sprigs and serve as a first course. Makes 4 servings.

Note: These make a delicious topping for open-faced grilled cheese sandwiches. Serve with knife and fork.

Mushroom Canapés

Slice large fresh mushrooms vertically through the stems and caps. Top each slice with Cream Cheese, Olive, and Nut Filling (page 192) or Chicken and Almond Filling (page 203). Sprinkle lightly with paprika or very finely chopped parsley. Serve at once, or cover with clear plastic wrap and chill up to 3 hours before serving.

Mushroom and Ham Canapés

Slice large fresh mushrooms vertically through the stems and caps. Set aside.

Spread thin slices of cooked ham with a thin coating of Spinach and Cheese Filling (page 198), then roll up tightly jelly-roll fashion. Cut crosswise into ¼- to ⅓-inch-thick slices. Place 2 or 3 slices on a mushroom slice. Serve at once, or cover with clear plastic wrap and chill up to 3 hours before serving.

Jicama Sandwiches

Spread slices of jicama with Cream Cheese and Avocado Filling (page 194). Sprinkle with chopped crisp cooked bacon, or cover with a thin slice of Swiss cheese or cooked ham cut to size.

Fennel Canapés

Spread wedges of crisp fennel with Swedish Cheese Filling (page 196). Serve as part of an appetizer tray.

Red Apple Sandwiches

Spread cored unpeeled red apple slices, each ¼ to ⅓ inch thick, with Roquefort Filling (page 196). Garnish with toasted slivered blanched almonds.

VARIATIONS:

Spread the slices with Ham, Cream Cheese, and Almond Filling (page 203) and garnish with paprika.

Spread the slices with Cream Cheese, Date, and Walnut Filling (page 209) and garnish with cinnamon.

Spread the slices with Lemon-Honey Cheese Filling (page 207). Garnish with chopped unsalted pistachio nuts.

Red Apple and Peanut Butter Triple–Decker

Core a medium-size red apple, but do not peel or stem it. Cut it horizontally into 4 thick slices. Spread peanut butter between the slices and stack them on a dessert plate with the stem end on top. Serve at once. Makes 1.

Green Apple Sandwiches

Select tart green apples such as Pippins or Granny Smiths. Core but do not peel them. Cut them into about ¼-inch-thick slices. Spread the slices with Cream Cheese and Nut Filling (page 191) and sandwich them together in pairs with a thin slice of prosciutto or Smithfield ham. Serve at once.

VARIATION:

Substitute Whipped Cream Cheese (page 191) for the Cream Cheese and Nut Filling, and very thin slices of Italian salami for the ham.

Pear and Cheese Sandwiches

Core an unpeeled Bartlett pear and cut lengthwise in half. Cover each half with a thin slice of any of the following cheeses: Dutch Leyden, Edam, or Gouda; Danish Tybo; French bonbel; Swiss Emmenthaler or Gruyère; Italian Fontina, Bel Paese, or provolone; and domestic baronet, Wisconsin Fontinella, and domestic or Canadian Cheddar. Makes 2 servings.

Pear and Prosciutto Sandwiches

Core an unpeeled Bartlett pear and cut lengthwise in half. Cover each half with a thin slice of prosciutto. Grind a light sprinkling of black pepper on top and squeeze over a little lemon juice. Serve at once. Makes 2 servings.

Pear, Ham, and Cheese Sandwiches

Core an unpeeled Bartlett pear and cut lengthwise in half. Cover each half with a thin slice of cooked ham and top with a thin slice of Dutch Leyden cheese. Serve at once. Makes 2 servings.

Pear and Salami Sandwiches

Core an unpeeled Bartlett pear and cut lengthwise in half. Cover with a thin slice of Italian salami. Serve at once. Makes 2 servings.

Dessert Pear Sandwiches

Core an unpeeled Bartlett pear and cut lengthwise in half. Using a pastry bag fitted with a small fluted tube, pipe Italian Cream Cheese Filling (page 207), Sweetened Yogurt Cheese Filling (page 209), or Bar-le-Duc Filling (page 207) over the pear half. Garnish with toasted slivered blanched almonds and serve. Makes 2 servings.

Peach, Nectarine, or Apricot Sandwiches

Follow the recipe for Dessert Pear Sandwiches (above), substituting peach, nectarine, or apricot halves for the pear halves. Use 4 apricot halves and omit the Bar-le-Duc Filling. Makes 2 servings.

Pineapple Sandwiches

Using a pastry bag fitted with a small fancy tube, pipe any of the following fillings over fresh pineapple sticks and serve:

Cream Cheese and Nut Filling (page 191)

Cream Cheese and Bacon Filling (page 193)

Chicken and Almond Filling (page 203)

Ham, Cream Cheese, and Almond Filling (page 203)

Cream Cheese, Date, and Walnut Filling (page 209)

10

Sandwich Fillings

Butter Spreads

Although regular butter, of course, makes an excellent spread for bread, many canapés and sandwiches take on extra character when the bread is spread with what the French call *beurres composés* or "compound butters," butter creamed with herbs, spices, nuts, vegetables, seafood, or other flavorings. These cold flavored butters can be used either alone or with compatible fillings, especially enhancing simple fillings such as sliced meat, poultry, cheese, or hard-cooked eggs. A few suggestions are included with each of the following recipes.

Use fresh, good butter and cream it before adding the flavoring. You can cream butter with an electric beater, in a blender or food processor, by pounding it in a bowl with a pestle, or by mashing it a little at a time with the back of a wooden spoon and then beating it vigorously until it is light and smooth. Next cream the butter and flavoring together and chill the mixture just until it is firm enough to be spread. One-half cup (1 stick) butter is sufficient to spread 18 to 24 regular-size open-faced sandwiches, 9 to 12 regular-size closed sandwiches, 36 to 48 small closed sandwiches, and 72 to 96 canapés. You may wish to apply a more generous amount, especially if no other filling is being used.

To decorate canapés and open-faced sandwiches with butter

182

spreads, fill a pastry bag with chilled but still malleable flavored butter and pipe it through a small fancy tube.

Butter spreads can be shaped into logs, wrapped securely in aluminum foil, and frozen up to 2 weeks. Simply open the frozen packages and slice off what you need. They can also be refrigerated up to 24 hours.

Parsley Butter

Cream ½ cup butter. Gradually beat in 1 teaspoon freshly squeezed and strained lemon juice, then beat in 3 tablespoons finely chopped parsley. Season to taste with salt and freshly ground pepper. For sandwiches with egg, seafood, poultry, or meat.

Tarragon Butter

Cream ½ cup butter. Gradually beat in 1 teaspoon freshly squeezed and strained lemon juice, then beat in 2 tablespoons finely chopped fresh tarragon or 1 teaspoon crushed dried tarragon. Season to taste with salt and freshly ground pepper. For sandwiches with seafood, poultry, or meat.

Dill Butter

Cream ½ cup butter. Gradually beat in 1 teaspoon freshly squeezed and strained lemon juice, then beat in 2 tablespoons finely chopped fresh dill or 1 teaspoon dried dill weed. Season to taste with salt. For sandwiches with cucumber, tomato, egg, seafood, or veal.

Mint Butter

Cream ½ cup butter. Gradually beat in 1 teaspoon freshly squeezed and strained lemon juice, then beat in 2 tablespoons finely chopped fresh mint. Season to taste with salt and freshly ground pepper. For sandwiches with cucumber, tomato, or lamb.

Oregano Butter

Cream ½ cup butter. Gradually beat in 1 teaspoon freshly squeezed and strained lemon juice, then beat in 2 tablespoons finely chopped fresh oregano or 1 teaspoon crushed dried oregano. Season to taste with salt. For sandwiches with cheese, tomato, egg, seafood, poultry, or meat.

Mixed Herb Butter

Cream ½ cup butter. Gradually beat in 1 teaspoon freshly squeezed and strained lemon juice, then beat in 3 tablespoons finely chopped mixed fresh herbs (parsley, basil, and chives). Season to taste with salt and freshly ground pepper. For sandwiches with cucumber, tomato, egg, seafood, or poultry.

VARIATION:

Instead of the above herbs you may substitute a combination of parsley, tarragon, basil or dill, and chives; parsley or chervil, tarragon, and basil; or a complementary mixture of your own choice.

Watercress Butter

Cream ½ cup butter. Gradually beat in 1 teaspoon freshly squeezed and strained lemon juice, then beat in ¼ cup finely chopped watercress leaves. Season to taste with salt. For sandwiches with cucumber, tomato, egg, or seafood.

Chive Butter

Cream ½ cup butter. Gradually beat in 1 teaspoon freshly squeezed and strained lemon juice, then beat in 2 tablespoons finely chopped chives. Season to taste with salt and freshly ground pepper. For sandwiches with egg or seafood.

Garlic Butter

Pound or cream together ½ cup butter and 1 to 3 garlic cloves, crushed. season to taste with salt and freshly ground pepper. For sandwiches with vegetables or seafood.

Note: Two tablespoons finely chopped parsley or mixed fresh herbs may be added. The garlic may be parboiled before combining it with the butter.

Mustard Butter

Cream ½ cup butter. Gradually beat in 2 to 3 tablespoons Dijon-style, Düsseldorf, or other prepared mustard. Season to taste with salt and freshly ground pepper and, if desired, beat in 2 tablespoons finely chopped parsley or mixed fresh herbs. For sandwiches with cheese, seafood, or meat.

Horseradish Butter

Cream ½ cup butter. Gradually beat in 1 teaspoon freshly squeezed and strained lemon juice, then beat in 2 to 3 tablespoons grated horseradish. Season to taste with salt. For sandwiches with seafood, ham, beef, or tongue.

Lemon Butter

Cream ½ cup butter. Gradually beat in 2 tablespoons freshly squeezed and strained lemon juice, then beat in 1 teaspoon finely grated lemon rind. Season to taste with salt. For sandwiches with seafood.

Paprika Butter

Cream ½ cup butter. Blend in 1½ teaspoons paprika. For sandwiches with egg, veal, or tongue. Good as a garnish for some canapés.

Curry Butter

Cream ½ cup butter. Gradually beat in ½ teaspoon freshly squeezed and strained lemon juice, then beat in ½ teaspoon curry powder and salt to taste. For sandwiches with vegetables, egg, seafood, poultry, or meat.

VARIATION:

Two tablespoons finely chopped parsley or chives or 2 tablespoons finely chopped shallots that have been sautéed in 2 teaspoons butter until soft may be added with the curry powder.

Nut Butter

Cream ½ cup butter. Beat in ½ cup very finely chopped or ground lightly toasted blanched almonds, hazelnuts, walnuts, pecans, cashews, or pistachios. Season with salt to taste. For sandwiches with vegetables, seafood, or poultry.

Sesame Butter

Cream ½ cup butter. Beat in ½ cup toasted sesame seeds and salt to taste. For sandwiches with vegetables or poultry.

Olive Butter

Cream ½ cup butter. Gradually beat in 1 teaspoon freshly squeezed and strained lemon juice, then beat in 2 tablespoons finely chopped pitted green or black olives. For sandwiches with cheese, egg, or seafood.

Caper Butter

Cream ½ cup butter. Beat in 2 tablespoons finely chopped capers. For sandwiches with seafood or meat.

Avocado Butter

Mash 1 large peeled and pitted avocado with 1 tablespoon freshly squeezed and strained lemon or lime juice. Cream ½ cup butter. Gradually beat in the mashed avocado and season to taste with salt and freshly ground pepper. For sandwiches with tomato, egg, seafood, poultry, ham, or beef.

VARIATIONS:

Avocado-Nut Butter

Add ½ cup finely chopped or ground macadamia nuts or cashews with the mashed avocado.

Parmesan Butter

Cream ½ cup butter. Beat in ¼ to ½ cup freshly grated Parmesan (or Romano) cheese. For sandwiches with tomato, eggplant, zucchini, or salami.

Egg Yolk Butter

Cream ½ cup butter. Beat in 3 or 4 sieved hard-cooked egg yolks and, if desired, 1 to 2 tablespoons finely chopped chives or mixed fresh herbs. Season to taste with salt and freshly ground pepper. For sandwiches with cucumber, tomato, seafood, ham, tongue, or salami; also used to decorate canapés and open-faced sandwiches.

Anchovy Butter

Cream ½ cup butter. Gradually beat in 2 tablespoons mashed anchovies, or 1 tablespoon anchovy paste and 1 teaspoon freshly squeezed and strained lemon juice. Season to taste with freshly ground pepper and, if desired, add 1 to 2 tablespoons finely chopped parsley or mixed fresh herbs. For sandwiches with tomato, egg, seafood, or veal.

Anchovy and Cream Cheese Butter

Cream ½ cup butter. Gradually beat in 4 ounces cream cheese, ½ teaspoon or more anchovy paste, 2 teaspoons freshly squeezed and strained lemon juice, and 1 tablespoon finely chopped fresh dill. For sandwiches with cucumber, tomato, or seafood.

Shrimp Butter

In a mortar pound 16 medium shrimp, cooked, shelled, and deveined, to a paste. Cream ½ cup butter. Gradually beat in the shrimp paste and 2 teaspoons freshly squeezed and strained lemon juice or 1 tablespoon tomato paste. Season to taste with salt and freshly ground pepper. For sandwiches with avocado or seafood.

VARIATIONS:

Lobster Butter

Substitute cooked lobster meat for the shrimp.

Crab Butter

Substitute cooked crabmeat for the shrimp.

Tuna Butter

Cream ½ cup butter. Gradually beat in ¼ cup drained and mashed canned tuna and 2 teaspoons freshly squeezed and strained lemon juice. Season to taste with salt and freshly ground pepper. For sandwiches with cucumber, tomato, olive, avocado, egg, sardines, or veal.

Smoked Salmon Butter

Cream ½ cup butter. Gradually beat in 2 tablespoons pounded smoked salmon and 1 teaspoon freshly squeezed and strained lemon juice. Season to taste with freshly ground pepper. For sandwiches with cucumber, tomato, olive, or avocado.

Prosciutto Butter

Cream ½ cup butter. Gradually beat in ½ cup ground or very finely chopped prosciutto, trimmed of all fat, until the mixture attains the consistency of a smooth paste. For sandwiches with cheese, cucumber, tomato, olive, or fruit.

VARIATION:

Substitute Westphalian ham for the prosciutto.

Deviled Ham Butter

Cream ½ cup butter. Beat in ½ cup deviled ham and, if desired, ½ teaspoon fresh lemon juice. For sandwiches with cheese or egg.

Rum Butter

Cream ½ cup butter. Beat in 1 tablespoon dark rum and ⅛ teaspoon freshly grated nutmeg or to taste. For sandwiches with ham.

Whipped Honey Butter

Cream ½ cup butter. Add 1 cup whipped honey and, if desired, ⅛ teaspoon nutmeg, preferably freshly ground, and beat until well blended and smooth. Use as a spread for toast.

VARIATION:

In a mixing bowl beat ¾ cup regular honey until light and fluffy, then gradually beat in the butter. Omit the nutmeg.

Cold Savory Fillings

Whipped Cream Cheese

3 ounces cream cheese, at room   1 tablespoon milk or cream
temperature   Salt to taste

In a small bowl beat together the ingredients until light and fluffy.
Cover and refrigerate. Makes about ½ cup.

Lemon Cream Cheese

3 ounces cream cheese, at room   2 teaspoons freshly squeezed and
temperature   strained lemon juice
¼ teaspoon finely grated lemon
rind

In a small bowl beat together the ingredients until well blended and
fluffy. Cover and refrigerate. Makes about ½ cup.

Cream Cheese and Nut Filling

3 ounces cream cheese, at room   ¼ cup finely chopped toasted
temperature   blanched almonds
1 tablespoon milk or cream   Salt to taste

In a small bowl beat the cream cheese with the milk or cream until
light and fluffy. Add the almonds and mix well. Taste and add salt, if
needed. Cover and refrigerate. Makes about ¾ cup.

Cream Cheese, Olive, and Nut Filling

3 ounces cream cheese, at room
  temperature
1 tablespoon milk or cream
¼ cup finely chopped pimento-
  stuffed olives

2 tablespoons finely chopped
  toasted blanched almonds
Salt to taste

In a small bowl beat the cream cheese with the milk or cream until light and fluffy. Fold in the olives and nuts. Taste and add salt, if needed. Cover and refrigerate. Makes about ¾ cup.

VARIATIONS:

Cream Cheese, Olive, and Nut Filling with Mayonnaise

Substitute 1½ tablespoons mayonnaise for the milk or cream. Use ¾ cup olives and ½ cup almonds.

Curried Cream Cheese and Olive Filling

3 ounces cream cheese, at room
  temperature
2 teaspoons milk or cream
¾ teaspoon freshly squeezed
  lemon or lime juice

1 teaspoon finely chopped chives
¼ teaspoon curry powder
Salt to taste
8 pitted black olives, finely
  chopped

In a small bowl beat the cream cheese with the milk or cream and lemon or lime juice until light and fluffy. Add the chives, curry powder, and salt and blend thoroughly. Fold in the olives. Taste and adjust the seasoning. Cover and refrigerate. Makes about ½ cup.

Cream Cheese, Olive, and Bacon Filling

3 ounces cream cheese, at room
   temperature
1 tablespoon milk or cream
¼ cup finely chopped pimento-
   stuffed olives

3 tablespoons cooked crisp,
   drained, and crumbled bacon

In a small bowl beat the cream cheese with the milk or cream until light and fluffy. Add the olives and bacon and mix well. Cover and refrigerate. Makes about 1 cup.

VARIATION:

Cream Cheese and Bacon Filling

Omit the olives and increase the bacon to ¼ cup.

Cream Cheese and Chives Filling

3 ounces cream cheese, at room
   temperature
2 teaspoons milk or cream

1 teaspoon finely chopped chives
   or scallion tops
Salt and Tabasco sauce to taste

In a small bowl beat the cream cheese with the milk or cream until light and fluffy. Add the remaining ingredients and blend thoroughly. Taste and adjust the seasoning. Cover and refrigerate. Makes ½ cup.

Herbed Cream Cheese

8 ounces cream cheese, at room
   temperature
1 tablespoon milk or cream
1 tiny garlic clove, crushed and
   finely chopped

¼ teaspoon crushed dried basil
¼ teaspoon dried dill weed
¼ teaspoon caraway seeds,
   crushed
Salt to taste

Combine all the ingredients in a bowl and beat until the mixture is well blended and fluffy. Taste and adjust the seasoning. Cover and refrigerate. Makes about 1¼ cups.

Cream Cheese and Mushroom Filling

1 tablespoon butter
4 ounces mushrooms, finely chopped
4 scallions, finely chopped, including 2 inches of the green tops
3 ounces cream cheese, at room temperature

1 tablespoon milk or cream
1½ tablespoons finely chopped fresh dill
2 tablespoons freshly grated Parmesan cheese
Salt and freshly ground pepper to taste

In a small, heavy skillet melt the butter over medium-high heat. Add the mushrooms and scallions and sauté until golden brown, stirring frequently. Remove from the heat and let cool to room temperature.

In a mixing bowl beat the cream cheese with the milk or cream until light and fluffy. Add the mushroom mixture, dill, Parmesan cheese, and salt and pepper and mix thoroughly. Taste and adjust the seasoning. Cover and refrigerate. Makes about 1½ cups.

Cream Cheese and Avocado Filling

1 large, ripe avocado
3 ounces cream cheese, at room temperature
2 teaspoons sour cream
1 tablespoon freshly squeezed and strained lemon juice

1 teaspoon very finely chopped scallion tops
Salt and Tabasco sauce to taste

Halve and pit the avocado. Peel off the skin. Place the avocado flesh in a bowl and mash it with a fork. Add the remaining ingredients and beat until smooth. Taste and adjust the seasoning. Cover and refrigerate. Makes about 1 cup.

VARIATION:

Cream Cheese, Gorgonzola, and Avocado Filling

Add 1 ounce Gorgonzola or other blue cheese, crumbled, and, if desired, ¼ teaspoon Worcestershire sauce.

Cream Cheese, Green Pepper, and Pimento Filling

6 ounces cream cheese, at room temperature
1½ tablespoons mayonnaise
2 tablespoons finely chopped green pepper
1 tablespoon drained diced pimento
1 tablespoon finely chopped parsley
Salt to taste

In a bowl mix the cream cheese with the mayonnaise until smooth. Add the remaining ingredients and blend thoroughly. Taste and adjust the seasoning. Cover and refrigerate. Makes ¾ to 1 cup.

Persian Yogurt Cheese Filling

½ cup Yogurt Cheese (page 266)
½ medium cucumber, peeled, seeded (if seeds are large), and finely chopped
1 tablespoon very finely chopped red onion
1 radish, grated
2 tablespoons finely chopped walnuts
1 tablespoon dried currents
1 teaspoon finely chopped fresh mint leaves
1 teaspoon finely chopped fresh basil
Salt to taste

Combine all the ingredients in a bowl and mix thoroughly. Taste and adjust the seasoning. Cover and refrigerate. Makes about 1¼ cups.

Swedish Cheese Filling

1 to 2 ounces Roquefort, Gorgonzola, or other blue cheese	2 tablespoons heavy cream, whipped
3 ounces cream cheese, at room temperature	

In a bowl mash together the blue cheese and cream cheese and beat until well blended and smooth. Fold in the whipped cream. Cover and refrigerate. Makes about ¾ cup.

VARIATIONS:

Radish Cheese Filling

Fold in ¼ cup finely chopped radishes with the whipped cream.

Pistachio Cheese Filling

Fold in 2 tablespoons finely chopped salted pistachio nuts and, if desired, 1 teaspoon finely chopped chives or scallion tops with the whipped cream.

Roquefort Filling

2 ounces Roquefort cheese	1 tablespoon finely chopped chives or scallion tops (optional)
4 ounces cream cheese, at room temperature	1 tablespoon dry sherry
1 tablespoon butter, at room temperature	

Combine all the ingredients in a bowl and beat until the mixture is well blended and smooth. Cover and refrigerate. Makes about 1 cup.

VARIATIONS:

Roquefort and Walnut Filling

Substitute Tawny Port or Amaretto liqueur for the sherry, if desired. Add 3 tablespoons finely chopped toasted walnuts and mix well.

Caucasian Walnut, Cheese, and Herb Filling

3 ounces cream cheese, at room
  temperature
½ cup grated or crumbled brindza
  or feta cheese
¼ cup unflavored yogurt
1 tablespoon finely chopped chives
2 teaspoons finely chopped fresh
  dill, or 1 teaspoon each finely
  chopped fresh dill and fresh
  mint leaves

2 tablespoons finely chopped
  toasted walnuts
1 tiny garlic clove, crushed and
  finely chopped
Salt to taste

Combine the cheeses and yogurt in a bowl and beat until the mixture is well blended and smooth. Add the remaining ingredients and mix thoroughly. Taste and adjust the seasoning. Cover and refrigerate. Makes about 1⅓ cups.

Curried Cheese Filling

3 ounces cream cheese, at room
  temperature
4 ounces small curd cottage
  cheese, drained
1½ tablespoons finely chopped
  chives

½ teaspoon curry powder
Salt and cayenne pepper to taste
6 tablespoons heavy cream,
  whipped

Combine the cream cheese and cottage cheese and force the mixture through a fine sieve into a mixing bowl. Add the chives, curry powder, and salt and cayenne pepper and mix well. Fold in the whipped cream. Taste and adjust the seasoning. Cover and refrigerate. Makes about 1¼ cups.

Cheddar Cheese and Olive Filling

½ cup grated sharp Cheddar
   cheese
¾ cup finely chopped black olives
1 tablespoon finely chopped onion
   or scallion (include 2 inches of
   the scallion tops)

3 tablespoons mayonnaise
⅛ teaspoon curry powder or to
   taste

Combine all the ingredients in a bowl and mix well. Taste and adjust the seasoning. Cover and refrigerate. Makes about 1¼ cups.

Spinach and Cheese Filling

1 pound spinach
⅓ cup cold water
2 tablespoons butter
4 scallions, finely chopped,
   including 2 inches of the green
   tops
Salt and freshly ground pepper
   to taste
6 ounces cream cheese, at room
   temperature

½ cup unflavored yogurt or sour
   cream
2 tablespoons finely chopped fresh
   dill, or 1 teaspoon dried dill
   weed
1 large garlic clove, crushed
⅓ to ½ cup freshly grated
   Parmesan cheese

Wash the spinach thoroughly under cold running water, discarding the stems and bruised leaves. Drain. Chop the spinach and combine with the water in a large saucepan. Bring to a boil over high heat. Reduce the heat to low, cover, and simmer 5 minutes, or until the spinach is wilted. Transfer to a colander and allow the spinach to drain and cool. Squeeze it dry, chop it finely, and reserve.

In a small, heavy skillet melt the butter over moderate heat. Add the scallions and sauté gently until golden, stirring frequently. Add the spinach and salt and pepper and cook, stirring, 2 minutes. Remove from the heat and set aside.

In a small bowl mash the cream cheese with a fork, gradually adding the yogurt or sour cream until the mixture is well blended and smooth. Add the spinach mixture, dill, garlic, and Parmesan cheese and mix thoroughly. Taste and adjust the seasoning. Cover and refrigerate. Makes about 1½ cups.

Curried Egg Filling

5 hard-cooked eggs, finely chopped
½ cup butter, at room temperature

1½ teaspoons curry powder
Salt and freshly ground pepper to taste

Combine all the ingredients in a bowl and mix thoroughly. Taste and adjust the seasoning. Cover and refrigerate. Makes about 1½ cups.

Curried Shrimp Filling

1 cup finely chopped cooked shrimp
⅓ cup mayonnaise
1 tablespoon finely chopped scallion tops

Dash Worcestershire sauce
1 teaspoon curry powder
Salt to taste

Combine all the ingredients in a small bowl and mix thoroughly. Taste and adjust the seasoning. Cover and refrigerate. Makes about 1⅓ cups.

Shrimp and Avocado Filling

8 ounces shrimp, cooked, shelled, deveined, and finely chopped
1 cup finely chopped avocado
2 hard-cooked eggs, sieved
½ cup mayonnaise
¼ cup finely chopped scallions, including 2 inches of the green tops

2 tablespoons freshly squeezed and strained lemon juice
¼ teaspoon crushed dried tarragon
Salt, freshly ground pepper, and Tabasco sauce to taste

Combine all the ingredients in a bowl and toss gently but thoroughly. Taste and adjust the seasoning. Cover and refrigerate. Makes about 2½ cups.

Curried Crabmeat Filling

Follow the recipe for Curried Shrimp Filling (page 199), substituting 1 cup finely chopped cooked crabmeat for the shrimp. Makes about 1⅓ cups.

Curried Lobster Filling

Follow the recipe for Curried Shrimp Filling (page 199), substituting 1 cup finely chopped cooked lobster meat for the shrimp. Makes about 1⅓ cups.

Smoked Salmon Filling

3 ounces smoked salmon
2 tablespoons sour cream
1 teaspoon freshly squeezed and strained lemon juice

2 teaspoons finely chopped fresh dill or to taste
Salt and white pepper (preferably freshly ground) to taste

Combine all the ingredients in the container of an electric blender and blend until smooth. Taste and adjust the seasoning. Cover and refrigerate. Makes about ½ cup.

VARIATION:

Smoked Salmon and Cream Cheese Filling

Substitute 8 ounces cream cheese, at room temperature, for the sour cream.

Swedish Anchovy and Egg Filling

12 anchovy fillets, chopped
2 hard-cooked eggs, sieved
2 tablespoons mayonnaise or sour cream

2 to 3 tablespoons finely chopped chives or fresh dill

Combine all the ingredients in a bowl and mix until well blended and smooth. Taste and adjust the seasoning. Cover and refrigerate. Makes about ¾ cup.

Sardine and Cream Cheese Filling

1 can (3 to 4 ounces) skinless and boneless sardines, drained
3 ounces cream cheese, at room temperature
1 tablespoon finely chopped chives or scallion tops

1 tablespoon finely chopped parsley (optional)
1 teaspoon freshly squeezed and strained lemon juice or to taste
Salt and freshly ground pepper to taste

Combine all the ingredients in a bowl and beat until well blended and smooth. Taste and adjust the seasoning. Cover and refrigerate. Makes about ¾ cup.

Greek Taramasalata

3 slices white bread, trimmed of
  crusts
¼ cup tarama (salted carp roe)° or
  red caviar

2 tablespoons freshly squeezed and
  strained lemon juice or to taste
2 tablespoons grated mild onion
⅓ to ½ cup olive oil

Dip the bread in water and squeeze dry. Place it and the tarama or red caviar in the container of an electric blender and blend until smooth. Keeping the motor running, remove the cover and add the lemon juice, onion, and enough olive oil in a slow, steady stream to make a rich, smooth texture. (Alternatively, dip the bread in water and squeeze dry. Place it in a shallow bowl. Add the tarama or red caviar a little at a time, mashing and mixing it with a spoon. Beat in the lemon juice, onion, and enough oil to achieve a thick, creamy mixture.) Taste and adjust the seasoning. Transfer to a glass jar, cover, and refrigerate. Makes about 1 cup.

Tarama and Caviar Filling

4 ounces cream cheese, at room
  temperature
6 tablespoons tarama (salted carp
  roe)°

2 tablespoons sour cream
2 ounces red caviar

In a mixing bowl beat together the cream cheese, tarama, and sour cream until thoroughly blended. Fold in the caviar. Cover and refrigerate. Makes about 1 cup.

°Available at Middle Eastern groceries and specialty shops.

Chicken and Almond Filling

1 cup ground cooked chicken
2 tablespoons butter, at room
   temperature
2 tablespoons finely chopped mild
   onion
1 tiny garlic clove, crushed and
   finely chopped

2 tablespoons finely chopped
   toasted blanched almonds
1 tablespoon dry sherry or to taste
1 teaspoon freshly squeezed and
   strained lemon or lime juice
Salt and Tabasco sauce to taste

Combine all the ingredients in a bowl and mix thoroughly. Taste and adjust the seasoning. Cover and refrigerate. Makes about 1⅓ cups.

Ham Filling

1 cup very finely chopped lean
   cooked ham
2 tablespoons finely chopped mild
   white onion

4 teaspoons Dijon-style mustard or
   to taste
Salt and cayenne pepper to taste
⅔ cup heavy cream, whipped

Combine the ham, onion, mustard, and salt and cayenne pepper in a bowl and mix thoroughly. Fold in the whipped cream until well blended. Taste and adjust the seasoning. Cover and refrigerate. Makes about 2¼ cups.

Ham, Cream Cheese, and Almond Filling

4 ounces cream cheese, at room
   temperature
4 ounces lean cooked ham, ground
   or very finely chopped
¼ cup finely chopped toasted
   blanched almonds

½ teaspoon dry mustard
⅛ teaspoon paprika
½ teaspoon Worcestershire sauce
2 drops Tabasco sauce
Salt and freshly ground pepper
   to taste

Combine all the ingredients in a bowl and mix until thoroughly blended. Taste and adjust the seasoning. Cover and refrigerate. Makes about 1¼ cups.

Ham and Pâté de Foie Gras Filling

6 ounces lean cooked ham, very finely chopped

2 ounces pâté de foie gras

3 tablespoons butter, at room temperature

1 tablespoon finely chopped chives

Combine all the ingredients in a bowl and mix until thoroughly blended. Cover and refrigerate. Makes about 1¼ cups.

VARIATION:

Use 3 ounces each ham and pâtè de foie gras. Omit the butter and chives.

Deviled Ham Filling

1 can (4½ ounces) deviled ham

1 tablespoon finely chopped onion

½ teaspoon Dijon-style or Düsseldorf mustard

1 tablespoon butter, at room temperature

⅛ teaspoon freshly ground pepper or to taste

Combine all the ingredients in a bowl and mix until thoroughly blended. Taste and adjust the seasoning. Cover and refrigerate. Makes about ½ cup.

Deviled Ham and Cream Cheese Filling

3 ounces cream cheese, at room temperature

1 can (4½ ounces) deviled ham

1 tablespoon finely chopped mild onion

1 teaspoon mayonnaise or ketchup

Combine all the ingredients in a bowl and beat until thoroughly blended. Cover and refrigerate. Makes about ¾ cup.

Chicken Liver Pâté

¾ cup butter
1 pound chicken livers, cleaned
   and dried with paper towels
2 medium garlic cloves, crushed

⅓ cup dry sherry or Madeira
½ teaspoon salt or to taste
¼ teaspoon freshly ground pepper

In a large, heavy skillet melt the butter over moderate heat. Add the chicken livers and garlic and sauté, stirring frequently, about 4 minutes, or until lightly browned outside but still pink inside. Remove from the heat and transfer the contents of the skillet into the container of an electric blender. Add the sherry or Madeira, salt, and pepper. Blend until a smooth paste is formed. Taste and adjust the seasoning. Transfer to a glass jar, cover, and refrigerate. Makes about 2½ cups.

Chicken Liver Pâté and Mushroom Filling

1 tablespoon butter
½ cup finely chopped mushrooms
1½ cups Chicken Liver Pâté
   (above)
2 tablespoons mayonnaise

1 tablespoon very finely chopped
   onion or scallions (include some
   of the green tops of the scallions)
¼ teaspoon salt or to taste

In a small, heavy skillet melt the butter over moderate heat. Add the mushrooms and sauté about 5 minutes or until tender, stirring frequently. Remove from the heat. Transfer the sautéed mushrooms to a mixing bowl and let cool. Add the remaining ingredients and mix thoroughly. Taste and adjust the seasoning. Cover and refrigerate. Makes about 2 cups.

Chicken Liver Pâté and Bacon Filling

Combine Chicken Liver Pâté (page 205) with 12 slices bacon, cooked until crisp, and crumbled. Cover and refrigerate. Makes about 2¾ cups.

Whipped Pâté de Foie Gras

Whip 1 cup pâté de foie gras until light and fluffy. Stir in 1 tablespoon Cognac and, if desired, 1 tablespoon chopped truffles. Makes about 1¼ cups.

Tongue and Ham Filling

½ cup finely chopped cooked tongue	1 tablespoon finely chopped chives
½ cup finely chopped cooked ham	1 teaspoon Dijon-style mustard
1 hard-cooked egg, finely chopped	¼ cup mayonnaise, or as needed
1 tablespoon finely chopped dill gherkin	Salt and freshly ground pepper to taste

Combine all the ingredients in a bowl and mix until thoroughly blended. Taste and adjust the seasoning. Cover and refrigerate. Makes about 1½ cups.

Cold Sweet Fillings

Italian Cream Cheese Filling

4 ounces mascarpone or cream
  cheese, at room temperature
3 to 4 tablespoons confectioners'
  sugar, sifted
¾ teaspoon finely grated orange
  rind

1 tablespoon Grand Marnier or
  other orange-flavored liqueur
¼ cup heavy cream, whipped

Combine the cheese, confectioners' sugar, orange rind, and orange liqueur in a bowl, and beat until well blended and smooth. Fold in the whipped cream. Cover and refrigerate. Makes about 1 cup.

Note: Mascarpone is a soft, creamy Italian cheese. Cream cheese makes a good substitute.

Lemon-Honey Cheese Filling

4 ounces cream cheese, at room
  temperature
2½ tablespoons honey

1 teaspoon finely grated lemon
  rind
¼ cup heavy cream, whipped

Combine the cheese, honey, and lemon rind in a bowl, and beat until well blended and smooth. Fold in the whipped cream. Cover and refrigerate. Makes about 1 cup.

Bar-le-Duc Filling

3 ounces cream cheese, at room
  temperature
2 teaspoons heavy cream

2 tablespoons red currant
  preserves

In a small bowl beat the cream cheese with the cream until light and fluffy. Add the preserves and blend thoroughly. Cover and refrigerate. Makes about ½ cup.

VARIATION:

Substitute apricot or other preserves of your choice for the currant preserves.

Cream Cheese and Marmalade Filling

3 ounces cream cheese, at room
  temperature
1 teaspoon freshly squeezed and
  strained orange juice

2 tablespoons Seville orange
  marmalade

In a small bowl beat the cream cheese with the orange juice until light and fluffy. Add the marmalade and blend thoroughly. Cover and refrigerate. Makes about ½ cup.

VARIATION:

Substitute pineapple or another marmalade of your choice for the orange marmalade.

Cream Cheese and Kumquat Filling

3 ounces cream cheese, at room
  temperature
2 to 3 teaspoons syrup from
  preserved kumquats
¼ cup finely chopped preserved
  kumquats or to taste

In a small bowl beat the cream cheese with the kumquat syrup until light and fluffy. Add the kumquats and mix well. Cover and refrigerate. Makes about ⅔ cup.

VARIATION:

Substitute 2 tablespoons each finely chopped preserved kumquats and toasted blanched almonds or hazelnuts for the kumquats.

Cream Cheese, Date, and Walnut Filling

3 ounces cream cheese, at room
   temperature
1 tablespoon honey

⅓ cup chopped dates
¼ cup chopped toasted walnuts

In a small bowl beat the cream cheese with the honey until light and fluffy. Add the dates and walnuts and mix well. Cover and refrigerate. Makes about 1 cup.

Sweetened Yogurt Cheese Filling

½ cup Yogurt Cheese (page 266)
1 tablespoon Grand Marnier
1 tablespoon sugar or to taste

2 tablespoons finely chopped
   toasted blanched almonds,
   walnuts, or hazelnuts (optional)

Combine all the ingredients in a bowl and mix thoroughly. Cover and refrigerate. Makes about ⅔ cup.

Crème Chantilly

1 cup chilled heavy cream
2 tablespoons confectioners' sugar
   or to taste, sifted

1 teaspoon vanilla extract

Pour the cream into a chilled bowl and beat until it begins to thicken. Add the confectioners' sugar and vanilla extract and continue to beat until the cream stands in stiff peaks. Use preferably at once. Makes about 2 cups.

VARIATIONS:

Substitute 1 to 2 tablespoons Cognac, rum, Grand Marnier, apricot liqueur, or other sweet liqueur for the vanilla extract.

Chocolate Crème Chantilly

Reduce the amount of vanilla extract to ½ teaspoon and add 4 teaspoons cocoa.

Pineapple Crème Chantilly

Place 1½ cups finely chopped and drained fresh pineapple in a bowl. Sprinkle with 1 tablespoon amber rum. Cover and chill. Just before serving, using a rubber spatula, fold the fruit into the Crème Chantilly, blending them together gently but thoroughly.

Fruit and Nut Tea Fillings

Apricot-Almond Filling

1½ cups dried apricots
1 cup water
½ cup firmly packed brown
   sugar or to taste

½ cup chopped toasted blanched
   almonds
Cinnamon or apricot liqueur to
   taste

In a small, heavy saucepan combine the apricots and water. Cover and simmer about 25 minutes, or until the apricots are very soft and almost all the water has evaporated (uncover if necessary during the last few minutes of cooking). Remove from the heat, mash the apricots, and stir in the sugar. Add the almonds and cinnamon or apricot liqueur and stir again. Makes about 1½ cups.

Date-Nut Filling

2 cups pitted dates
¾ cup water
1 teaspoon grated lemon rind
3 tablespoons freshly squeezed and
   strained lemon juice

⅓ cup firmly packed brown
   sugar or to taste
½ cup chopped toasted walnuts
Cinnamon or orange liqueur to
   taste

In a small, heavy saucepan combine the dates, water, lemon rind, and lemon juice. Cover and simmer about 25 minutes or until the dates are very soft and almost all the water has evaporated (uncover if necessary during the last few minutes of cooking). Remove from the heat, mash the dates, and stir in the sugar. Add the nuts and cinnamon or orange liqueur and stir again. Makes about 1½ cups.

Prune-Nut Filling

Follow the directions for Date-Nut Filling (page 211), substituting 1½ cups pitted prunes for the dates. Use almonds or hazelnuts instead of the walnuts. Makes about 1½ cups.

Hot Cream Fillings

Cream Filling with Cheese

4½ tablespoons butter
3 tablespoons all-purpose flour
1½ cups hot milk or heavy cream
Pinch freshly grated nutmeg
Dash cayenne pepper
Salt and freshly ground pepper to
  taste

1 egg yolk
1 cup grated Swiss cheese, or ½
  cup each freshly grated
  Parmesan and Swiss cheese

In a heavy saucepan melt 2½ tablespoons of the butter over low heat. Add the flour and cook 1 to 2 minutes, stirring constantly with a wire whisk. Add the hot milk or cream, nutmeg, cayenne pepper, and salt and pepper and cook, stirring, about 1 minute, or until the mixture comes to a boil and is thick and smooth. Taste and adjust the seasoning. Remove from the heat. Place the egg yolk in the center of the sauce and beat it vigorously with a wire whisk, then beat in the cheese and, finally, the remaining 2 tablespoons butter. Taste again for seasoning. Makes about 2 cups.

VARIATIONS:

Cream Filling with Ham and Cheese

Use only ½ cup cheese. Add 3 ounces chopped cooked ham sautéed in ½ tablespoon butter to the sauce along with the cheese.

Cream Filling with Mushrooms and Cheese

Use only ½ cup cheese. Add 4 ounces diced mushrooms sautéed in 1 tablespoon butter to the sauce along with the cheese.

Cream Filling with Shellfish

4 tablespoons butter
2 tablespoons chopped shallots or
scallions (include 2 inches of the
scallion tops)
10 ounces diced or flaked cooked
shellfish
¼ cup dry white wine, Madeira, or
sherry
1 tablespoon finely chopped fresh
tarragon, or 1 teaspoon crushed
dried tarragon

Salt and freshly ground pepper to
taste
2½ tablespoons all-purpose flour
1 cup hot milk
1 egg yolk
¼ cup heavy cream
¼ cup grated Swiss cheese

In a heavy skillet melt 2 tablespoons of the butter over low heat. Add the shallots or scallions and sauté about ½ minute, stirring frequently. Add the shellfish and sauté 2 minutes, stirring frequently. Add the wine, cover, and simmer 1 minute. Uncover, increase the heat to high, and cook until most of the liquid in the skillet has evaporated. Stir in the tarragon and salt and pepper. Remove from the heat and set aside.

In a heavy saucepan melt the remaining 2 tablespoons butter over low heat. Add the flour and cook 1 to 2 minutes, stirring constantly with a wire whisk. Add the hot milk and salt and pepper and cook, stirring, about 1 minute, or until the mixture comes to a boil and is thick and smooth. Remove from the heat and keep warm.

In a mixing bowl beat the egg yolk with the cream, then beat in the sauce, 1 tablespoon at a time. Return to the saucepan and boil, stirring, 1 minute, or until very thick. Fold in the shellfish mixture and cheese. Taste and adjust the seasoning. Makes about 2 cups.

Cream Filling with Chicken

Follow the recipe for Cream Filling with Shellfish (above), substituting 8 ounces diced cooked chicken (or turkey) for the shellfish. Makes about 2 cups.

Cream Filling with Chicken Livers and Mushrooms

4½ tablespoons butter
1 tablespoon all-purpose flour
⅔ cup half-and-half
⅛ teaspoon grated nutmeg (preferably freshly grated)
Salt, freshly ground pepper, and cayenne pepper to taste
⅓ cup freshly grated Parmesan or Romano cheese
1 egg yolk

4 shallots, finely chopped
1 medium garlic clove, very finely chopped
8 medium mushroom caps, chopped
¾ pound chicken livers, cleaned and dried with paper towels
2 tablespoons Cognac
2 tablespoons finely chopped parsley

In a small saucepan melt ½ tablespoon of the butter. Add the flour and cook over low heat about 1 minute, stirring constantly. Gradually stir in the half-and-half, then add the nutmeg and salt, pepper, and cayenne pepper. Bring to a boil, stirring. Add the cheese, mix well, and remove from the heat.

In a small bowl beat the egg yolk lightly. Add a small quantity of the hot sauce to the egg yolk and return the mixture to the saucepan.

In a small, heavy skillet melt 2 tablespoons of the remaining butter over moderate heat. Add the shallots and garlic and sauté until tender but not browned, stirring frequently. Add the mushrooms and cook 2 minutes. Increase the heat and add the remaining 2 tablespoons butter. When the butter is melted add the chicken livers and cook, turning to brown on all sides. Transfer the mixture onto a chopping board and chop finely. Add the Cognac, parsley, and salt and pepper to taste. Stir into the cheese sauce. Makes about 2½ cups.

Salad Fillings

Middle Eastern Vegetable Salad

1 medium cucumber, peeled, seeded (if seeds are large), and diced

2 medium tomatoes, seeded and diced

½ medium green pepper, seeded, deribbed, and diced

2 scallions, finely chopped, including 2 inches of the green tops

2 tablespoons finely chopped fresh mint leaves

2 tablespoons olive oil

2 tablespoons freshly squeezed and strained lemon juice

Salt and freshly ground pepper to taste

Combine the cucumber, tomatoes, green pepper, scallions, and mint in a bowl. Beat together the remaining ingredients with a fork or whisk until blended and pour over the salad. Toss gently but thoroughly. Taste and adjust the seasoning. Drain well and use at once.

Curried Egg Salad

4 hard-cooked eggs, diced

½ cup diced celery

1 scallion, finely chopped, including 2 inches of the green top

3 tablespoons mayonnaise

½ teaspoon curry powder or to taste

Salt and freshly ground pepper to taste

Combine all the ingredients in a bowl and mix well. Taste and adjust the seasoning. Cover and refrigerate.

VARIATION:

Egg Salad

Substitute ½ teaspoon Dijon-style mustard, or to taste, for the curry powder.

Swiss Cheese and Egg Salad

8 ounces Swiss cheese, cut into strips about 1 inch long and ⅜ inch wide
8 hard-cooked eggs, finely chopped
¾ cup sour cream
2 teaspoons Dijon-style mustard

1 tablespoon capers
3 tablespoons finely chopped parsley
3 tablespoons finely chopped scallions, including 2 inches of the green tops
Salt to taste

In a mixing bowl combine the cheese and eggs. Mix together the remaining ingredients. Pour over the cheese and eggs and toss gently but thoroughly. Taste and adjust the seasoning. Cover and refrigerate.

Shrimp, Asparagus, and Egg Salad

1 pound diced cooked shrimp
1½ pounds fresh asparagus, cooked, drained, and cut into ½-inch lengths
4 hard-cooked eggs, chopped
1 cup sour cream, or ½ cup each sour cream and unflavored yogurt

2 tablespoons finely chopped scallions, including 2 inches of the green tops
2 tablespoons Dijon-style mustard
Salt to taste

Combine the shrimp, asparagus, and eggs in a bowl. Mix together the remaining ingredients until well blended. Add to the shrimp mixture and toss gently but thoroughly. Taste and adjust the seasoning. Cover and refrigerate.

Curried Shellfish Salad

8 ounces cooked shrimp, shelled, deveined, and cubed
8 ounces cooked lobster meat, cubed
8 ounces cooked crabmeat, cubed
2 hard-cooked eggs, chopped
⅓ cup pitted black olives
⅓ cup finely chopped green pepper

2 scallions, finely chopped, including 2 inches of the green tops
¾ cup Curry Mayonnaise (page 262)
Salt and freshly ground pepper to taste

Combine all the ingredients in a bowl and toss gently but thoroughly. Taste and adjust the seasoning. Cover and refrigerate.

VARIATION:

Curried Lobster Salad

Substitute 1½ pounds cubed lobster meat for the shrimp, lobster, and crabmeat.

Salade Provençale

2 jars (6 ounces each) marinated artichoke hearts
⅓ cup olive oil
3 tablespoons white wine vinegar
1 medium garlic clove, finely chopped
2 teaspoons finely chopped fresh tarragon, or ½ teaspoon crushed dried tarragon
1 can (2 ounces) anchovy fillets with capers, drained and chopped

Salt to taste
8 ounces mushrooms, thinly sliced
1 medium red onion, thinly sliced
1 can (6½ ounces) tuna, drained and broken into chunks
1½ cups cherry tomatoes, quartered

Drain the marinade from the artichoke hearts into a mixing bowl. Add the oil, vinegar, garlic, tarragon, anchovy fillets, and salt, and beat with a fork or whisk until well blended. Stir in the mushrooms and set aside.

Cut each artichoke heart in thin lengthwise slices. Combine the artichoke hearts, onion, tuna, and tomatoes in a salad bowl. With a slotted spoon lift out the mushrooms from the dressing and add them to the salad bowl. Beat the dressing again and spoon evenly over the ingredients in the bowl. Toss gently but thoroughly. Taste and adjust the seasoning, cover, and refrigerate. Drain well before using.

Salmon Salad

1 can (7¾ ounces) salmon, drained, any bones or skin removed, and flaked
2 hard-cooked eggs, finely chopped
⅓ cup finely chopped green pepper or celery
¼ cup finely chopped mild onion or scallions (include 2 inches of the scallion tops)

¼ cup mayonnaise
2 teaspoons freshly squeezed and strained lemon juice
½ teaspoon Dijon-style mustard
1 tablespoon finely chopped fresh dill or to taste
Salt and freshly ground pepper to taste

Combine all the ingredients in a bowl and mix thoroughly. Taste and adjust the seasoning. Cover and refrigerate.

220 / The Complete International Sandwich Book

Other Fillings

Ratatouille

The memory of this Provençal specialty will linger long after your Riviera suntan has faded.

½ pound eggplant, peeled and cut into ½-inch cubes
½ pound zucchini, cut into ½-inch cubes
Salt
9 tablespoons olive oil
3 medium onions, thinly sliced
1 large green pepper, seeded, deribbed, and cut into strips
1 large garlic clove, crushed and finely chopped
2 large, ripe tomatoes, peeled, seeded, and thinly sliced
1½ teaspoons finely chopped fresh basil, or ½ teaspoon crushed dried basil
Freshly ground pepper to taste

Place the eggplant and zucchini on paper towels and sprinkle generously with the salt. Let stand 30 minutes. Rinse and dry with paper towels.

In a large, heavy skillet heat 4 tablespoons of the oil over medium-high heat. Add the eggplant and zucchini and sauté until golden brown, stirring frequently. With a slotted spoon transfer the vegetables to a bowl and set aside.

Add 3 tablespoons of the remaining oil to the skillet and heat over moderate heat. Add the onions, green pepper, and garlic and sauté, stirring frequently, until soft. Stir in the tomatoes, basil, and salt and pepper, cover, and cook 5 minutes. Raise the heat to medium-high and cook the vegetables, uncovered, stirring, about 5 minutes, or until almost all the liquid in the pan has evaporated.

Pour the remaining 2 tablespoons oil into a heavy flameproof casserole. Spread half the tomato mixture in the bottom. Spread the eggplant and zucchini over it and top with the remaining tomato mixture. Cover and cook over very low heat 15 minutes. Baste the vegetables with the juices in the casserole and cook them, uncovered, 15 minutes more, or until most of the liquid has evaporated. Serve hot or cold.

Peperonata

Wonderful on hero sandwiches with sliced cold meats or sausages, *peperonata* also goes well with scrambled egg sandwiches.

2 large green peppers
2 large red bell peppers
3 tablespoons olive oil
1 cup sliced onions
4 medium, ripe tomatoes, peeled, seeded, and cut into ⅛-inch-wide strips

2 teaspoons finely chopped fresh basil, or ¾ teaspoon crushed dried basil
Salt and freshly ground pepper to taste

Roast the peppers as directed in the recipe for Marinated Roasted Peppers (page 228), then cut them into ¼-inch-wide strips. Set aside.

In a large, heavy skillet heat the oil over moderate heat. Add the onions and sauté, stirring frequently, until they are golden brown. Stir in the peppers, tomatoes, basil, and salt and pepper. Cook, uncovered, about 15 minutes, or until almost all the liquid in the pan has evaporated. Remove the pan from the heat and cool the peperonata to room temperature. Transfer to a bowl, cover, and refrigerate several hours until well chilled. Makes about 3 cups.

Frijoles Refritos
Refried Beans

5 tablespoons flavorless vegetable oil
2 tablespoons butter
1 large yellow onion, finely chopped
1 large garlic clove, finely chopped (optional)

4 cups cooked pinto or kidney beans
1 cup cooking liquid from the beans, or as needed
Salt to taste

In a large, heavy skillet heat the oil and butter over moderate heat. Add the onion and garlic, if used, and sauté until golden brown, stirring frequently. Add the beans, 1 cup of the bean liquid, and the salt. Cook, stirring and mashing the beans with a wooden spoon or a fork until the mixture is thickened, adding more liquid, a little at a time, if it seems too dry. Use as directed in individual recipes. Makes 4 to 6 servings.

Swiss Meat Loaf

The good meat loaf entrée of today can make the great meat loaf sandwich of tomorrow.

2 pounds lean beef, ground twice
1 large garlic clove, crushed and finely chopped
¾ cup soft bread crumbs
2 eggs, lightly beaten
⅓ cup tomato juice
2 tablespoons finely chopped parsley
½ teaspoon crushed dried oregano
½ teaspoon crushed dried basil
Salt and freshly ground pepper to taste
8 thin slices prosciutto
1 cup grated Swiss cheese
¼ cup freshly grated Parmesan cheese

Combine the beef, garlic, bread crumbs, eggs, tomato juice, parsley, oregano, basil, and salt and pepper in a large mixing bowl and knead until thoroughly blended. On a flat surface covered with a piece of aluminum foil or waxed paper, pat the meat mixture into a 12-by-10-inch rectangle. Lay the prosciutto slices on the rectangle of meat, leaving a ½-inch margin around the edge. Sprinkle the cheeses over the prosciutto. Starting at one of the short ends, carefully roll up the meat, using the foil or waxed paper to lift. Pinch together the edges and ends to seal. Place the meat roll, seam side down, in a buttered 9-by-5-inch loaf pan. Bake in a preheated 350° F. oven 1 hour and 15 minutes, or until nicely browned. Serve hot or cold.

11

Garnishes and Relishes

Good sandwiches can become even better in partnership with the appropriate garnishes and relishes. When choosing them, however, be sure to keep in mind complementary flavors, colors, and textures.

Learning how to make attractive garnishes for sandwiches is not difficult. This chapter includes suggestions for a number of interesting ones. Although a multitude of commercial relishes are available, those made at home are often superior in taste and certainly more economical. On the following pages you will find a small sampling of my favorites. Some of them can be served within a matter of hours or even sooner. Others mature more slowly and keep for a considerable length of time.

Garnishes

Radish Chrysanthemums

Select large, round radishes. Trim off the top and bottom of each radish to make a ½-inch-thick circle. Place the circle on a cutting board. Using a sharp knife, make a series of closely spaced cuts, slicing almost to the bottom. Cut another series across them. Place in ice water to open. Drain well on paper towels before using. If desired, place a tiny piece of carrot or green pepper in the center of each.

Radish Accordions

With a sharp paring knife cut long, narrow radishes crosswise into thin parallel slices without cutting all the way through. Place in ice water at least 1 hour to allow the radishes to fan out, accordion-style. Drain well on paper towels before using.

Radish Roses

Select large, round radishes. Trim off the root of each radish. Leave on some green leaves at the stem for trim, if desired, or cut off the stem end so the radish sits flat. Starting from the root end, cut 4 or 5 thin petals around the radish, cutting down almost to the base (stem end), leaving a little red between the petals. Place the radishes in ice water until the petals spread open like a flower. Drain well on paper towels before using.

Tomato Roses

Select firm, ripe tomatoes. With the stem end of each tomato pointing down and using a sharp paring knife, peel the skin in one spiral by cutting circular fashion around the tomato, making a continuous strip about ¾ inch wide. Beginning with one end of the strip, roll tightly to form the center. Roll the remaining end of the strip around the center, folding back the edges as you roll to give a petal effect.

Cherry Tomato Rosettes

Select large firm, ripe cherry tomatoes. With the stem end of each tomato pointing down and using a sharp paring knife, cut 5 petals, cutting through the skin but not into the seed pocket. Carefully separate the petals slightly. Season with salt and freshly ground pepper to taste. If desired, sprinkle the center with sieved hard-cooked egg yolks.

Cucumber Twists

Select an unwaxed firm, seedless cucumber. Cut crosswise into very thin slices, using a fluted vegetable knife, if desired. Cut each slice halfway and twist, spreading out the cucumber slice as much as possible.

Cucumber Boats

Select very small cucumbers. Cut each unpeeled cucumber in half lengthwise. Scoop out the seeds with a grapefruit spoon and discard. Fill the cucumber boats with olives, chopped raw or pickled vegetables, or any preferred condiment.

Cucumber Roses

Roll cucumber peelings as for Tomato Roses (page 224).

Pickle Accordions

With a sharp paring knife cut off the ends of pickled gherkins, then cut crosswise into thin parallel slices without cutting all the way through. Bend each gherkin gently so the slices separate at the top.

Pickle Fans

Slice pickled gherkins lengthwise almost to the stem ends, making thin parallel slices. Spread out each gherkin into a fan shape and press the uncut end of the gherkin so that the fan will hold its shape.

Carrot Curls

Using a vegetable peeler, cut thin, wide lengthwise strips from a peeled carrot. Roll up into circles and secure each with a food pick. Place in ice water to crisp. Drain well on paper towels. Remove the food pick before serving.

Carrot Accordions

Using a vegetable peeler, cut thin, wide lengthwise strips from a peeled carrot. Thread each on a food pick accordion fashion. Place in ice water to crisp. Drain well on paper towels. Remove the food pick before serving.

Fluted Carrots

Cut peeled carrots in sticks or slices with a French-fry cutter.

Celery Curls

Wash celery stalks and remove the leaves. Cut the stalks into 1½-inch pieces. Using a paring knife, cut very thin ½-inch-long slices at each end of the celery pieces, leaving ½ inch intact in the center. Place in ice water at least 1 hour to curl. Drain well on paper towels before using.

Celery Fans

Cut pieces of celery into 2-by-½-inch pieces. Cut a point at one end of each piece. Beginning at the other end, make 4 or 5 lengthwise cuts to within about ½ inch of the pointed end. Place in ice water at least 1 hour to spread and curl to form fans.

Scallion Flowers

See page 160.

Stuffed Olives

Stuff chilled, drained, and pitted black olives with toasted slivered blanched almonds or carrot sticks.

Lemon, Lime, or Orange Twists

Cut an unpeeled lemon, lime, or small orange crosswise into very thin slices, using a fluted vegetable knife, if desired. Cut each slice halfway and twist, spreading out the slice as much as possible.

Lemon or Lime Rose

Starting at the stem end of a lemon or lime, and using a sharp paring knife, cut the peel around the fruit in a continuous spiral. With the stem end in the center, curl into a rose shape. Secure with a food pick.

Parsleyed Lemon Slices

Dip lemon slices with pinked edges in finely chopped parsley.

Frosted Grapes

Beat an egg white until it is frothy but not stiff. Dip clusters of grapes into the egg white and place on a rack. Sprinkle with granulated sugar and let stand until dry.

VARIATION:

Substitute cranberries for the grapes.

Cold Scrambled Eggs

Scramble eggs in butter with a minimum of stirring so that they set almost like a custard, then cool. Cut into strips or other shapes, or use to garnish *smørrebrød*.

Mimosa

Mix together sieved hard-cooked egg and finely chopped parsley (use 2 tablespoons parsley for each egg). A popular garnish for canapés and hors d'oeuvre.

Relishes

Marinated Roasted Peppers

These zesty peppers enhance grilled fish or meat sandwiches. Thin marinated pepper strips may be added to pizza toppings before baking. Or you may top cheese sandwiches with the strips before toasting.

6 medium red bell peppers	½ teaspoon crushed dried oregano
1 cup olive oil	½ teaspoon crushed dried basil
½ cup white wine vinegar	½ teaspoon salt
1 large garlic clove, finely chopped	¼ teaspoon freshly ground pepper

Impale the peppers, one at a time, on the tines of a long-handled fork and turn them over a gas flame until the skins are evenly blistered and charred. Or, arrange the peppers on a broiler pan and broil about 2 inches from the heat, turning frequently, until they are evenly browned on all sides.

Cool the peppers slightly, then peel off the charred skins. Cut the peppers in half and remove and discard the stems, seeds, and ribs. Cut the halved peppers into ½- to 1-inch-wide strips or larger pieces as desired.

In a bowl mix together the oil, vinegar, garlic, oregano, basil, salt, and pepper. Add the peppers and toss gently but thoroughly. Cover and chill several hours or as long as 5 days. Makes about 4 cups.

Ajvar

Yugoslav Vegetable Relish

This spirited salad-like relish is a choice partner for grilled fish, chicken, or meat sandwiches.

2 medium eggplants (about 1¼ pounds each)

6 tablespoons olive oil

2 medium green peppers, cut in half and seeded

2 large, firm ripe tomatoes, peeled, seeded, and chopped

3 medium garlic cloves, crushed and finely chopped

1 can (7 ounces) peeled green chilies, seeded and chopped

2 teaspoons salt or to taste

½ teaspoon freshly ground pepper

2 tablespoons red wine vinegar

Cut the stem and hull from the top of each eggplant and discard. Cut each eggplant in half lengthwise. Rub the cut surfaces with about 2 tablespoons of the oil. Arrange the eggplants and peppers, cut sides down, on a rimmed baking pan. Bake in a preheated 400° F. oven about 45 minutes, or until the eggplants are very soft and the skins of the peppers are blistered and charred.

Cool the vegetables slightly, then peel off the skins. Slit the eggplants open. Scoop out the seeds and discard. Coarsely chop the vegetables and place them in a bowl. Add the tomatoes, garlic, chilies, salt, pepper, the remaining 4 tablespoons oil, and vinegar. Toss gently but thoroughly. Cover and chill about 2 hours or as long as overnight. Makes about 8 cups.

Caponata

Another richly flavored relish-salad, this popular Sicilian specialty is memorable on a hero sandwich with sliced cold meats, or spread it over a cheese pizza for an exceptional treat.

2 small eggplants (about 1 pound each)
Salt
½ cup olive oil
2 cups finely chopped celery
¾ cup finely chopped onions
⅓ cup red wine vinegar
4 teaspoons sugar
3 cups peeled, seeded, and chopped tomatoes

2 tablespoons tomato paste
6 large green olives, pitted, rinsed, and cut into slivers
2 tablespoons capers, rinsed and drained
4 flat anchovy fillets, rinsed and mashed (optional)
Freshly ground pepper
2 tablespoons pine nuts

Remove the stems and hulls from the eggplants. Cut the eggplants into ½-inch cubes. Sprinkle the cubes liberally with salt and place them in a colander to drain 30 minutes. Rinse under cold running water and dry with paper towels.

In a large, heavy skillet heat ¼ cup of the oil over moderate heat. Add the celery and cook about 10 minutes, stirring frequently. Add the onions and cook, stirring, about 8 minutes, or until the celery and onions are golden brown. With a slotted spoon transfer them to a bowl. Add the remaining ¼ cup oil to the skillet and heat. Add the eggplant cubes and sauté, stirring constantly, until they are golden brown. Mix the vinegar with the sugar and add to the skillet along with the celery and onion mixture, tomatoes, tomato paste, olives, capers, anchovy fillets (if used), salt, and pepper. Bring to a boil, reduce the heat, and simmer, uncovered, about 15 minutes, stirring frequently. Stir in the nuts. Taste and adjust the seasoning. Remove the skillet from the heat and cool the *caponata* to room temperature. Transfer to a serving bowl, cover, and refrigerate until chilled. Makes about 8 cups.

Italian Vegetable Relish

1 small head cauliflower, separated into flowerets

2 stalks celery, cut diagonally into 1-inch pieces

2 large carrots, peeled and cut lengthwise into 2-inch strips

2 medium green peppers (or 1 green and 1 red bell pepper), seeded, deribbed, and cut into 2-inch strips

¼ pound green beans, trimmed and cut in half crosswise

1 bunch scallions (white portions only), cut into 1-inch pieces

1 can (4 ounces) pitted black olives, drained

1¼ cups water

1¼ cups red or white wine vinegar

1¼ cups olive oil

1 tablespoon sugar

1 large garlic clove, crushed

1½ teaspoons crushed dried oregano

Salt and freshly ground black pepper to taste

Combine all the ingredients in a large, heavy skillet. Bring to a boil over high heat. Reduce the heat to low, cover, and simmer 6 minutes. Remove from the heat and cool to room temperature. Transfer to a large jar or glass bowl. Cover and chill at least 12 hours. Drain well before serving. This relish will keep for a week in the refrigerator. Makes 4 pints.

Tomato Relish

Excellent served with hamburgers or meat patties.

3 medium onions, diced

3 large, tart apples, peeled, cored, and diced

4 medium tomatoes, peeled, seeded, and diced

2 small green peppers, seeded, deribbed, and diced

2 small red bell peppers, seeded, deribbed, and diced

1¼ cups sugar

1 cup cider vinegar

1½ teaspoons salt

In an enameled or stainless steel saucepan combine all the ingredients. Bring to a boil, reduce the heat, and simmer about 1 hour or until thick, stirring from time to time. Remove from the heat. Pack into hot, sterilized jars (below) and seal. This will keep several weeks in the refrigerator. Makes 3 pints.

To sterilize jars: Wash Mason jars and their lids in hot, soapy water and rinse well in scalding water. Place the jars in a large kettle with a rack on the bottom. Cover them completely with hot (not boiling) water and boil 20 minutes, then reduce the heat. Leave the jars in the hot water until ready to use, then remove them with tongs and drain. Do not boil the self-sealing lids. Place them in a bowl, pour boiling water over them, and leave until ready to use. Wipe the jar rims with a clean, damp cloth. Fill and seal the jars while they are still hot so that they will not break when the hot ingredients are poured into them. Allow the jars to cool thoroughly before storing.

Pickled Mixed Vegetables

Vividly colorful and piquant, these Middle Eastern pickles can enliven many fish, poultry, and meat sandwiches as well as meat pastries.

4 carrots, quartered lengthwise and cut into approximately 3-inch lengths
4 small pickling cucumbers
¼ pound green beans, trimmed
1 small head cauliflower, separated into flowerets
2 green, yellow, or red bell peppers, quartered, seeded, and deribbed
4 1-inch pieces hot red pepper
4 medium garlic cloves, peeled
4 heads fresh dill
4 cups water
1 cup cider vinegar
¼ cup salt (not iodized)

Wash the vegetables and pack into 4 hot, sterilized pint jars (above), adding 1 piece hot pepper, 1 garlic clove, and 1 head dill to each jar. In an enameled or stainless steel saucepan bring the water, vinegar, and salt to a boil. Remove from the heat and pour over the vegetables in the jars, covering them completely. Seal and store in a cool place 1 month. Makes 4 pints.

Pickled Cherries

Serve these exquisite pickles with liver pâté, veal, pork, or poultry sandwiches.

1¼ cups light brown sugar, firmly
  packed
1 cup cider or white wine vinegar
2 sticks cinnamon, 3 inches long,
  broken

1 teaspoon whole cloves
1 quart pitted sour cherries

In an enameled or stainless steel saucepan combine the sugar, vinegar, cinnamon, and cloves. Bring to a boil over high heat. Reduce the heat to low and simmer 3 minutes. Strain to remove the cinnamon and cloves. Return the strained liquid to the saucepan. Add the cherries and cook gently about 5 minutes, or until heated through. Remove from the heat. Ladle the cherries into hot, sterilized jars (page 232). Cover with the hot liquid and seal. Makes about 1½ pints.

Pickled Peaches

2 cups sugar
¼ cup cider vinegar
2 sticks cinnamon, 2 inches long
1½ teaspoons whole allspice

1½ teaspoons whole cloves
1 quart peaches, peeled, pitted,
  and halved

In a large enameled or stainless steel saucepan combine the sugar, vinegar, cinnamon sticks, allspice, and cloves. Bring to a boil, stirring constantly to dissolve the sugar. Reduce the heat and simmer a few minutes. Add the peaches and simmer, uncovered, 10 minutes, stirring occasionally.

With a slotted spoon ladle the peaches into hot, sterilized jars (page 232). Put a cinnamon stick into each jar. Pour the sugar syrup into the jars over the fruit, filling them to within ½ inch of the tops. Seal at once. Makes 2 pints.

Pickled Pineapple

Splendid as a relish for poultry, ham, or pork sandwiches.

1 large pineapple, peeled and cored	1¼ cups white wine vinegar
1 cup water	1 stick cinnamon, 2 inches long
2 cups sugar	1 tablespoon whole cloves

Cut the pineapple into 1-inch cubes. In an enameled or stainless steel saucepan combine the water, sugar, and vinegar. Tie the cinnamon and cloves in a piece of cheesecloth and add. Bring to a boil, reduce the heat, and boil gently 15 minutes. Add the pineapple, cover, and simmer about 20 minutes or until the fruit is tender and translucent. Remove the fruit and place in hot, sterilized jars (page 232). Discard the spices. Pour the syrup over the fruit and seal the jars. Makes about 2 pints.

Apple Chutney

Delightful with poultry, ham, or pork sandwiches.

1 cup cider vinegar	½ teaspoon dry mustard
1½ cups plus 2 tablespoons firmly packed brown sugar	½ teaspoon allspice
½ cup chopped onion	¼ teaspoon cinnamon
1 small garlic clove, crushed and finely chopped	⅛ teaspoon cloves
2 small dried hot chili peppers, crushed	½ teaspoon salt
¼ lime, finely chopped	1 cup seedless raisins or currants
1½ teaspoons peeled and very finely chopped ginger root	5 cups pared, cored, and chopped tart green apples

In a heavy enameled kettle combine the vinegar, sugar, onion, garlic, chili peppers, lime, ginger root, dry mustard, allspice, cinnamon, cloves, salt, and raisins or currants. Bring to a boil over medium-high heat, stirring constantly. Add the apples and return to a boil. Reduce the heat and simmer, uncovered, about 40 minutes or until thickened, stirring frequently to prevent sticking.

Remove the chutney from the heat, ladle it into hot, sterilized jars (page 232) to within ¼ inch of the tops, and seal. Makes about 2¼ pints.

Cranberry Chutney

A natural with poultry or ham sandwiches.

1 cup cider vinegar
3¼ cups sugar
⅔ cup chopped onions
1 tablespoon peeled and very
 finely chopped ginger root
1 teaspoon allspice

¼ teaspoon cinnamon
1 cup seedless raisins or currants
2 pounds cranberries, picked over
 and washed
¾ cup chopped walnuts or
 blanched almonds (optional)

In a heavy enameled kettle combine the vinegar, sugar, onions, ginger root, allspice, cinnamon, and raisins or currants. Bring to a boil over medium-high heat, stirring constantly. Add the cranberries and return to a boil. Reduce the heat and simmer, uncovered, about 15 minutes or until thickened, stirring frequently to prevent sticking. Stir in the nuts, if you like.

Remove the chutney from the heat, ladle it into hot, sterilized jars (page 232) to within ¼ inch of the tops, and seal. Makes about 3 pints.

Tomato Ketchup

4 pounds ripe tomatoes, peeled,
seeded, and chopped
1 large green or red bell pepper,
seeded, deribbed, and chopped
2 medium onions, chopped
1½ cups cider vinegar or distilled
white vinegar
1½ cups sugar
1½ tablespoons salt

1½ teaspoons dry mustard
⅟₁₆ teaspoon cayenne pepper or
to taste
1 cinnamon stick, 2 inches long,
broken into pieces
¾ teaspoon whole allspice
¾ teaspoon whole cloves
¼ teaspoon celery seeds

Purée the tomatoes, pepper, and onions in batches in an electric blender. Transfer to a heavy enameled kettle and stir in the vinegar, sugar, salt, dry mustard, and cayenne pepper. Tie the cinnamon stick, allspice, cloves, and celery seeds in a piece of cheesecloth and add to the kettle. Bring the mixture to a simmer over medium-high heat, stirring frequently. Reduce the heat and simmer, uncovered, stirring often, about 1½ hours or until the ketchup is very thick. Discard the spice bag. Taste and adjust the seasoning.

Remove the ketchup from the heat, ladle it into hot, sterilized jars (page 232) to within ¼ inch of the tops, and seal. Makes about 4 cups.

12

Breads

Since good bread may be difficult to find in some areas or only a limited selection may be available, or simply because many readers enjoy making their own bread, I have in this chapter provided a modest sampling of basic breads, more unusual ethnic breads, and tea breads.

Choosing a bread for a particular filling is a matter more of personal taste than of hard and fast rules. For instance, some breads that are traditionally partnered with certain types of foods in their country of origin can be surprisingly compatible with fillings created in kitchens halfway around the world.

The recipes that follow are for light and delicate breads, earthy peasant breads, crisp breads, flat breads, puffy fried breads, chewy rolls, and moist, fruity breads. Experiment with them for their flavors and textures, and pair them with the fillings of your choice.

White Bread

Firm-textured and pleasantly flavored, this basic white bread is ideal for sandwiches and toasting. It is remarkably versatile, as the following variations attest. For a heavier, crisper crust use water instead of milk.

¼ cup warm water (110° F.)
1 package active dry yeast
2 cups warm milk or water
(110° F.)
2 tablespoons melted butter or
flavorless vegetable oil

1 tablespoon salt
2 tablespoons sugar
6 cups sifted all-purpose flour
(approximately)

Pour the water into a large mixing bowl and sprinkle with the yeast. Let the mixture rest 5 minutes, then stir to dissolve the yeast. Stir in the milk or water, then add the melted butter or oil, salt, and sugar, and continue stirring until well blended. Stir in 3 cups of the flour, 1 cup at a time, and beat with a large spoon until smooth. Add the remaining 3 cups flour, a little at a time, mixing first with the spoon and then with your hands until thoroughly blended.

Turn out the dough onto a lightly floured board and knead thoroughly, sprinkling occasionally with just enough flour to keep it from sticking. When it is smooth and elastic in texture, form it into a lump and place in a lightly greased bowl. Turn the dough over to grease the top. Cover loosely with a kitchen towel and let rise in a warm place free from drafts about 1½ hours, or until the dough has doubled in size.

Punch down the dough and knead 1 to 2 minutes to eliminate any air bubbles. Divide the dough into 2 equal parts. Shape each part into an oval loaf about 8 inches long, folding and pinching the seam securely closed.

Place each loaf, seam side down, in a greased 8½-by-4½-inch loaf pan. Cover and let rise in a warm place about 45 minutes or until almost doubled in size. Bake in a preheated 375° F. oven about 45 minutes or until nicely browned and just beginning to pull away from the pan sides. Remove the loaves from the oven, turn them out of the pans, and cool on wire racks. Makes 2.

VARIATIONS:

Swiss Egg Braid

In a small bowl break 2 eggs. Beat in enough of the warm milk to make 2 cups, and use this mixture in place of all milk. Divide the dough for each loaf into 3 parts. Roll each part into a strand. Braid each trio of strands together, pinching the ends to seal. Let rise on a lightly greased baking sheet. Brush with 1 lightly beaten egg and bake in a 375° F. oven 30 to 35 minutes, or until nicely browned.

French Bread

Use water in place of milk and reduce the amount of sugar to 2 teaspoons. Omit the butter or oil. Shape the dough into 2 oblong loaves and let rise on a lightly greased baking sheet. Brush with water, and with a sharp knife make diagonal slashes on top of each loaf about ½ inch deep and 2 inches apart. Put the loaves in a preheated 400° F. oven with a shallow pan of hot water placed on the bottom rack. Bake about 45 minutes or until nicely browned and crusty.

Herb Bread

To make 2 kinds of herb bread, after all the flour has been added divide the dough into 2 equal parts. Knead each part separately, kneading a different herb into each. Choose from these crushed dried herbs, using the following amounts for each half of the dough: 1 tablespoon dill weed; 1 tablespoon savory; 1½ teaspoons basil; 1½ teaspoons oregano; 1½ teaspoons thyme; or 2 teaspoons marjoram.

100% Whole Wheat Bread

Substitute stone ground whole wheat flour for the all-purpose flour. Omit the sugar. Use ½ cup honey or molasses with 1½ cups milk instead of all milk.

Light Rye Bread

Use 2 cups rye flour and 4 cups all-purpose flour.

Dark Rye Bread

Use 3 cups rye flour and 3 cups all-purpose flour. Omit the sugar. Use ½ cup light or dark molasses with 1½ cups milk instead of all milk.

Swedish Orange Rye Bread

Use 2 cups rye flour and 4 cups all-purpose flour. Add 2 tablespoons grated orange rind and 1 tablespoon caraway, anise, or fennel seed with the melted butter or oil, salt, and sugar.

Brioches

Brioche dough, rich, buttery, and light-textured, is formed into a number of traditional shapes, among them a ringed and slashed crown (*brioche couronne*), a top-knotted muffin that can range in size from tiny to large (*brioche à tête*), and a tall cylinder (*brioche mousseline*). It can also be shaped into a loaf that is marvelous for sandwiches and canapés using such delicacies as smoked salmon and various pâtés. In addition, brioche dough is ideal for encasing foods that are baked in a crust (*en croûte*), for example beef Wellington and coulibiac.

Here are three popular shapes for brioche.

Small Brioches à Tête

Pâte a Brioche (page 241)	1 egg yolk
Butter	1 tablespoon milk

Prepare the Pâte à Brioche. Butter well 12 3½-inch petite brioche molds or 3-inch muffin cups and set aside.

Punch down the chilled dough and knead it briefly on a lightly floured board to release air. Divide into 12 equal pieces. (Dough is easier to handle when chilled; therefore it is best to shape a few brioches at a time, keeping the remaining dough covered and refrigerated.) Working quickly, shape each brioche as follows: Pinch off about ⅙ of each piece of dough and set aside. With lightly floured hands, form the large piece of dough into a smooth ball and place it in a well-buttered petite brioche mold or muffin cup. Shape the small piece of dough into a teardrop. With your finger make an indentation in the center of the large ball and firmly insert the teardrop's pointed end into it. Cover the filled molds or cups with a kitchen towel and set them in a warm place free from drafts about 1½ hours, or until the dough has almost doubled in size.

Beat the egg yolk with the milk. With a soft brush paint the tops of the brioches with the mixture. Bake in a preheated 425° F. oven about 20 minutes, or until a rich golden brown. Remove the brioches from the molds or cups and serve warm, or let cool on wire racks. Makes 12.

Tiny Brioches à Tête

Prepare as above, substituting the smallest brioche molds you can find or 1¼-inch muffin cups for the larger brioche molds or muffin cups, and dividing the dough equally into as many pieces as there are molds or cups. Decrease the baking time to about 10 minutes. Makes 30 or more, depending on the size of molds or cups used.

Brioche Sandwich Loaf

Form the brioche dough into a loaf and place it in a well-buttered 5-by-9-inch loaf pan. Bake in a preheated 375° F. oven about 50 minutes. Makes 1.

Pâte à Brioche
Brioche Dough

½ cup warm water or milk
  (110° F.)
1 package active dry yeast
2 teaspoons sugar
1 teaspoon salt

2½ cups unsifted all-purpose flour
3 eggs
½ cup butter, at room
  temperature, cut into small
  pieces

Pour the warm water or milk into a large mixing bowl and sprinkle it with the yeast. Let the mixture stand 5 minutes, then stir to dissolve the yeast. Add the sugar, salt, and ½ cup of the flour and beat thoroughly. Add the eggs, one at a time, beating thoroughly after each addition until smooth. Add the butter and remaining 2 cups flour, a little at a time, beating vigorously until the mixture is thoroughly blended and forms an elastic dough. Place the dough in a lightly greased bowl and turn over to grease the top. Cover loosely with a kitchen towel and let rise in a warm place free from drafts about 1½ hours, or until doubled in bulk.

Punch down the dough, transfer to a lightly floured board, and knead briefly to release air. Return to the lightly greased bowl and turn to grease the top. Cover with clear plastic wrap and refrigerate 6 hours or overnight.

Pumpernickel Bread

Excellent for sandwiches when thinly sliced, this firm-textured, chewy bread has a rich flavor and an authoritative personality.

Be sure that your kitchen is well ventilated while you make the caramel coloring. The sugar will smoke as it turns black, and there may be spattering when the boiling water is added.

½ cup plus 1 teaspoon sugar
½ cup boiling water
1½ cups warm water (110° F.)
3 packages active dry yeast
½ cup unsulfured dark molasses
3 tablespoons caraway seeds
3 tablespoons butter, at room
temperature

1 tablespoon salt
2¾ cups sifted pumpernickel rye
meal or rye flour
3½ cups unsifted all-purpose flour
2 tablespoons cornmeal

To make the caramel coloring, in a heavy, 10-inch skillet cook ½ cup of the sugar over medium-high heat, stirring constantly with a fork until it is melted. Cook about 2½ minutes, or until the sugar turns black. Slowly add the boiling water and cook, stirring constantly, until the sugar is dissolved and the liquid is reduced to ¼ cup. Remove the caramel liquid from the heat and allow to cool. Pour ¾ cup of the warm water into a small bowl and sprinkle with the yeast and the remaining 1 teaspoon sugar. Let the mixture stand 5 minutes, then stir to dissolve the yeast.

In a large bowl combine the remaining ¾ cup warm water, the yeast mixture, molasses, caraway seeds, the caramel coloring, butter, and salt. Stir in the pumpernickel rye meal or rye flour and beat thoroughly. Stir in the all-purpose flour, ½ cup at a time, until a stiff dough is formed.

Turn out the dough onto a lightly floured board. Invert the mixing bowl over the dough and let rest 15 minutes. Knead the dough thoroughly, sprinkling occasionally with a little flour until it is smooth but slightly sticky. Form the dough into a lump and place it in a lightly greased bowl. Turn it over to grease the top. Cover loosely with a kitchen towel and let rise in a warm place free from drafts 1 hour and 15 minutes or until almost doubled in size.

Punch down the dough and knead it briefly on a lightly floured board. Divide the dough in half and form each half into an oval loaf. Place the loaves about 8 inches apart on a greased baking sheet sprinkled with the cornmeal. Cover and let rise in a warm place about 50 minutes or until almost doubled in size. Pierce each loaf in 4 places with a floured skewer to prevent cracking. Bake in a preheated 375° F. oven, brushing 3 times with hot water to obtain a chewy crust, about 45 minutes or until the loaves are browned and sound hollow when tapped on the bottom. Transfer the loaves to wire racks to cool. Makes 2.

Italian Cheese Bread

With this golden bread, some assorted Italian cold cuts and relishes, fresh fruits in season, and a bottle of wine (and a little help from the weatherman) you're set for a memorable picnic.

¾ cup warm water (110° F.)
1 package active dry yeast
2 tablespoons sugar
¾ teaspoon salt
4½ cups unsifted all-purpose flour (approximately)
5 eggs

¼ pound butter, at room temperature, cut into small pieces
1 cup freshly grated Parmesan cheese
1 cup shredded Swiss or Gruyère cheese

Pour the water into a large mixing bowl and sprinkle with the yeast. Let the mixture stand 5 minutes, then stir to dissolve the yeast. Add the sugar, salt, and 1 cup of the flour and beat thoroughly. Add 4 of the eggs, one at a time, and beat until smooth. Beat in the butter, then gradually beat in the remaining 3½ cups flour to make a soft dough.

Turn out the dough onto a lightly floured board and knead thoroughly, sprinkling occasionally with just enough flour to keep it from sticking. When it is smooth and elastic in texture, form it into a lump and place in a lightly greased bowl. Turn the dough over to grease the top. Cover loosely with a kitchen towel and let rise in a warm place free from drafts about 1½ hours or until doubled in size.

Punch down the dough, turn out onto a lightly floured board, and knead briefly. Divide the dough in half. Form each half into a ball. Roll out 1 of the balls into a 10-by-14-inch rectangle. In a mixing bowl beat the remaining egg and mix in the cheeses. Spread half of the cheese mixture over the dough, covering it to within 1 inch of the edges. Beginning from a long side, roll up and pinch the seam firmly to seal. Shape the roll into a ring, pinching the ends together firmly to seal. Place in a greased 2-quart round baking dish. Repeat this procedure with the second ball of dough and the remaining cheese mixture. Let the loaves rise in a warm place until doubled. Bake in a preheated 350° F. oven about 45 minutes, or until the loaves are golden and sound hollow when tapped on the bottom. Transfer the breads to wire racks and let cool slightly. Serve warm, or let the breads cool to room temperature before serving. Makes 2.

Norwegian Lefse

When freshly baked, this thin, flat unleavened bread is soft enough to be rolled or wrapped around cheese, preserves, or other foods. Toasted, *lefse* makes a crisp bread that is delicious served with butter.

3½ cups unsifted all-purpose flour
3 teaspoons baking powder
½ teaspoon salt
¼ cup sugar

1½ teaspoons baking soda
1½ cups buttermilk or unflavored
    yogurt
Flavorless vegetable oil

Sift 2½ cups of the flour with the baking powder, salt, and sugar into the large bowl of an electric mixer. Mix together the baking soda and buttermilk or yogurt until foamy and add to the flour mixture. Beat at medium speed about 5 minutes or until the batter is smooth. Measure the remaining 1 cup flour and mix into the batter, using a dough hook or wooden spoon, until thoroughly blended. Cover the bowl tightly and refrigerate 1 to 2 hours.

Spread a pastry cloth on a board and sprinkle it with flour. Remove half of the dough at a time from the refrigerator. Form it into a cylinder, then divide it into 18 equal pieces. With floured hands shape each piece into a ball, flattening it out to an even circle on the cloth. Flour the dough well on both sides, then roll it out to about 6 inches in diameter.

To cook the lefse, preheat an electric griddle or skillet to 375° F., or use a griddle or large skillet over moderate heat. Lightly grease the griddle or skillet with oil. Shake the excess flour off each circle of dough and place it on the hot griddle or skillet. It should begin to bubble at once. Bake about 1½ minutes, or until the bubbles are golden brown. Turn and brown the other side. Repeat the rolling and baking procedure with the remaining balls of dough, lightly greasing the griddle or skillet each time.

If you wish to serve the lefse immediately, stack them as they are baked, wrap in aluminum foil, and keep warm in a preheated 200° F. oven. To serve later, cool each lefse as it is baked and stack. Wrap securely and store at room temperature up to 1 week.

For crisp lefse, spread the breads out on a large baking sheet and bake in a preheated 425° F. oven about 5 minutes. Or toast the lefse 4 inches from the heat about ½ minute on each side. Serve the crisp lefse in a basket.

For soft lefse, sprinkle each bread with a little water, then stack about 18 lefse, wrap them in aluminum foil, and heat in a preheated 300° F. oven 10 to 15 minutes. Wrap the stack of lefse in a napkin to keep them warm and soft for serving. Makes 36.

Lavash

This thin, crisp, cracker-like Armenian bread is made in various sizes, from small cocktail rounds for canapés to circles 16 or more inches in diameter, the version in which it is becoming widely available commercially. Homemade *lavash* is, however, thinner and more flavorful. When softened, the bread can be wrapped around cheese, meat, or other foods to make a leakproof sandwich.

1 package active dry yeast	¼ cup butter or margarine,
1 cup warm water (110° F.)	melted and cooled
2 teaspoons sugar	3 cups unsifted all-purpose flour
1½ teaspoons salt	(approximately)

In the large bowl of an electric mixer soften the yeast in the water about 5 minutes. Stir in the sugar, salt, and butter or margarine. Add 2 cups of the flour and stir until moistened, then beat at medium speed about 4 minutes, pushing the dough down as necessary. (If you do not have a mixer, beat vigorously with a wooden spoon until the dough begins to pull away from the bowl.) Stir in the remaining 1 cup flour to make the dough stiff enough to knead.

Transfer the dough onto a lightly floured board and knead thoroughly until smooth and elastic, sprinkling occasionally with just enough flour to keep it from sticking. Form the dough into a ball and place it in a lightly greased bowl. Turn it over to grease the top. Cover with a kitchen towel and let rise in a warm place free from drafts 1 to 1½ hours, or until doubled in bulk.

Punch down the dough. Knead lightly to release any air bubbles, then divide into 6 equal parts. Form each into a ball and place 2 inches apart on a lightly floured surface. Cover with a kitchen towel and let rest at room temperature 45 minutes.

On a lightly floured board roll out 1 ball of dough at a time into a very thin sheet 12 to 14 inches in diameter, sprinkling lightly with flour only if needed to keep it from sticking. Carefully roll it onto a rolling pin and unroll onto an ungreased baking sheet. Prick the surface of the dough in 4 or 5 places with a fork.

Bake the bread on the lowest shelf of a preheated 400° F. oven 4 minutes. Raise it to the top shelf and bake about 4 minutes longer or until golden brown and puffed, watching closely to prevent burning.

Repeat this procedure with the remaining balls of dough. Cool the breads on a rack, then stack. Store in a dry place, wrapped securely in aluminum foil.

Serve the lavash crisp, or about 30 minutes before serving sprinkle it lightly with water, then shake off the excess. Wrap in a kitchen towel and set aside to absorb the water and soften. Makes 6.

VARIATIONS:

Substitute 1½ cups each unsifted all-purpose flour and whole wheat flour for the all-purpose flour.

Cocktail-Size Lavash

Using a cookie cutter, cut out circles 2 to 3 inches in diameter from each sheet of dough. Prick the surface of each circle once or twice with a fork and bake as above.

Pita Bread

Pita is variously known as pocket bread or Arab, Armenian, Syrian, or Middle Eastern bread. In my mind it still remains synonymous with the word bread, being the loaf I consumed more regularly than any other while growing up in Beirut, Lebanon. Rarely found outside of communities with large Middle Eastern populations a decade ago, this flat, age-old bread with a chewy texture is now available in many supermarkets across America, with demand for it increasing regularly.

Pita can be made with different types of wheat flour. Coarse flour produces earthy, dark bread, while a refined white one yields a lighter, more delicate loaf. During baking pita puffs up like a balloon, forming a pocket, but flattens as it cools. It is best eaten freshly baked and warm. Once cooled, however, reheating will help to revive its flavor. The outer crust of pita is soft and smooth, not crisp, while the inside is coarse-textured, making it highly absorbent and thus an ideal bread for holding moist fillings.

Besides being more economical, good homemade pita is superior in flavor and texture to the store-bought version. For sandwiches made with pita, please consult Chapter 4.

1½ cups warm water (110° F.)   1½ teaspoons salt
½ package active dry yeast   1½ teaspoons flavorless vegetable
1 teaspoon sugar   oil
4½ cups unsifted all-purpose flour

Pour the water into a small bowl. Sprinkle it with the yeast and sugar. Let the mixture stand 5 minutes, then stir to dissolve the yeast.

Place the flour in a large bowl. Make a well in the center and add the salt, oil, and the yeast mixture. Mix until the ingredients are well blended and form a moderately firm dough.

Transfer the dough onto a lightly floured board and knead thoroughly, sprinkling occasionally with just enough flour to keep it from sticking. When it is smooth and elastic in texture, form it into the shape of a log, then cut into 10 equal pieces. Knead each piece, shaping it into a smooth, round ball. Place the balls 2 inches apart on cloth-lined trays. Cover loosely with a kitchen towel and let rise in a warm place free from drafts 1 to 1½ hours, or until puffed.

With a rolling pin flatten each of the balls on a lightly floured board until it is ¼ inch thick and about 6 inches in diameter. Arrange the rounds 1 inch apart on a floured wooden surface or on floured towels. Cover with a floured cloth and let rest 1 hour or until slightly puffed.

Place a large baking sheet on the lowest shelf of your oven and preheat the oven to 500° F. When the oven is ready, remove the baking sheet. Gently lift and place 3 or 4 rounds of dough, upside down and about 1 inch apart, on the hot baking sheet, being careful not to dent or stretch them. It is important that they remain smooth; otherwise they may not puff up properly. Bake on the lowest shelf of the oven 5 to 6 minutes or until the breads puff up and the bottoms are lightly browned. Immediately switch the oven to broil and transfer the pan of breads to the top shelf, 4 inches from the broiler unit. Bake about 1 minute or until the tops are very lightly browned, watching closely.

Remove the breads from the baking sheet and cool on wire racks. Repeat the above procedure with the remaining rounds of dough. To store the pitas, gently flatten each one, stack together, and place in airtight plastic bags. Refrigerate or freeze. Makes 10.

Armenian Peda Bread

A crusty white yeast bread, *peda* is made in several sizes and shapes. In the following form it makes a delectable covering for skewered meats and meatballs.

½ cup warm water (110° F.)
2 packages active dry yeast
2 teaspoons plus 1½ tablespoons sugar
5¾ cups unsifted all-purpose flour (approximately)

1 tablespoon salt
1¾ cups warm milk (110° F.)
4 tablespoons olive oil
1 egg yolk
1 tablespoon water
¼ cup sesame seeds

Pour the warm water into a small bowl and sprinkle with the yeast and 2 teaspoons sugar. Let stand about 5 minutes, then stir to dissolve the yeast.

Combine the flour, remaining 1½ tablespoons sugar, and salt in a large mixing bowl. Make a well in the center and pour in the yeast mixture, warm milk, and 3 tablespoons of the oil. With a large wooden spoon stir the center ingredients together, then gradually mix into the flour. Beat until the ingredients are thoroughly blended and form a dough. Transfer the dough onto a lightly floured board and knead thoroughly, sprinkling occasionally with just enough flour to keep it from sticking. When it is smooth and elastic in texture, form it into a lump and place in a lightly greased bowl. Turn the dough over to grease the top. Cover loosely with a kitchen towel and let rise in a warm place free from drafts about 1 hour or until doubled in size.

Punch down the dough and knead a minute or so, then divide into 2 equal parts. Shape each part into a ball, and with a rolling pin flatten it into a round loaf about 8 inches in diameter. Place each loaf on a greased baking sheet. With a 3-inch cookie cutter cut a circle out of the center of each loaf, then put the circle back into the hole. Brush the loaves with the remaining 1 tablespoon oil, cover lightly with a kitchen towel, and let rise again in a warm place about 1 hour or until doubled in size.

Beat the egg yolk with the water and brush the loaves with the mixture. Sprinkle evenly with the sesame seeds. Bake in a preheated 350° F. oven about 35 minutes, or until golden brown. Transfer the loaves to wire racks and let cool slightly. Serve, preferably warm. Makes 2.

Poori

This small, unleavened Indian bread made of whole wheat flour puffs up when deep-fried. It tastes best when eaten warm.

½ cup unsifted whole wheat flour
½ cup unsifted all-purpose flour
⅛ to ¼ teaspoon salt (optional)
1½ tablespoons flavorless
  vegetable oil or melted butter

¼ cup water or more
Flavorless vegetable oil for
  deep-frying

Sift the 2 flours and salt, if used, into a bowl. Add the 1½ tablespoons oil or melted butter, then gradually stir in enough water to form a dough. Turn out onto a lightly floured board and knead 5 to 7 minutes, or until smooth. Form into a ball, cover with a damp kitchen towel, and let rest about 1 hour.

Knead the dough again and divide it into 14 equal pieces. Form each piece into a ball. Cover the balls with a damp kitchen towel. On a lightly floured board roll each ball into a circle about 4 inches in diameter, sprinkling with a little whole wheat flour if necessary to keep it from sticking. Cover with a damp kitchen towel.

In a deep-fryer or heavy saucepan heat 2 to 3 inches of vegetable oil to a temperature of 375° F. Fry the *pooris,* one at a time, in the hot oil about ½ minute or until they puff up, working quickly and using a large slotted spoon to ladle the oil over each poori constantly as it cooks. Turn over and fry about ½ minute more, or until golden and puffy. Remove with the slotted spoon and drain on paper towels. Serve at once. Makes 14.

Note: If not serving immediately, place the fried pooris on a baking sheet and keep them warm in a preheated 300° F. oven, or cool them on a wire rack. Reheat by placing the pooris on a baking sheet and heating them in a preheated 350° F. oven about 5 minutes.

Navajo Fry Bread

2 cups unsifted all-purpose flour
½ cup nonfat dry milk powder
1 tablespoon baking powder
¾ teaspoon salt

2 tablespoons shortening
¾ cup warm water (110° F.)
Shortening for shallow-frying

Combine the flour, nonfat dry milk powder, baking powder, and salt and sift them into a mixing bowl. Cut in the 2 tablespoons shortening with a pastry blender, 2 knives, or your fingers, working quickly until the mixture resembles coarse crumbs. Add the water and stir until the mixture clings together and forms a dough. Turn out onto a lightly floured board and knead thoroughly until smooth. Divide the dough into 8 balls. Cover and let rest 10 minutes.

On a lightly floured board roll out each ball into a circle about 7 inches in diameter. Place the circles on a floured surface and cover with a kitchen towel. In a large, heavy skillet heat 1½ to 2 inches shortening to 375° F. Drop 1 circle of dough at a time into the hot oil and fry. As soon as the circle rises to the surface, turn it over and fry about 1 minute. Turn over again and fry about 50 seconds longer or until lightly browned, crisp, and puffy. Drain on paper towels. Serve warm. Makes 8.

Nepalese Bread

Although this deep-fried bread is traditionally served at dinner with butter and, sometimes, chutney, it can be split open and stuffed with curries and assorted condiments.

2 cups unsifted whole wheat flour
2 tablespoons sugar
½ teaspoon baking powder
½ teaspoon salt
¼ teaspoon cinnamon
¼ teaspoon nutmeg

¼ teaspoon cloves
1 egg
½ cup milk
Peanut oil or flavorless vegetable
    oil

Combine the flour, sugar, baking powder, salt, cinnamon, nutmeg, and cloves in a mixing bowl and stir together. Lightly beat the egg, then stir in the milk. Add the mixture to the dry ingredients and blend thoroughly until a soft but not sticky dough is formed.

Divide the dough into 4 equal portions. Form each portion into a ball, cover loosely with clear plastic wrap, and let rest about 30 minutes. On a lightly floured board roll out each ball into an 8-inch circle. Cut each circle into quarters.

In a deep, heavy skillet heat 1½ to 2 inches oil to 400° F. Lower a single wedge of dough at a time into the hot oil, using 2 slotted spoons. Cook, turning frequently, about 2 minutes or until puffed, crisp, and nicely browned. Lift out and drain thoroughly on paper towels. Makes 16.

Sopaipillas

A favorite of New Mexican cooks, *sopaipillas* are golden deep-fried breads that make wonderful pockets for both savory and dessert fillings.

¼ cup warm water (110° F.)	2 tablespoons sugar
1 package active dry yeast	1 cup unsifted whole wheat flour
1½ cups milk	4 cups unsifted all-purpose flour
3 tablespoons lard or shortening	Corn oil or flavorless vegetable oil
1½ teaspoons salt	for deep-frying

Pour the warm water into a large mixing bowl and sprinkle it with the yeast. Let the mixture stand 5 minutes, then stir to dissolve the yeast. Combine the milk, lard or shortening, salt, and sugar in a saucepan. Heat to 110° F. and add to the dissolved yeast. Beat in the whole wheat flour. Gradually beat in 3 cups of the all-purpose flour. With a heavy-duty mixer or a wooden spoon, gradually beat in the remaining 1 cup all-purpose flour or enough to make a stiff dough. Turn out the dough onto a lightly floured board and knead thoroughly, sprinkling occasionally with just enough flour to keep it from sticking. When it is smooth and non-sticky in texture, form it into a lump and place in a lightly greased bowl. Turn the dough over to grease the top. Cover loosely with a kitchen towel and let stand at room temperature 1 hour.

Punch down the dough and knead briefly on a lightly floured board to expel air. Roll out the dough, a portion at a time, to ⅛- to ¹⁄₁₆-inch thickness. Cut into 3½-by-5-inch rectangles. Arrange on lightly floured pans, cover loosely with kitchen towels, and refrigerate the sopaipillas until all are ready to fry.

Fry the sopaipillas, 2 or 3 at a time, in hot deep oil (350° F.). To help them puff more evenly, with a perforated spoon gently push that part of the bread where the air bubble is forming into the hot oil several times. Turn the sopaipillas a few times and fry about 1 minute or until golden. Drain on paper towels. Makes 24.

Crusty Hamburger Buns

Hamburgers couldn't find a better home.

2 cups warm water (110° F.)	5¼ cups unsifted all-purpose flour
2 packages active dry yeast	plus 2 teaspoons for glaze
2 tablespoons sugar	½ cup cold water
1 tablespoon salt	Toasted sesame seeds (optional)
3 tablespoons melted butter or	
flavorless vegetable oil	

Pour the warm water into a large mixing bowl and sprinkle with the yeast. Let the mixture stand 5 minutes, then stir in the sugar, salt, and melted butter or oil. Add 4 cups of the flour, 1 cup at a time, beating thoroughly with a large spoon or an electric mixer at medium speed until well blended and smooth. Gradually add 1¼ cups more flour, mixing it in with a spoon or a heavy-duty mixer.

Turn out the dough onto a lightly floured board and knead thoroughly, sprinkling occasionally with just enough flour to keep it from sticking. When it is smooth and elastic in texture, form it into a lump and place in a lightly greased bowl. Turn the dough over to grease the top. Cover loosely with a kitchen towel and let rise in a warm place free from drafts about 1 hour or until doubled in size.

Punch down the dough and divide it into 12 equal pieces. Form each piece into a smooth ball and place about 4 inches apart on greased and floured baking sheets. Cover lightly with kitchen towels and let rest 30 minutes at room temperature, then flatten each ball to a circle about 4½ inches in diameter. Cover and let rise in a warm place 45 to 55 minutes, or until doubled in size.

Meanwhile, in a small saucepan blend the remaining 2 teaspoons flour with the cold water until smooth. Bring to a boil over moderate heat, stirring constantly, until the mixture thickens. Remove the flour glaze from the heat, cover, and set aside.

Bake the buns in a preheated 425° F. oven about 15 minutes or until golden brown. Remove from the oven and immediately brush the tops and sides of the buns lightly with the flour glaze. If you wish to put on the seeds, brush each bun again lightly with the glaze and immediately sprinkle evenly with the seeds. Serve warm or let cool on wire racks. Makes 12.

VARIATION:

Crusty Whole Wheat Hamburger Buns

Substitute 2½ cups all-purpose flour, 2¼ cups whole wheat flour, and ½ cup wheat germ for the 5¼ cups all-purpose flour. Add all of the whole wheat flour and wheat germ and 1 cup of the all-purpose flour in the first mixing stage. Mix in the remaining 1½ cups all-purpose flour and finish as directed above.

Bagels

These glossy, chewy rolls are a delicatessen staple, but they can easily be made at home. Their characteristic texture is achieved by boiling them before baking. Although they can be eaten plain in their traditional doughnut form, they lend themselves to a variety of both flavors and shapes.

Bagels, open-faced or closed, are excellent for sandwiches. Besides smoked salmon and cream cheese, their classic companions, fillings can consist of such items as ham, corned beef, Swiss cheese, and tuna or egg salad. Or simply enjoy them alone, split, toasted if you wish, and spread with butter.

2 cups warm water (110° F.)
2 packages active dry yeast
4 tablespoons sugar
3 teaspoons salt
5½ cups unsifted all-purpose flour
   (approximately)

3 quarts water plus 1 tablespoon
   for glaze
Cornmeal
1 egg yolk

Pour the water into a large mixing bowl and sprinkle with the yeast. Let the mixture stand about 5 minutes, then stir in 3 tablespoons of the sugar and the salt. Gradually add 4 cups of the flour, 1 cup at a time, beating thoroughly with a large spoon or an electric mixer at medium speed until well blended and smooth. Gradually add the remaining 1½ cups flour, mixing it in with a spoon to make a stiff dough.

Turn out the dough onto a lightly floured board and knead thoroughly, sprinkling occasionally with just enough flour to keep it from sticking. When it is smooth and elastic in texture, form it into a lump and place in a lightly greased bowl. Turn the dough over to grease the top. Cover loosely with a kitchen towel and let rise in a warm place free from drafts about 40 minutes or until doubled in size.

Punch down the dough and knead briefly to eliminate any air bubbles. Divide the dough into 12 equal pieces. Form each piece into a ball. Holding the ball with both hands, push your thumbs through the middle. With one thumb in the hole, work around the circumference, forming the bagel into a doughnut shape about 3½ inches across. Arrange the bagels on a lightly floured baking sheet, cover loosely with a kitchen towel, and let stand in a warm place about 20 minutes.

In a deep, heavy pot bring the 3 quarts water and remaining 1 tablespoon sugar to a boil. Regulate the heat to keep the water boiling gently. Carefully lift 1 bagel at a time and drop it into the water. Boil about 4 bagels at a time, turning frequently, 5 to 6 minutes. Lift out with a slotted spatula, drain a few minutes on a kitchen towel, and arrange slightly apart on a lightly greased baking sheet sprinkled with the cornmeal.

Beat the egg yolk with the remaining 1 tablespoon water and brush the bagels with the egg glaze. Bake in a preheated 400° F. oven about 35 minutes or until nicely browned and crusty. Serve warm or let cool on a wire rack. Makes 12.

Note: You may sprinkle each glazed bagel with ½ teaspoon sesame or poppy seeds or ¼ teaspoon coarse salt before baking.

VARIATIONS:

Miniature Bagels

Instead of dividing the dough into 12 pieces, divide it into 48. Bake the bagels about 20 minutes, or until browned and crusty.

Crusty Sausage Buns

Instead of shaping the pieces of dough into balls, roll them between your palms into 5-inch-long logs, smoothing the ends.

Whole Wheat Bagels

Substitute 3 tablespoons honey for the 3 tablespoons sugar added to the yeast. Instead of using only all-purpose flour, use 2¼ cups whole wheat flour, ½ cup wheat germ, and 2¾ cups all-purpose flour (approximately). Stir in the whole wheat flour, wheat germ, and 1¼ cups of the all-purpose flour before beating the dough. Then mix in the remaining 1½ cups all-purpose flour, knead, and proceed as directed.

Pumpernickel Bagels

Substitute 3 tablespoons dark molasses for the 3 tablespoons sugar added to the yeast. Instead of using only all-purpose flour, use 2 cups each rye flour and whole wheat or graham flour and 1½ cups all-purpose flour (approximately). Add the rye flour and 1 cup each of the whole wheat or graham and all-purpose flour before beating the dough. Then mix in the remaining 1 cup whole wheat or graham flour and ½ cup all-purpose flour, knead, and proceed as directed. If you wish to put on seeds, sprinkle each glazed bagel with ½ teaspoon caraway seeds before baking.

Tea Breads

Although these fragrant and flavorful breads can be sliced as soon as they are cool, they taste better when allowed to mellow for a day or two. Highly versatile, they are delicious spread with cream cheese and are excellent choices not only for teatime but for any other time of day, and travel well in lunch boxes and picnic baskets. All can be made ahead, tightly wrapped in aluminum foil, and refrigerated for about a week, or they can be stored in the freezer for longer periods.

Cranberry Bread

A memory not quickly faded.

2 cups unsifted all-purpose flour	1 egg
1 cup sugar	Grated rind of 1 orange
1½ teaspoons double-acting baking powder	½ cup freshly squeezed and strained orange juice
½ teaspoon baking soda	¼ cup butter, melted
½ teaspoon salt	1½ cups cranberries, picked over, washed, and coarsely chopped
¼ teaspoon cinnamon	½ cup chopped pecans or walnuts
¼ teaspoon cloves	

In a large mixing bowl sift together the flour, sugar, baking powder, baking soda, salt, cinnamon, and cloves. In a small bowl lightly beat together the egg, orange rind, orange juice, and melted butter. Stir the mixture into the dry ingredients. Add the cranberries and nuts and blend thoroughly.

Pour the batter into a greased and flour-dusted 9-by-5-by-3-inch loaf pan. Bake in a preheated 350° F. oven about 1 hour, or until a food pick inserted in the center comes out clean. Remove from the oven and cool in the pan 10 minutes. Turn out on a wire rack and let cool thoroughly. Makes 1.

Orange, Date, and Nut Bread

Anything this good should be more difficult to produce.

2 cups unsifted all-purpose flour	¼ cup butter, at room temperature
1 teaspoon double-acting baking powder	1 cup sugar
1 teaspoon baking soda	1 egg
¾ teaspoon salt	1 cup freshly squeezed and strained orange juice
1 cup chopped pitted dates	
½ cup finely chopped pecans or walnuts	

In a medium bowl sift together the flour, baking powder, baking soda, and salt. Combine 2 tablespoons of this mixture with the chopped dates and nuts in a small bowl. Stir well and set aside.

In a large mixing bowl cream the butter and the sugar until light and fluffy. Beat in the egg. Add the flour mixture to the creamed mixture in 3 parts, alternating with the orange juice and beating well after each addition. Stir in the date and nut mixture. Turn into a greased and flour-dusted 9-by-5-by-3-inch loaf pan. Bake in a preheated 350° F. oven about 55 minutes, or until a food pick inserted in the center comes out clean. Remove from the oven and cool in the pan 10 minutes. Turn out on a wire rack and let cool thoroughly. Makes 1.

Banana-Prune Bread

You will be amply rewarded for the short time it takes to make this moist, subtly-flavored bread.

2 cups unsifted all-purpose flour	1 cup sugar
1½ teaspoons double-acting baking powder	1½ tablespoons milk
½ teaspoon baking soda	1 teaspoon freshly squeezed and strained lemon juice
¼ teaspoon salt	½ teaspoon vanilla extract
3 medium bananas	1 cup chopped pitted prunes
2 eggs	½ cup chopped walnuts
½ cup butter, melted	

In a medium bowl sift together the flour, baking powder, baking soda, and salt. Set aside.

In a large mixing bowl mash the bananas. Add the eggs, melted butter, sugar, milk, lemon juice, and vanilla extract and beat until well blended. Gradually add the dry ingredients and mix until smooth. Stir in the prunes and walnuts. Turn into a greased and flour-dusted 9-by-5-by-3-inch loaf pan. Bake in a preheated 350° F. oven about 1 hour, or until a food pick inserted in the center comes out clean. Remove from the oven and cool in the pan 10 minutes. Turn out on a wire rack and let cool thoroughly. Makes 1.

VARIATION:

Banana, Apricot, and Raisin Bread

Substitute ½ cup each chopped dried apricots and seedless raisins for the prunes.

California Fruit Bread

Rum and Grand Marnier perform their magic for this delightful bread.

3 cups unsifted all-purpose flour
1¼ cups brown sugar
3 teaspoons baking powder
¼ teaspoon baking soda
½ teaspoon salt
½ cup chopped pitted dates or prunes
½ cup chopped dried apricots

½ cup chopped walnuts
1 egg
1 cup milk or freshly squeezed and strained orange juice
¼ cup dark rum
3 tablespoons Grand Marnier or other orange-flavored liqueur
¼ cup butter, melted

In a large mixing bowl combine the flour, brown sugar, baking powder, baking soda, and salt and mix well. Stir in the dates or prunes, apricots, and walnuts. Set aside.

In a medium bowl beat the egg, then stir in the milk or orange juice, rum, orange liqueur, and melted butter. Add the mixture to the dry ingredients and stir just until moistened. Turn into a greased and flour-dusted 9-by-5-by-3-inch loaf pan. Let stand 20 minutes. Bake in a preheated 350° F. oven about 1 hour, or until a food pick inserted in the center comes out clean. Remove from the oven and cool in the pan 10 minutes. Turn out on a wire rack and cool thoroughly. Makes 1.

Carrot-Coconut Bread

This could turn any rabbit into a gourmet (and it can grow on people, too!).

3 eggs	½ cup chopped walnuts or pecans
½ cup flavorless vegetable oil	2 cups unsifted all-purpose flour
2 teaspoons vanilla extract	½ teaspoon salt
2 cups grated carrots	2 teaspoons baking soda
¾ cup grated coconut	2 teaspoons cinnamon
½ cup seedless raisins or currants	1¼ cups sugar

In a large mixing bowl beat the eggs until light in color. Stir in the oil, vanilla extract, carrots, coconut, raisins or currants, and nuts. Set aside.

In a medium bowl sift together the flour, salt, baking soda, cinnamon, and sugar. Add these dry ingredients to the carrot mixture and stir until thoroughly blended. Turn the mixture into a greased and flour-dusted 9-by-5-by-3-inch loaf pan. Bake in a preheated 350° F. oven about 1 hour, or until a food pick inserted in the center comes out clean. Remove from the oven and let cool in the pan 10 minutes. Turn out on a wire rack and cool thoroughly. Let this particular bread age 2 or 3 days in the refrigerator before serving. Makes 1.

13

Basics

French Dressing

2 tablespoons wine vinegar
¼ to ½ teaspoon salt
½ teaspoon Dijon-style mustard
  (optional)

Freshly ground pepper to taste
6 to 8 tablespoons olive oil

Combine the vinegar, salt, mustard (if used), and pepper in a small bowl. Stir well to dissolve the salt, then gradually beat in the oil. Makes about ½ cup.

VARIATIONS:

Lemon French Dressing

Substitute 3 tablespoons or more freshly squeezed and strained lemon juice for the vinegar. If desired, add 1 tablespoon finely chopped scallion (include 2 inches of the green top) to the dressing. Mix well.

Herb French Dressing

Add ½ teaspoon each crushed dried oregano and basil and 1 medium garlic clove, crushed and finely chopped. Mix well.

Mayonnaise

1 egg	¼ cup olive oil
¾ teaspoon salt	¾ cup flavorless vegetable oil
½ teaspoon dry mustard	
2 tablespoons freshly squeezed and	
strained lemon juice, or	
1 tablespoon each lemon juice	
and white wine vinegar	

Place the egg, salt, mustard, lemon juice or lemon juice and vinegar, and olive oil in the container of an electric blender. Cover and whirl at high speed until the ingredients are blended. Immediately remove the lid and slowly pour in the vegetable oil in a steady stream until the mixture is thickened. Use the mayonnaise at once, or transfer to a clean jar, cover, and refrigerate for future use. Makes about 1¼ cups.

VARIATIONS:

Green Mayonnaise

Add 2 tablespoons each finely chopped fresh parsley, chives, and tarragon or dill. Mix well.

Curry Mayonnaise

Add 1 teaspoon curry powder or to taste. Mix well.

Thousand Island Dressing

Add 3 tablespoons chili sauce or ketchup, 1 hard-cooked egg, finely chopped (optional), 2 tablespoons finely chopped pimento-stuffed olives, 1 tablespoon finely chopped green pepper, 2 teaspoons finely chopped chives or scallion tops, 2 teaspoons finely chopped parsley, ¼ teaspoon paprika (optional), and salt to taste. Mix well.

Russian Dressing

Add 3 tablespoons chili sauce or ketchup, 1 teaspoon grated horse-radish, and 2 teaspoons grated mild white onion. Mix well.

Hollandaise Sauce

½ pound butter
2 egg yolks
1½ tablespoons boiling water
1 tablespoon freshly squeezed
   and strained lemon juice

Salt, freshly ground white
pepper, and cayenne pepper to
taste

Melt the butter over low heat. Remove from the heat and set aside. Place the egg yolks in the container of an electric blender. Cover and blend on low speed 1 minute while gradually adding the boiling water through the center cap. Slowly add the melted butter, then add the lemon juice and salt, pepper, and cayenne pepper until just mixed. Taste and adjust the seasoning. Use within ½ hour of making. Makes about 1¼ cups.

Béchamel Sauce

3 tablespoons butter
3 tablespoons all-purpose flour
2 cups milk

3 egg yolks
Salt and cayenne pepper to taste

In a heavy saucepan melt the butter over low heat. Add the flour and cook 1 or 2 minutes, stirring constantly with a wire whisk. Gradually add the milk and cook, stirring, until the mixture is thickened. Remove from the heat and keep warm. In a bowl beat the egg yolks, then gradually beat in some of the hot mixture from the saucepan. Return to the saucepan and boil, stirring, 1 minute. Stir in the salt and cayenne pepper and remove from the heat. Taste and adjust the seasoning. Makes 2 cups.

Mornay Sauce

Follow the recipe for Béchamel Sauce (page 263), adding 1 to 1½ cups freshly grated Swiss cheese or a combination of Swiss and Parmesan cheese to the hot sauce and stir over low heat until it is melted. Season to taste with salt, freshly ground pepper, and cayenne pepper. Makes about 3 cups.

Tomato Sauce

¼ cup olive oil
1 large onion, finely chopped
2 medium garlic cloves, finely chopped
4 large, ripe tomatoes, peeled, seeded, and finely chopped
⅓ cup tomato paste
1 tablespoon finely chopped fresh basil, or 1½ teaspoons crushed dried basil

1½ teaspoons crushed dried oregano
1 tablespoon finely chopped parsley
Salt and freshly ground pepper to taste

In a heavy saucepan heat the oil over moderate heat. Add the onion and garlic and sauté until golden and soft, stirring frequently. Add the remaining ingredients and cook, uncovered, about 45 minutes or until the mixture is thickened, stirring frequently. Put through a food mill or sieve and keep warm. Makes about 2 cups.

Salsa Mexicana Cruda

1 large, firm ripe tomato, finely chopped
¼ cup finely chopped mild onion or scallions (include 2 inches of the green tops of the scallions)
1 tablespoon finely chopped fresh coriander leaves or parsley

2 serrano or green chilies, finely chopped
Juice of 1 lime, freshly squeezed and strained
½ teaspoon salt or to taste

Combine all the ingredients in a small bowl and stir until well mixed. Taste and adjust the seasoning. Makes about 1 cup.

Guacamole

1 large, ripe avocado
1 small tomato, peeled, seeded, and finely chopped
1 tablespoon freshly squeezed and strained lime or lemon juice
1½ teaspoons olive oil (optional)

2 tablespoons finely chopped mild white or red onion
1 tiny garlic clove, crushed
½ teaspoon chili powder or to taste
¾ teaspoon salt or to taste

Halve and pit the avocado. Peel off the skin. Place the avocado flesh in a bowl and mash it with a fork. Add the remaining ingredients and mix thoroughly. Taste and adjust the seasoning. Cover and chill. Makes about 1½ cups

Plum Sauce

1 cup plum preserves
½ cup chutney, finely chopped

1 tablespoon cider vinegar
1 tablespoon sugar

Combine all the ingredients in a small saucepan. Cook over low heat, stirring constantly until heated through. Serve hot or cold. Makes about 1½ cups.

Horseradish Cream

½ cup chilled heavy cream, whipped

1 tablespoon grated horseradish or to taste
¼ teaspoon salt or to taste

Mix together the ingredients just before using. Makes about 1 cup.

VARIATION:

Sour cream may be substituted for the heavy cream.

Yogurt Cheese

With this you won't even know that you're dieting.

4 cups unflavored whole milk (not low-fat) yogurt

Line a colander or strainer with a clean muslin cloth wrung out in cold water, or with a few layers of dampened cheesecloth. Pour the yogurt into the cloth. Tie opposite corners of the cloth together securely to form a bag. Suspend the bag from a hook several hours or overnight, placing a bowl underneath to catch the drippings. The whey will drain off, leaving a soft, creamy white cheese. When the yogurt has become firm enough to spread, remove it from the bag and place it in a dish. Cover and refrigerate. Makes about 2 cups.

Clarified Butter

Since it burns less easily than ordinary butter, clarified butter is preferable to use for sautéing sandwiches. It is simple to make and keeps well.

2 pounds butter

In a heavy saucepan melt the butter over low heat, taking care not to allow it to burn. Skim off the foam with a spoon as it rises to the top. Remove from the heat and set aside about 3 minutes, then slowly and carefully pour the clear liquid into a container, discarding the creamy residue at the bottom of the pan. Cover and refrigerate. Makes about 1½ pounds.

Index